At Worship

With

Mary

*For my sister, Máire O'Donnell, RSHM,
in appreciation of family bonds
and of her deep zeal for Christian unity.*

At Worship

With

Mary

A Pastoral and Theological Study

Christopher O'Donnell, O. Carm.

Illustrated by Placid Stuckenschneider, OSB

Michael Glazier
Wilmington, Delaware

Our thanks to Dominican Publications, Dublin, and Costello Publishing Company, Long Island, NY, for permission to quote from *Vatican II: The Conciliar and Postconciliar Documents* edited by Austin Flannery, OP.

First published in 1988 by Michael Glazier, Inc., 1935 West Fourth Street, Wilmington, Delaware 19805. Copyright 1988 by Michael Glazier, Inc. All rights reserved.

Library of Congress Cataloging-in-Publication Data:

O'Donnell, Christopher.
    AT WORSHIP WITH MARY.

    Bibliography.
    1. Mary, Blessed Virgin, Saint—Feasts. 2. Catholic
Church—Liturgy. I. Title.
BT645.5.036   1988   263'.9   88-82465
ISBN 0-89453-738-5

Typography by Laura Kay Burke and Angela Meades.
Printed in the United States of America.

CONTENTS

ABBREVIATIONS

AAS	*Acta Apostolicae Sedis*
Brown	R.E. Brown, *The Birth of the Messiah. A Commentary on the Infancy Narratives in Matthew and Luke* (Garden City, NY: Doubleday, 1979).
Byzantine Daily Worship	Edited by the Most Reverend J. Raya and J. de Vinck (New Jersey: Alleluia, 1969).
Carol	J.P. Carol, ed., *Mariology*. 3 vols. (Milwaukee: Bruce, 1954-1960).
DBT	X. Léon-Dufour, ed., *Dictionary of Biblical Theology* (London-Dublin: Chapman, 1973²).
De Fiores	*Maria nella teologia contemporanea* (Rome: Centro "Mater Ecclesiae," 1987²).
DS	H. Denzinger and A. Schönmetzer, eds., *Enchiridion symbolorum, definitionum et declarationum* (Herder: Barcelona, 1973³⁵).
EnMar	D. Casagrande, ed., *Enchiridion marianum biblicum patristicum* (Rome: Ed. Cor Unum, 1974).
HBdMK	W. Beinert and H. Petri, eds., *Handbuch der Marienkunde* (Regensburg: Pustet, 1984).
Laurentin	R. Laurentin *Les évangiles de l'enfance du Christ* (Paris: Desclée, 1982²).
LG	*Lumen gentium*. Vatican II, Constitution on the Church.
McHugh	J. McHugh, *The Mother of Jesus in the New Testament* (London: Darton, Longman & Todd, 1975).
MaryNT	R.E. Brown, K.P. Donfried, J.A. Fitzmyer and J. Reumann,

9

	eds., *Mary in the New Testament. A Collaborative Assessment by Protestant and Roman Catholic Scholars* (London: Chapman—Philadelphia: Fortress, 1978).
MC	Pope Paul VI, Apostolic Exhortation, *Marialis cultus* (*To Honour Mary*. London: CTS, 1974).
Mhe	W. Beinert, ed., *Maria heute ehren* (Freiburg-Basel-Vienna: Herder, 1979).
NDizM	S. De Fiores and S. Meo, eds., *Nuovo dizionario di mariologia* (Turin-Milan: Ed. Paoline, 1985).
O'Carroll	M. O'Carroll, *Theotokos. An Encyclopedia of the Blessed Virgin Mary* (Wilmington: Glazier, 1983^2).
RM	Pope John Paul II, Encyclical, *Redemptoris Mater* (*On the Blessed Virgin Mary in the Life of the Pilgrim Church*. Vatican City, 1987).
Roschini	G.M. Roschini, *Maria santissima nella storia della salvezza*. 4 vols. (Isola del Liri: Pisani, 1969).
TCC	J. Neuner, H. Roos and K. Rahner, eds., *The Teaching of the Catholic Church* (New York: Alba, 1967).

PREFACE

This book arose to answer a simple need: to have one volume that gives the history and meaning of the various festivals of Mary. It began therefore from a pastoral concern to make available to celebrants some material on the marian feasts and to give them and others some help in their personal reflections on the significance of Mary's feasts throughout the liturgical year.

Teaching experience at seminary and post-graduate levels moreover brought home the fact that the Missal and the Lectionary are ideal text books for a course on the Blessed Virgin. But it was also clear that these admirable books are insufficient without some further help. Eventually the work assumed a multipurpose character. It seeks to retain the original impulse of a book that might assist liturgical celebration of the feasts of the Mother of God and prayerful reflection on them. Hence there are historical introductions, some exegesis of the scriptural texts used for the feasts, and prayers of the faithful. The addition of Church documents related to each feast is an attempt to penetrate more deeply the meaning of the liturgical celebration under the guidance of the magisterium. These texts will, it is hoped, supply additional material for reflection and prayer, as well as further theological insights. The reflections accompanying each feast, when taken together, deal with most of the outstanding issues concerning marian theology and devotion. In many cases they arise directly from the texts of the liturgy. In a few cases they are appended to feasts which do not have any theological problems. Finally, notes and further bibliography are supplied for each chapter. These may be of help to those who wish to pursue a particular question in mariology. With some hesitation, titles in languages other than English have been included: they acknowledge the author's debt to others; they may be useful to theologians and others who have not specialized in marian theology; in many cases these foreign language references themselves cite further useful works in English.

The success of combining various elements in a pastoral handbook, which is at the same time an introduction to mariology, must be judged by others. The work has been improved through the patient and discerning reading of the typescript by my friends, Sr. Teresa Clements, D.M.J., and Pat O'Kelly, and by my sister, Sr. Máire O'Donnell, R.S.H.M. To them my thanks.

25 March 1988.

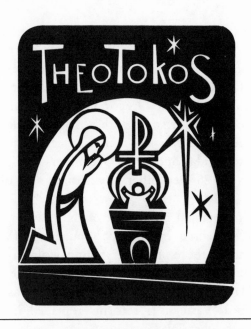

THE SOLEMNITY OF MARY, MOTHER OF GOD
(1 January)

LITURGICAL HISTORY

The Solemnity of the Mother of God is an example of the way the revised liturgy reinstates what was very ancient and disregards more recent developments. Before 1969 the feast celebrated on 1 January was the Circumcision of Jesus. It originated in the Gallican liturgy, spread throughout Europe and was firmly established by the Tridentine reform. It was not, however, devoid of some marian characteristics.

The origins of the feast of Mary's maternity are obscure. There is evidence of various dates on which a major feast of Mary was held. A celebration in Jerusalem on 15 August dates from around 428 and this had spread in the Armenian Church and the church at

Gethsemane by 458. The East's marian celebration came somewhat later ("Day of Theotokos") being held either before or after Christmas. From about 600 the Gregorian and Roman calendars marked the octave day of Christmas with a strong marian emphasis and in many places there was also a marian celebration during advent—on the 4th Sunday and/or 18 December—while the East had marian feasts on 26 December (Byzantine) and 16 January (Coptic)[1]

A movement in Portugal for a feast of the Divine Maternity culminated with a decree from Pope Benedict XIV in 1751 allowing a celebration there on the first Sunday of May. By 1914 this had been extended to various dioceses and religious congregations with the date of 11 October. In 1931 the feast was extended universally but post-Vatican II reforms replaced it with the restored 1 January celebration.[2]

THEMES

The celebration of Mary as mother focuses also on her child: "Hail holy Mother! The child to whom you gave birth is the king of heaven and earth forever" (entrance antiphon). In the opening prayer we have reference to Mary's intercession because she is the mother of the One who is life and salvation. On this day we ask for salvation with particular insistence for we are celebrating the prolongation of Christmas the beginning of salvation (prayer over gifts). Finally, we pray that communion with her Son may bring us salvation.

> Mary gave birth to the king whose name is eternal. She united the joy of a mother with the honour of a virgin. (Morning Prayer)
> O wonderful exhange! The creator of human nature took on a

[1] B. Kleinheyer, *HBdMK* 419-21.

[2] D. Sartor, *NDizM* 825-26.

human body and was born of the Virgin. He became man without having a human father and bestowed on us his divine nature. (Evening Prayer)

He who before the birth of the Morning Star was born of the Father without a mother, became incarnate on earth of you, O Mother of God, without a father. Wherefore a star announces to wise men that you have given birth without human seed, and angels and shepherds glorify you. O Woman full of grace! (*Byzantine Daily Worship* 572)

SCRIPTURE READINGS

a) Numbers 6:22-27

The lovely priestly blessing has three short elements: *bless/keep; face shine/be gracious; show his face/bring peace.*. Some of the Fathers of the Church have re-read this blessing in trinitarian terms. Two reasons can be suggested for the choice of this reading. Firstly, it is through the Incarnation that the blessing is most fully realized: it is the Father's great blessing; the Son reflects the Father's glory (see Heb 1:1-3); the Spirit reveals the Son and the eternal plan of God (see Jn 14:26; 15:26-27; 16:13-15). The second reason is probably the concurrence of this feast of Mary with New Year's Day on which people wish others well and exchange greetings.

The *response* to this reading is: "O God be gracious and bless us."

b) Galatians 4:4-7

In this reading we have Paul's only direct reference to Mary. It is a dense passage which sums up salvation history. The *Son* was *sent* and was *born of a woman*. The reasons are given: *to redeem* those under the law, and *so that we could receive adoption* as God's sons and daughters. Moreover, because *God has sent into our hearts the Spirit of his Son*, we can use the familiar word for father, *Abba*. We are therefore no longer *slaves*, but sons and daughters and thus *heirs*.

This text gives us an insight into the heart of the divine plan:

through a woman God became man, and we are brought into the fullness of divine blessings. It is not clear that Paul is asserting a virginal conception.[3]

c) Luke 2:16-21[4]

The gospel gives us the scene at Bethlehem to which the shepherds *hurried*. They had heard the angels and are now going to see the *sign* (2:12). The task of proclaiming the birth of the Messiah was given to a group which was generally despised by the Jewish authorities: shepherds were illiterate, outside the law, and they were often considered dishonest.[5] They respond to the angelic message. Spiritually then they are open to God's revelation; along with Zechariah, Elizabeth, Simeon, Anna, and of course Mary, they are figures of the *anawîm*, the poor who place their trust in God. On arriving they *found Mary and Joseph and the baby lying in the manger*. Mary is placed first, even though the *sign* was the *child lying in the manger*. The shepherds *repeated what they had been told* about the child. (Literally "the word spoken to them," where "word" can mean what is spoken or what is done). The gospel then gives three reactions, patterned on the foundational parable of the sower (see Lk 8:4–15). One group comprising *everyone who heard it*: is *astonished*. But like the seed sown on the path (see Lk 8:12) they do not figure again, and there is no indication that the event had a particular significance for them. The *shepherds* went back *glorifying and praising God*. The response of praise is typically lucan. But they have no further role and the word seems to have had no sustained effect on them: they believe for a time (see Lk 8:13–14). *Mary* is singled out: she *treasured all these things and pondered them*. Once again "things" has

---

[3]For denial of virgin birth here see *Mary NT* 41–45; O. Knoch, *HBdMK* 23; for assertion see M. Miguens, *The Virgin Birth. An Evaluation of Scriptural Evidence* (Boston: St. Paul, 1981[2]) 44–59 and P. Scott, *A Virgin Called Woman. Essays on N.T. Marian Texts* (Portglenone, N. Ireland: Bethlehem Abbey, 1986) 10–30; A. Serra *NDizM* 1425–26 exposes the view of A. Vanhoye and A. Vincent Cernuda who are open to an assertion of virginity.

[4]On this passage see Brown, 406–407, 427–433; *Mary NT* 143–52; McHugh 87–98.

[5]See Brown 420.

the Hebrew meaning of both words and actions. Mary is like the seed on good soil (see Lk 8:15) or like the wise scribe who ponders (see Sir 39:1-3). The pondering is *in her heart*. In scripture *heart* is the core, the depths of a person's being.[6] Mary is thus profoundly involved in both the retention and the interpretation of the event. Faith needs love to penetrate divine truth; time is also required for a person to enter contemplatively into truth.

The gospel concludes with a reference to the *circumcision* of Jesus. As he was born under the law (2nd reading), so his parents fulfil the law in his regard. Jesus thus becomes a member of the chosen people. *He was given the name Jesus*: in Luke it was Mary who was told the name chosen by God (1:31), whilst in Matthew it was Joseph (1:21.25). The Hebrew form of the name, *Jehoshua* means "Yahweh help," in popular etymology, "Yahweh saves."

CHURCH DOCUMENTS[7]

The expression of the Council of Ephesus (431) remains classical:

> If anyone does not confess that Emmanuel is truly God and therefore that the blessed Virgin is truly Mother of God (*Theotokos*) for she bore according to the flesh him who is the Word from God, let him be anathema.[8]

Like many conciliar affirmations before Vatican II, the statement is put in negative form. The assertion is against Nestorius who separated excessively the divine and the human in Christ, thereby ascribing to him a dual personality. *Theotokos* consists of two elements: *Theos* (God) and *tokos* (any creature who gives birth). It is a bold contraction, analogous to John 1:14: "The *Word* was made *flesh*" (Jn 1:14). It is not certain who first used the expression

---

[6]J. de Fraine and A. Vanhoye, "Heart" in *DBT* 228-229.

[7]See also E.R. Carroll, "Mary in the Documents of the Magisterium" in Carol 1:5-10.

[8]DS 252/TCC 234.

Theotokos; it was certainly used by Alexander of Alexandria (c. 319).[9]

Vatican II takes up the thought of the second reading and weaves into a summary of salvation history the words of early councils:

> Wishing in his supreme goodness and wisdom to effect the redemption of the world, 'when the fullness of time came, God sent his Son, born of a woman . . . that we might receive the adoption of sons (Gal 4:4). He for us men and for our salvation, came down from heaven, and was incarnated by the Holy Spirit from the Virgin Mary. This divine mystery of salvation is revealed to us and continued in the Church, which the Lord established as his body. (LG 52)

This mystery communicated to the Church will be discovered in the Church, not only in its official teaching, but also in liturgy, piety, art, and in the religious experience of its members. Later the Council remarks that Mary "joyfully showed her firstborn son to the shepherds and the Magi" (LG 57), and develops the idea of the Fathers of the Church that it was through her faith and obedience that Mary gave birth to the Son of God (see LG 63).

In his apostolic constitution, *Marialis cultus* ("To Honour Mary") Pope Paul VI wrote:

> In the revised ordering of the Christmas period it seems to us that the attention of all should be directed towards the restored Solemnity of Mary the holy Mother of God. This celebration, placed on 1 January in conformity with the ancient indication of the city of Rome, is meant to commemorate the part played by Mary in this mystery of salvation. It is meant also to exalt the singular dignity which this mystery brings to the 'holy Mother . . . through whom we are found worthy to receive the author of life' (Missal). It is likewise a fitting occasion for renewing adoration to the newborn Prince of Peace, for listening once more to the glad

[9]P.L. 18:567/*EnMar* 178.

tidings of the angels (see Lk 2:14), and for imploring from God, through the Queen of Peace, the supreme gift of peace. It is for this reason that, in the happy concurrence of the Octave of Christmas and the first day of the year, we have instituted the World Day of Peace, an occasion that is gaining support and already bringing forth fruits of peace in the hearts of many. (MC 5)

REFLECTION

From the scriptures it is clear that Mary is the mother of Jesus. But it would take several centuries for the Church to clarify the person, role and mission of Jesus. Parallel to this development there was a deepening understanding of Mary's motherhood. There was no mention of Mary in the first ecumenical council of the Church, Nicea (325). The problem there was to assert against Arius that Jesus was divine, "of one being with the Father" (*homoousios*). The second council, Constantinople 1, was largely concerned with the Holy Spirit, but it gave approval, in a manner not yet agreed by scholars, to the "Nicene" Creed. It stated that the Son was incarnate "from the Holy Spirit and Mary the Virgin." There is only one "from" (*ek*) in the Greek text, so we are encouraged to see the Holy Spirit and Mary as two principles of the Incarnation. Mary is described as "the Virgin." In this council we have a clear expression of the maternity of Mary with respect to Jesus, who is Son of God.

The next council, Ephesus (431) had a different problem. In trying to grasp the meaning of the scriptures and the "Nicene" Creed two viewpoints had emerged: one asserted the legitimacy of the title *Theotokos* (God-bearer), whilst the other dissented. It was not, however, a question of mariology, but rather of christology. The underlying question could be formulated in this way: Could everything about Christ in the scriptures be asserted about one entity or two? If there was only one entity who was divine and human, then Mary could be called "God-bearer" or *Theotokos*, not in the sense that she was mother of the divinity, but because she was the mother of one who was truly God.[10] Nestorius denied the

[10]See 2nd letter of Cyril approved by Nicea DS 251/TCC 246.

propriety of the title *Theotokos*, and wished to call Mary "Christ-bearer" but not "God-bearer." He was condemned, and the title *Theotokos* entered firmly into christian theology and liturgy.

The fourth council was at Chalcedon twenty years later (451). A new problem of understanding and expression had arisen: the complexity of the mystery of the incarnation had been simplified by Monophysitism: there was only one nature in Christ after the union of the divine and human. The Council of Chalcedon defined two distinct natures in one person:

> the Son, Our Lord Jesus Christ, is one and the same, the same perfect in divinity, the same perfect in humanity, true God and true man, . . . born of the Father before all time as to his divinity, born in recent times for us and for our salvation from the Virgin Mary, Mother of God, as to his humanity.[11]

Much of the language used about Christ was rather fluid up to Chalcedon. The difficult terminology of this council can be put into simple, if somewhat inelegant, English: in Christ there were two *hows*, but only one *what*. The *how* refers to nature—the way in which Christ was, the principle of his operations—he was God, he was man. But there is only one *what*, that is one subject, one entity, one person. The things said about his human nature (he walked, he wept . . .), and the things said about his divine nature (he was eternal, forgave sins on his own authority . . .), are all said about one *him* ("what"), the one entity or person. Pope John Paul II summarizes this teaching in his encyclical *Redemptoris Mater* (n. 39): "Her election to the supreme office and dignity of Mother of God refers on the ontological level to the very reality of the union of the two natures in the person of the Word (hypostatic union)."

There are theologians today who do not find the language of the Council of Chalcedon very helpful in speaking about Christ. They should not, however, reject the central affirmation of the Council:

---

[11]DS 301/TCC 254.

Jesus is fully human and fully divine; he is, however, not two, but one.[12]

It will be clear too that any flaw in orthodoxy with regard to Christ will have repercussions on Mary as *Theotokos*, and vice versa. The catholic faith gives affirmative answers to these three questions: Can Mary be said in the true sense of the word to be Mother of God? Did she really conceive and give birth to God according to his human nature? Can we say, "God is Son of Mary—Mary gives birth to God"?[13]

The early councils were mainly concerned with questions about the Trinity and the incarnation. Mary was mentioned in the context of clarifying issues about her Son. We can go further and say that the marian statements of the first councils are in relation to salvation. The divine maternity is not a personal privilege of Mary; it is rather for our salvation. Nor is the perspective of Vatican II any different: this council wished to show the role of Mary in relation to Christ the redeemer and to the Church.

But whereas the earlier councils were almost solely interested in Mary as virginally conceiving and bringing forth Jesus, Son of God and truly man, Vatican II further sees Mary as close associate of Jesus throughout his entire redeeming life. This association is described as her "pilgrimage of faith" (LG 58). Again, some aspects of the human side of her maternity have not been of much interest to theologians,[14] but are nonetheless important for the living faith of the Church. A fine passage from an early work of E. Schillebeeckx can serve as an introduction for further reflection:

> Mary was Jesus' mother. That means that Jesus, as a man, was brought up by Mary and Joseph. This is, of course, a great mystery and difficult for the human mind to grasp. Nonethe-

[12]See on this entire issue J.T. O'Connor, "Modern Christologies and Mary's Place Therein: Dogmatic Aspect," *Marian Studies* 32 (1981) 51-75.

[13]See D. Bertetto, *Maria, Madre universale nella storia della salvezza*. "Nouva collana di teologia cattolica 7" (Florence: Fiorentina, 1969) 81.

[14]See M. O'Carroll, *Theotokos*, "The Personality of Mary" 385-86.

less, we must affirm the dogma that Christ was a true human being and, as such, had to be brought up and educated, in the strictest sense of the word, by his mother. His human qualities and character were formed and influenced by his mother's virtues. And when we read in Scripture that Christ went around in the land of Palestine doing good, and realize that this human goodness was God's love, we are bound to acknowledge too that Mary had a maternal share in this christian interpretation of God's love. It is common human experience that the mother's features are recognizable in the child, and this was also true in the case of Mary and Jesus. Mary's function in the Incarnation was not completed when Jesus was born. It was a continuous task, involving the human formation of the young man, as he grew up from infancy to childhood and from childhood to adulthood. How this was accomplished is hidden from us.[15]

Following D. Sartor we can bring together various themes from the liturgy, Church documents, and the doctrine of the Theotokos.[16] The first of January is a rich meeting of various ideas. Firstly, it is the octave day of Christmas. It therefore prolongs the solemnity of 25 December, and it should not dislodge the centrality of the incarnation. Secondly, again as the octave of the birth of Christ, we commemorate his circumcision and thus his submission to the Law. Thirdly, the time of circumcision is the occasion for giving a child a name; he is called Jesus. The former feast of the Holy Name of Jesus is thus suppressed. Fourthly, the feast occurs on the first day of the civil year when people exchange good wishes. In the Church these good wishes are given a deeper religious meaning. Finally, as we saw in the excerpt from Paul VI, it is the World Day of Peace. In this rich cluster of themes it is important to hold on to what is most central: the virginal motherhood of Mary and the incarnation of her Son born to be our Saviour. From a pastoral point of view it would be preferable to

---

[15]*Mary, Mother of the Redemption* (London-New York, 1964) 144–45.

[16]See D. Sartor, "Madre di Dio," *NDizM* 827–28.

touch on the pluralism of themes in the introduction to the Mass and in the Prayer of the Faithful, and focus on the heart of the celebration in the homily. Pope John Paul II says that as a result of being Mother of the Son of God, "she is also the favourite daughter of the Father and the temple of the Holy Spirit. Because of this gift of sublime grace she far surpasses all other creatures, both in heaven and on earth" (RM 9).

PRAYER OF THE FAITHFUL

Jesus is the Emmanuel, God-is-with-us; in his name we pray to our Father in heaven:

- that the full meaning of the coming of the Lord at Christmas may take root in the hearts of christians;
- that as Jesus was subjected to the Law of Moses, we might always be submissive to the New Law of love;
- that those in need and in darkness may experience the power of Jesus, their Lord and Saviour;
- that as the New Year begins we may find new incentives for being loving and caring towards those around us;
- that nations, peoples and families may through Mary's intercession come into a new experience of peace.
  Loving Father, we come with these our needs; our prayer is confident and trusting because we rely on the prayers of the Mother of your Son, and because we pray in his name. Amen.

ADDITIONAL READING

De Fiores, 478-495.

E.A. Johnson, "Mary and Contemporary Christology: Rahner and Schillebeeckx," *Eglise et theologie* 15 (1984) 155-182.

T. Koehler, "Qui est Marie—Theotokos dans la doctrine christologique et ses difficultés actuelles," *Etudes mariales* 38 (1981) 11-35.

S. Meo, *La "Theotokos" al concilio ecumenico di Efesi a. 431* (Rome: Marianum, 1979).

C.W. Neumann, "The Virginal Conception and Divine Motherhood. A Modern Reappraisal," *Marian Studies* 33 (1982) 90-120 at 108-120.

J.T. O'Connor, "Mary, Mother of God and Contemporary Challenges," *Marian Studies* 29 (1978) 26-45.

K. Rahner, *Mary Mother of the Lord. Theological Meditations* (Freiburg: Herder—Edinburgh/London: Nelson, 1963) 53-62.

Roschini, 2:9-110.

G. Söll, *Storia dei dogmi mariani.* "Accademia mariana salesiana 15" (Rome: LAS, 1981) 108-113.

M. Thurian, *Mary. Mother of the Lord. Figure of the Church* (London: Faith Press, 1963) 74-83.

G. van Ackeren, "Mary's Divine Motherhood" in Carol 2:177-227.

THE PRESENTATION OF THE LORD
(Feast—2 February)

LITURGICAL HISTORY

The earliest account of the feast is found in the diary of Egeria, a fourth-century Spanish pilgrim who describes what she saw in Jerusalem, probably between 381 and 384 A.D.

Note that the fortieth day after Epiphany is observed here with special magnificence. On that day they assemble at the Anastasis (place of the resurrection). Everyone gathers, and things are done with the same solemnity as at the feast of Easter. All the presbyters preach first, then the bishop, and they interpret the passage from the Gospel about Joseph and Mary taking the Lord to the Temple, and about Simeon and the prophetess Anna, daughter of Phanuel, seeing the Lord, and about the sacrifice offered by his parents. When all the rest is done in the proper way, they celebrate the sacrament and have their dismissal. (n. 26)[1]

The special solemnity at the tomb of Christ suggests that there was a vigil followed by Mass.

Later this celebration spread from Jerusalem, with lights and candles appearing from the 5th century. By the 7th century it had reached Rome. The Syro-Sicilian Pope Sergius I (687-701) established a procession for the feast which later took on a penitential character. Up to 1960 the vestments for the blessing of candles and the procession were violet. The blessing of candles and the singing of the *Nunc dimittis* were added about the 10th century. The feast has had several names: the *Hypapante* (Meeting of the Infant Jesus and Simeon), Presentation of the Lord, Purification of the Blessed Virgin Mary. In the 1969 reform of the calendar the old name, Presentation of the Lord, was restored. It is a feast we share with the Orthodox and Anglicans.

THEMES

Though it has many marian features, the feast is now more a celebration of the Lord. The liturgical introduction to the blessing of candles and the procession recalls the meeting of Simeon and Anna with Christ, and it looks to the Church's eucharistic meeting with the Lord until he comes. A dominant theme is light symbolized by the candles and the refrain taken from Simeon's canticle,

> Christ is the light of the nations
> and the glory of Israel his people.

The opening prayer of the Mass asks that we be purified from sin, as we continue on our way to meet the Lord (post-communion prayer). The preface of the Mass takes up again the theme of the

---

[1] *Egeria's Travels.* Tr. John Wilkinson (London: SPCK, 1973) 128.

revelation of Christ as the glory of Israel and the light of all peoples.

> The old man held the child, but the child was his king; the virgin bore the child, yet remained a virgin after the birth; she adored as her God the child she bore. (Evening Prayer 1) When his parents brought in the child Jesus, Simeon took him in his arms and gave thanks to God. (Morning Prayer) Today the Blessed Virgin Mary presented the child Jesus in the temple; there Simeon took him in his arms and gave thanks to God. (Evening Prayer 2)

SCRIPTURE READINGS

a) Malachi 3:1-4

This prophecy dates from the early 5th century B.C., a time of lessened religious fervour. The prophet foretells the Day of the Lord which will be both terror and renewal. A *messenger* will be sent *to clear a way before* the Lord. The New Testament sees this fulfilled in John the Baptist, the new Elijah (see Mt 11:10). The *Lord whom* we *seek will come to his Temple*. He will bring about renewal of the people like a *refiner's fire, like fuller's alkali* for *he will purify* the priests, the *sons of Levi*. They will then be able to *make the offering to the Lord with uprightness*. With the renewal of the temple priesthood, *the offering of Juda and Jerusalem will then be acceptable*.

The choice of this text for the feast indicates that the Presentation is an anticipation of the future ministry of Jesus: coming as a baby to the temple, he already begins his mission to the temple and thus to the whole people; he will later establish a new and authentic worship to the Father (see Jn 4:21-23); there is even a hint of the opposition he will encounter for *who will remain standing when he appears?*

The *response* to this reading is, "Who is the king of glory? It is the Lord."

b) Hebrews 2:14-18

This letter dating from the 70's A.D. was probably written for Jews, perhaps priests, whose faith was weak, and who looked back longingly to the splendour of the temple ritual. The author presents Christ as the great *high priest.* He is the one who can set them free from the *power of death, namely the devil.* To be such a *high priest* it was necessary that he become flesh *in the line of Abraham,* so that in this way he should be *made completely like his brothers.* Thus he is *a compassionate and trustworthy high priest* for the people *in their relationship with God, able to expiate* their *sins.* His own experience of *being put to the test enables him to help others* in the same situation. This text brings out another aspect of the ministry of Jesus, one that is the result of christian reflection rather than explicit in his own direct teaching: he is truly a priest in offering himself for the sins of the people. The Presentation in the Temple can then be seen as an initial foreshadowing of the definitive offering he would later make to the Father on the cross. He is to be priest of a new cult.

c) Luke 2:22-40[2]

The gospel narrative is somewhat compressed at the beginning. There were two different ceremonies involved. In Israelite law the woman was to be *purified* after childbirth. An offering of a lamb was made, but the poor could give instead *a pair of turtledoves or two young pigeons* (see Lev 12:1-8). Mary obeys the law, even though we know that it did not apply to her, for one of the doves was a sin offering, the other being a burnt offering. The event pictures Mary as an Israelite faithful to the Law, as the mother of a baby, and as a poor person.

The second ceremony was the ransoming of the first-born, for *every first-born male must be consecrated to the Lord.* (We might note in passing that the Greek text says "every male opening a womb," meaning "first-born." But this text would hardly have been used

[2]On this text see Brown 433-470; *Mary NT* 152-157; McHugh 99-112.

by Luke if he thought that the actual birth of Jesus was miraculous,[3] that is with no physical change in Mary. We return later to this point). The first-born male was either to be offered in sacrifice, or an alternative offering was to be made (see Ex 13:2.11). At the time of Jesus this offering was five shekels, that is about twenty days' wages of a labourer. The presentation of the child was not prescribed, but was fitting (see Nb 18:15), and it was done by Elkanah and his wife Hannah in the case of Samuel (see 1 Sm 1:24-28).

Luke hurries over the details of the ceremonies; indeed it would seem that he himself was not too clear about them.[4] The focus of the narrative now becomes Simeon. Luke tells us three times about his docility to the Spirit. This is one of the author's devices to emphasize something, for example the triple account of the conversion of Paul in Acts. Simeon had been promised that *he would not see death until he had set eyes on the Christ of the Lord*, that is, the one whom the Lord anointed. *He took* the child *into his arms and blessed God* and said his *Nunc dimittis*, thus named because his canticle begins in Latin with the words "Now dismiss." Simeon is being presented as one of the *anawîm*, the poor of the Lord who trust in him alone: *he looked forward to the restoration of Israel*. The word translated by "restoration" is in Greek *paraclēsis*, a word reminiscent of the Holy Spirit (see Jn 14:26) and Jesus (see Jn 14:26; 1 Jn 2:1), both of whom are called paracletes, that is advocates, supporters, counsellors.

Prompted by the Spirit Simeon *came to the Temple*. He can now accept death, he can *go in peace* for his *eyes have seen the salvation* of the Lord. The words *you are letting your servant go in peace* evoke the idea of manumission, that is, the freeing of a slave in the ancient world. A key word here is to *see*. Simeon would not *see death* until he would *see* the Christ. So with Jesus in his arms he proclaims that he has *seen the salvation* of the Lord. The idea is continued as he speaks of the destiny of the child: this *salvation* has been *made*

[3]Brown 437.

[4]Idem. 447-50.

ready in the sight of the nations. The role of Jesus is not restricted to the *glory* of the *people Israel* for it is *a light of revelation for the gentiles.* In the gospel of Matthew the Magi symbolize the fact that Jesus is for the non-Jewish world too (see Mt 2:1-12); the point is explicit in Luke, since Jesus is *salvation* for all.

Simeon's first prophecy surprises Joseph and Mary: they *were wondering at the things that were being said about him.* We can see Simeon's words as giving new insight to them about their child. In the annunciation he was foretold as the king of Israel (see Lk 1:33). But now the vision extends beyond the Chosen People to the whole world. The latter part of Isaiah had already broken out of the narrow exclusivism of the earlier prophets and had seen God as saving also the pagans (see Is 52:9-10; 49:6; 42:6; 40:5—all texts that lie behind the *Nunc dimittis*). It is this new revelation that puzzles Mary and Joseph. Simeon *blessed them;* he gives God thanks for them, and invokes his favour on them.

He now begins to speak more clearly about the future of the child: *he is destined for the fall and for the rise of many in Israel.* Jesus will in time be a source both of rising (Greek *anastasis,* the resurrection word) and of destruction. He will then be a challenge, a test whereby people will rise or fall. The idea that the Messiah will be the cause of ruin for some is developed in the next line, *destined to be a sign that is opposed.* Jesus will meet with hostility from his own people. This theme of hostility is present also in Matthew's gospel when Herod persecutes the child (Mt 2). A further notion is that the *secret thoughts* (Greek, "the thoughts of the heart," *of many may be laid bare.* The expression "thoughts of the heart," or innermost attitudes, is always negative in Luke (see 5:22; 6:8; 9:46; 47; 24:38): it refers to thoughts, or a frame of mind, hostile to Jesus or questioning him. The prophecy of *secret thoughts* being *laid bare* was fulfilled during the ministry of Jesus. Before he came proclaiming the reign of God, the scribes (learned people) and the pharisees (strict observers of the law) were held in high regard. But the preaching and ministry of Jesus showed them up, so that their inmost being was seen to run counter to the plan of God. This opposition to Jesus will be a source of distress for his mother, a point we develop in treating of the sorrows of Mary (15 September).

Then a *prophetess, Anna came up*. The term "prophetess" implies holiness of life, spelled out by Luke who observed that *she never left the Temple, serving God night and day with fasting and prayer*. It also indicates that she would correctly interpret God's plan for the child when *she spoke of the child to all who looked forward to the deliverance of Jerusalem*. She is described as arriving on the scene and beginning *to praise God*. Her prophecy seems more concerned with the positive effects of Jesus' ministry than with the negative consequences indicated by Simeon. Like him, Anna is herself a figure of the *anawîm*, and resembles the *anaw* personage of Judith in the Old Testament. Judith prayed and trusted in the Lord, and she had occasion to praise the power of his deliverance (see Jud 8:1-8; 15:14-16:17). Like Judith who lived on as a widow to be 105, Anna was also of great age, being either 84 years old, or else a widow for 84 years. Anna also shows many of the characteristics of the ideal of widowhood in the New Testament (see 1 Tm 5:3-16).

The scene of the Presentation in the Temple thus moves from an observance of Jewish rituals on the part of Joseph and Mary to be a profound revelation of the future destiny of Jesus. The scene closes with a brief statement that in Nazareth he *grew to maturity, he was filled with wisdom; and God's favour was on him*. He was thus gradually being prepared for the mission which the Father had planned for him. In time he will appear as *salvation, light* and *glory* for Israel and for the gentiles, even though as a child he is brought to the house of the Father by his humble parents who could afford only the offering of the poor, *a pair of turtledoves or two young pigeons*.

CHURCH DOCUMENTS

Pope Paul VI wrote in his exhortation *Marialis cultus*, n.9:

The Feast of 2 February, which has been given back its

ancient name, the Presentation of the Lord, should also be considered as a joint commemoration of the Son and of the Mother, if we are fully to appreciate its rich content. It is the celebration of a mystery of salvation accomplished by Christ, a mystery with which the Blessed Virgin was intimately associated as the Mother of the Suffering Servant of Yahweh, as one who performs a mission belonging to ancient Israel, and as the model for the new People of God, which is ever being tested in its faith and hope by suffering and persecution (see Luke 2:21-35).

REFLECTION

The long exposition of the scripture reading for this feast has highlighted its central meaning. We have already noted that the feast is of eastern origin, a fact that invites us to look at the picture of Mary which emerges in oriental theology, spirituality and liturgy. When we turn to the eastern liturgy of this feast we find the same themes, but with a special flavour. We can find the difference of approach in that greatest of all hymns to Mary, the incomparable *Akathistos Hymn* (probably from St. Romanus the Melodist, who died about 560):

> As Simeon drew near to the time of his departure from this world of error, he received thee as an infant in his arms, but he knew thee to be perfect God; and, struck with wonder at thine ineffable wisdom, he cried: Alleluia![5]

To a much greater extent than the West, the East celebrates the glory of the *Theotokos* in the liturgy, often with her full title:

[5]Kontakion Six—*The Akathistos Hymn to the Most Holy Mother of God*. Tr. Mother Mary and Bishop Kallistos. (The Ecumenical Society of the Blessed Virgin Mary, 1986) 21.

Our All-Holy, immaculate, most blessed and glorified Lady,
Mother of God and Ever-virgin Mary.[6]

For though in the western Church Mary is invoked in almost all
liturgical functions, there is in the eastern Church a greater fre-
quency with more striking invocations, such as the oft-repeated,

> O you higher in honour than the cherubim and more glorious
> and beyond compare than the seraphim, you gave birth to
> God the Word in virginity. You are truly Mother of God:
> you do we exalt.

It is often said that *Theotokos*, Mother of God, is the central
marian affirmation of the East. But this needs to be seen in the
wider context of eastern liturgy and spirituality. At the heart of
eastern spirituality is the glory of the incarnation, the immense
condescension of the divine majesty that allows the creator of the
world to be the crucified one in order that divine life might erupt
into the world. Glory and beauty surround his whole visible life,
and especially his passion, death and resurrection. Thus for the
feast of the Presentation we read:

> 'Search the scriptures' said Christ our God in his Gospel.
> There we shall see our God being born, and wrapped in
> swaddling clothes; we shall find him feeding on milk, being
> circumcised, being carried in Simeon's arms, appearing in
> the world as real man—no imagination or dream, but solid
> reality. Wherefore we cry out to Him and say: 'O God who
> exist from eternity, glory to You!'
>
> *(Byzantine Daily Worship* 628)

Mary is intimately bound up in this mystery:

> The One who comes forth from the Father in all eternity,
> and from a Virgin's womb in time, is carried to the Temple

[6]Timothy Ware (Bishop Kallistos), *The Orthodox Church* (Harmondsworth: Penguin,
1986[6]) 262.

by his Mother all-pure. The Lawmaker of Mount Sinai, submitting to the Law, is presented to the elderly and holy Simeon, to whom it had been revealed that he would see Christ the Lord. When Simeon received him in his arms, he leaped for joy and said: 'This is God, One in eternity with the Father, the Saviour of our souls!'

(Byzantine Daily Worship 629)

Perhaps the nearest expression in the West to the vision of the East is to be found in that superb gem of the Roman liturgy, the first Christmas Preface:

In the wonder of the incarnation your eternal Word brought to the eyes of faith a new and radiant vision of your glory. In him we see our God made visible and so are caught up in love of the God we cannot see.

The theology of the East developed above all in a liturgical setting. It was in prayer that Mary became known and venerated. The distinguished Orthodox theologian A. Schmemann noted:

Thus when investigating the history of Mariological piety, one discovers that it is rooted not in any special revelation but, primarily, in the experience of liturgical worship. In other terms, it is not a theological reflection on Mary that gave birth to her veneration; it is the liturgy as the experience of 'heaven on earth,' as communion with and knowledge of heavenly realities, as an act of love and adoration, that little by little revealed the unique place of Christ's Mother in both the economy of salvation and the mystery of the 'world to come.' Mary is not part of the Church's *kerygma* whose only content is Christ. She is the inner secret of the Church as communion with Christ. The Church preaches Christ, not Mary. But communion with Christ reveals Mary as the secret joy within the Church. 'In her,' says a hymn, 'rejoices the whole creation.'[7]

[7]"Mary in Eastern Liturgy," *Marian Studies* 19 (1968) 76–86 at 79.

Mary's role in the life of the christian East is summed up in the tradition of icons. Mary appears in a privileged place on the iconastasis, the screen in front of the altar which depicts Christ, the angels, the patriarchs and saints. She is at the heart of the Communion of Saints: in the liturgy which unites heaven and earth she is present to the Church. There are several icon traditions of particular importance: firstly, there is the *Theotokos*, an icon of majesty with Mary dressed in subdued purple, whilst her Son is in royal gold; secondly, we have the *Deesis* (Mary in supplication), with the Virgin's hands upraised in intercession; thirdly, there is the *Hodegetria* (pointing the way) in which Mary holds the child Jesus in one arm and points to him with her other hand; fourthly, we note the *Eleousa* (the Mother of Tenderness), familiar especially in the St. Vladimir icon which shows Mary's eyes as seeming to look forward to the passion whilst she holds the child to her cheek.[8]

We cannot explain devotion to the Mother of God in the East, a characteristic of oriental spirituality, by making a superficial reference to the more 'sentimental' mentality of the East. T. Špidlík suggests that the deeper reason for the extraordinary esteem for Mary in the East lies in the fact that devotion to the *Theotokos* resonates with the essential characteristics of eastern spirituality. Firstly, from an anthropological viewpoint, she is the human being who most resembles the perfect image of God, the incarnate Word. In her then the divine image can be contemplated; in her we find a model to imitate as we seek to be like God. Secondly, we look to that central idea of eastern spirituality which is the theology of deification by grace. Of all humans she has been most endowed with divine glory and has already reached the final glorification towards which the Church aspires. Thirdly, for the contemplative East, Mary is the one *par excellence* who has contemplated God. "Through contemplation, the Logos born of

---

[8]See T. Špidlík, "Teologia dell'iconografia mariana" in *La Madre del Signore*. "Parola spirito e vita. Quaderni di lettura biblica 6" (Bologna: Centro Dehoniano, 1986) 243–254 or more briefly, M. O'Carroll, *Theotokos* 176-177; K; Kolb, *HBdMK* 849-860.

her body rests forever in her heart, as is illustrated by the *Znamenye* icon, the praying Virgin with the divine Word on her heart."[9] We might note also that not only in its marian masterpiece, the *Akathistos Hymn*,[10] but quite generally in its hymnology, Mary is seen in the East as a symbol of the Temple, where God dwelt. The Temple with all its furnishings foretells the various dimensions of the mystery of Mary.[11]

Finally, in this reflection which began with some consideration of the presentation in the East, but has moved to the wider question of Mary in the East, we should compare the doctrinal[12] and liturgical positions of East and West. Both traditions celebrate a feast of the *Theotokos* (1 January in the West, 26 December in the East), the Nativity of the Virgin, the Presentation of Mary in the Temple, the Annunciation, the Presentation of the Lord and the Assumption (West) or Dormition (East).

The East treasures the marian dogmas of the divine motherhood, perpetual virginity, and assumption of Mary. The dogma of the Immaculate Conception is not however found there. The main reason for its absence is the fact that there was never a major controversy about original sin in the East. It was Pelagianism in the West that was responsible for this latter development. Once the doctrine of original sin was established in the 4th and 5th centuries, it was inevitable that Mary's situation would surface: Did she too have original sin? In the West the Church came gradually to grasp her Immaculate Conception. In the East it is

[9]T. Špidlík, *The Spirituality of the Christian East. A Systematic Handbook.* "Cistercian Studies 79" (Kalamazoo, Mi., 1986) 158-159; with short bibliography 388.

[10]See above n.5 for two translations: one rather liturgical (Mother Mary and Bishop Kallistos), the other more free (R. Green). A translation is to be found also in D. Flanagan, *In Praise of Mary* (Dublin: Veritas, 1975) 82-95.

[11]See A. Schmemann, art. cit. (n.7) 79; J. Ledit, *Marie dans la liturgie de Byzance.* "Théologie historique 39." (Paris: Beauchesne, 1976) 81-82; 115-126.

[12]See P.N. Trembelas, *Dogmatique de l'Eglise Orthodoxe Catholique.* "Textes et études théologiques" 3 vols. (Bruges: Ed. de Chevetogne—Desclée de Brouwer, 1967) 2:222-234; T. Ware, op.cit. (n.6) 258-265; N. Nissiotis, "Mary in Orthodox Theology," *Concilium* 168 (1983) 25-39

more usual to speak of Mary as "All-holy" (*Panagia*). These necessarily brief indications concerning the mariology of the East find confirmation in a long section of the encyclical of Pope John Paul II, *Redemptoris Mater* (31-34) in which he treats of the Churches of the East:

> The Greek Fathers and the Byzantine tradition, contemplating the Virgin in the light of the Word made flesh, have sought to penetrate the depth of that bond which unites Mary, as Mother of God, to Christ and the Church: the Virgin is a permanent presence in the whole reality of the salvific mystery.... Such a wealth of praise, built up by the different forms of the Church's great tradition, could help us to hasten the day when the Church can begin once more to breathe fully with her 'two lungs,' the East and the West. (RM 31 and 34)

PRAYER OF THE FAITHFUL

As Jesus was presented to his Father by Mary and Joseph, we rely on their intercession in our prayers to our common Father.

- Jesus was proclaimed as light of revelation to the gentiles: may the Church always reflect his light to the world.
- Simeon longed to see the Christ: may the Church continue to bring him to all peoples.
- Simeon's heart was filled with peace: may the peace of God be shared amongst the nations and within each country and race.
- Mary and Joseph were puzzled at Simeon's words—may those in doubt or distress be guided into light by the Holy Spirit.
- Today the Churches of both East and West celebrate the same feast of the Presentation—may unity grow between them and among all the followers of Christ.
  Father in heaven, we give you thanks for the light you gave to

the world in your Son, Jesus Christ; may we always walk in
his light, for he is Lord for ever and ever. Amen.

ADDITIONAL READING

a) Presentation

G. Mealo, "Presentazione del Signore," *NDizM* 1148-55. H. Urs
    von Balthasar, *The Threefold Garland. The World's Salvation
    in Mary's Prayer* (San Francisco: Ignatius, 1982) 51-57.

b) Eastern Christianity

G. Gharib, "Oriente cristiano," *NDizM* 1030-43. C. Gumbinger,
    "Mary in the Eastern Liturgies," Carol 1:185-244.

G.A. Maloney, "Russian Devotion to Mary the Mother of God"
    in *Mary the Womb of God,* (Denville, N.J.: Dimension,
    1976) 185-201.

T. Špidlík, "Maria e lo Spirito Sancto nella Chiesa orientale" in
    AA.VV. *Maria e lo Spirito Sancto* (Rome: Marianum—Bo-
    logna: Ed. Dehoniane, 1984) 104-132.

A. Stacpoole, ed., *Mary's Place in Christian Dialogue* (Slough: St.
    Paul, 1982): K. Ware, "The Mother of God in Orthodox
    Theology" 157-168; S. Brock, "Mary in Syriac Tradition"
    169-181.

E. Toniolo, *"Akathistos"*, *NDizM* 16-25.

OUR LADY OF LOURDES
(Optional Memorial—11 February)

LITURGICAL HISTORY

The story of Lourdes is well known and amply documented.[1] There were eighteen apparitions to Bernadette Soubirous from 11 February to 16 July 1858. The feast was established by Pius X in 1907 and survives in the revised liturgy as the sole celebration of the universal Church that is linked directly with an apparition.

---

[1]See T.F. Casey, "Lourdes," *New Catholic Encyclopedia* 8:1031-33; M. O'Carroll, *Theotokos* 224-225. The essential documentation is to be found in R. Laurentin—B. Billet, *Lourdes. Dossier des documents authentiques.* 7 vols. (Paris: Lethiellieux, 1957-61).

THEMES

The only special texts supplied for this memorial are the opening prayer and two scripture passages. In the prayer there is an indirect allusion to Mary's own self-description at Lourdes ("I am the Immaculate Conception"), in the words "we celebrate the feast of the sinless Mother of God." The prayer has an ecclesial focus: "may her prayers help us" stresses Mary's intercession for us; the phrase "to rise above our human weakness" is an indication of the healing we all need. The Latin text is rather stronger than "weakness" ("*a nostris iniquitatibus*"), and points to difficulties, even sin, rather than mere weakness.

> Bright dawn of salvation, Virgin Mary; from you rose the Sun of justice, the Rising Sun who came to visit us from on high. (Morning Prayer)
> Hail Mary, full of grace: the Lord is with you. You are the most blessed of all women and blessed is the fruit of your womb. (Evening Prayer)

SCRIPTURE READINGS

a) Isaiah 66:10-14

The text chosen for the celebration has several echoes of the Lourdes experience. It is a prophecy of restoration, having as its immediate context the return after the captivity (582-538 B.C.). The people are depressed and cynical about any deliverance, but the prophet gives a message of hope. Jerusalem, here standing for the people as well as the city, is to *rejoice*: the people are to be *suckled and satisfied*. The vision of Jerusalem as mother caring for her children merges into an account of God's loving plan: he will send *peace* flowing like a *river*; indeed the *glory* of the city will be like a *river in spate*—one is reminded of the swift-flowing Gave river at Lourdes. In the restoration God will be like a mother of his people who will be *suckled, carried, fondled, comforted*. The divine blessing will cause the people to *rejoice* for their *limbs* will *regain vigour like the grass*—an image of health and well-being.

The *response* focuses on Mary as it takes up the praise of Judith, "you are the highest honour of our race."

b) John 2:1-11[2]

The memorial of Our Lady of Lourdes is the only marian celebration in the revised Missal and Lectionary to use this account of the wedding at Cana. It is otherwise found only in Year A at the end of the Epiphany cycle which commemorates the epiphanies, or manifestations, of Christ, as in the hymn of the Liturgy of the Hours:

> Manifested by the star
> To the sages from afar...
> Manifest at Jordan's stream,
> Prophet, priest and king supreme;
> And at Cana wedding guest
> In thy Godhead manifest. (C. Wordsworth 1807-85)

The Gospel of this manifestation in which Jesus *revealed his glory, and his disciples believed in him*, is not without difficulties. These centre on Mary's words, his enigmatic reply, and the meaning of the *sign* which is the miracle of the wine.

The text opens with the words, *On the third day*. Many scholars see in the first two chapters of the gospel a week having a climax in Cana on the third day after the meeting with Philip and Nathanael (Jn 1:43-51). We should also be alert to the quite

---

[2]On the text see R.E. Brown, *The Gospel According to John.* "The Anchor Bible." 2 vols. (Garden City, NY: Doubleday, 1966—London: Chapman, 1971) 1:95-111 (abbreviated below Brown, *John*); McHugh 351-403; X. Léon-Dufour, "Le signe de Cana ou les noces de Dieu avec Israël," *La vie et la Parole. Études offertes à Pierre Grélot* (Paris: Desclée, 1987) 229-40; M. O'Carroll, *Theotokos* 95-97 with extensive bibliography; R. Schnackenburg, *The Gospel According to St. John.* 3 vols. (New York: Herder and Herder—London: Burns and Oates, 1968-82) 1:323-340.

common symbolism of the third day being a decisive one (e.g. Ex 19:16; Hos 6:2 and of course the resurrection).[3]

The text tells us that *the mother of Jesus was there* and that *Jesus and his disciples had also been invited*. Perhaps a relative of Mary, and hence of Jesus, was being married, we do not know. For the long wedding celebrations that lasted several days, it was customary for guests to bring a gift of wine.[4] It would be unlikely that Jesus and his disciples brought any. He is pictured in the gospel as living austerely (see Mt 8:20, though 11:19 and Lk 7:34 should also be kept in mind). The augmented number of guests, as commentators and preachers often suggest, could have contributed to the shortage.

Mary approaches Jesus and says to him, *they have no wine*. The words themselves do not imply a request for a miracle, though a similar phrase used by the sisters of Lazarus implies that they hoped for an intervention from Jesus: "Lord, the man you love is ill" (Jn 11:3 with v. 21: "Lord, if you had been here . . . "). However the reply of Jesus does seem to indicate that Mary was requesting Jesus to intervene: *Woman, what do you want from me? My hour has not come yet*. There are several problems about this response. *Woman* is a normal respectful address of Jesus recorded elsewhere in the Gospels (e.g. Mt 15:28; Lk 13:12; Jn 4:21; 8:10). But it is quite an extraordinary expression from a son to his mother, and scholars have not found a similar filial address in Hebrew or Greek.[5] The only parallel is to be found in John 19:26 when Jesus says from the cross, "Woman, this is your son." R.E. Brown notes that whilst Catholic exegetes usually read too much into this text Protestant exegetes pass over the verse as if it were unthinkable that Mary played a role in Johannine theology.[6] If we

---

[3]See Brown, *John* 1:105-107 for views. Léon-Dufour prefers "third day" as being a decisive one, art.cit. 234.

[4]See J.D.M. Derrett quoted in Brown, *John* 1:102.

[5]See Brown, *John* 1:99.

[6]Ibid. 1:107 where he also praises the treatment of the text by M. Thurian, as being not only the best Protestant evaluation, but far superior to many Catholic ones—see

bring together John 2:4 and 19:26 we find a distinctive Johannine procedure. Here as in other texts we find Jesus (and others) "seeing through" a person to a deeper truth about them than what is apparent.[7] Jesus sees his *mother*, but calls her *woman*: he sees beyond her immediate presence to the role she will after- wards play. Though the full doctrine of Mary as the New Eve (in contrast with the woman in Genesis 3) is not fully articulated by John, there are indications that Mary has a deeper role than merely being the one who bore Jesus.[8]

The statement of Jesus, *Woman, what do you want from me?* means literally "what to me and to you?" It is a Hebrew expression that should have one of two meanings.[9] Firstly, when someone is unjustly bothering another, the injured party means to say, "what have I done that you should do this to me?" (e.g. Jdg 11:12; 2 Ch 35:21). There is some hostility implied in the idiom used in this way. Secondly, the phrase is used when someone is asked to get involved in a situation, and they answer, "This is your business, how am I involved?" (e.g. 2 Kgs 3:13; Hos 14:8). The answer of Jesus belongs somehow to this second usage; there is no hostility in Jesus' attitude, but there is some reluctance. And the reason he gives is, *my hour has not come yet.*

His *hour*, here as elsewhere in John, is the climactic hour of his passion and glorification. Nonetheless, the reference is not clear. He is implying that had his hour come, things might have been different. It is only with his exaltation that there will be a defini-

---

Marie, Mère du Seigneur, Figure de l'Église published in England as *Mary, Mother of the Lord. Figure of the Church* (London: Faith Press, 1963) but in the USA as *Mary, Mother of All Christians* (New York: Herder and Herder, 1964) 117-144.

[7]See Jn 1:42 where Jesus sees Peter, but recognises in him the rock (Cephas); 1:47 Nathanael is proclaimed as an Israelite without guile; 1:29 John the Baptist sees Jesus but recognises in him the Lamb of God. Here we have a notion of transparency (the *Durchsichtigkeit* so prominent in H. Urs von Balthasar): the eyes of Jesus, our eyes of faith, can penetrate appearances. Making a somewhat similar point is M. de Groedt, "Un schéma de révélation dans le Quatrième Evangile," *NTStudies* 8 (1962) 142-150.

[8]Brown, *John* 1:108-109.

[9]Ibid. 1:99.

tive overcoming of evil. For an absence of wine is no mere embarrassment; it is rather a symbol of desolation. In Isaiah 24:6-11 lack of wine sums up the utter distress of the people, while an abundance of wine signifies the return of God's blessing (25:6-11). The temporary upset of the wedding is a symbol of the much deeper misfortunes of the Old Testament peoples. It will be at the *hour* of Jesus that deliverance is to come. Then Mary will share in the work of Jesus, uniting herself in mind and heart with his mission (see Vatican II, LG 58). Indeed Jesus distances himself from his family during his public mission, and even earlier at the age of twelve (see Lk 2:41-50). Just as there was in his youth a superior call of his heavenly Father, so too in his ministry he pointedly states on several occasions that faith, and doing the will of God, are decisive, and not blood relationship (see Mk 3:31 and par.; Lk 11:27-28). With the coming of Jesus' hour, Mary, who heard the word and kept it (see Lk 2:19.51 with 8:15) will have a new and special role in the christian community. She will then again be "Woman" (see Jn 19:26) at the "hour" of Jesus.[10]

We do not really have a sufficiently detailed account of the incident to understand Mary's response to Jesus' apparent refusal to become involved. She is not put off, however, for she asks the servants, using words also found in Genesis 41:55, to do all that Jesus will ask.[11] Though she senses that he will act, she does not anticipate what his action might be, but merely says *Do whatever he tells you.* And we are told that he changes the contents of *six stone water jars* into wine, that is, he provided in excess of 120 gallons of wine.

The account of the wedding at Cana is not the description of a prodigy for the evangelist is concerned to highlight theological implications of the miracle. With reasonable probability we can point out several of these. Firstly, the jars of Old Testament

[10]Ibid. 1:109.

[11]See J. McPolin, *John.* "New Testament Message 6" (Wilmington: Glazier—Dublin: Veritas, 1979, 1982²) 25.

purification become vessels of New Testament wine.[12] Secondly, Mary stands at the junction of the two Testaments. She recalls the great act of faith and commitment of her people at Sinai, "Whatever Yahweh has said, we will do" (Ex 19:8). She points out her Son at the wedding feast, and to all of us. She asks obedience to him. As Pope John Paul II states:

> The Mother of Christ presents herself as the spokeswoman of her Son's will, pointing out those things that must be done so that the salvific power of the Messiah may be manifested. (RM 21)

Here we see Mary acting out one of the classical poses of the icon tradition, the *Hodegetria*, "Mary pointing the Way" which is her Son. This *first of Jesus' signs*, one in which the mission and meaning of Jesus is revealed, shows his mother as involved:

> Mary is present in Cana of Galilee as Mother of Jesus, and in a significant way she contributes to the 'beginning of the signs' which reveal the messianic power of her Son ... At Cana, thanks to the intercession of Mary and the obedience of the servants, Jesus begins 'his hour.' At Cana Mary appears as believing in Jesus. Her faith evokes his first 'sign' and helps to kindle the faith of the disciples. (RM 21)

Thirdly, we see the theme of superabundance of wine, itself a sign in the Old Testament of God's blessing (see Amos 9:13-14; Hos 14:8; Jer 31:12). St. Thomas notes that Jesus did not create the wine, but changed Old Testament water into wine:

> He did not wish to make wine from nothing (*ex nihilo*), but he made wine from water, to show that he was not establishing a completely new doctrine; he was not destroying

---

[12]See Léon-Dufour, art. cit. 231 and 235, which stresses that it is the *jars* for ablution, rather than the water that are singled out by the evangelist. On other replacement themes in John (Temple, living bread, real Light, etc.) see Brown, *John* 1:109.

the old, but fulfilling it, as we find in Matthew 5:17, 'I did not come to abolish, but to complete.'[13]

Thus we can conclude with R. Schnackenburg, "The significance of the wine is that it is Jesus' gift, a sign that comes from him, and points to him."[14] Fourthly, in the first chapter of John, Jesus has been proclaimed Messiah, the one who also was eternally with God. In this incident there is an emphasis on "now" as the time to accept him (see "hour" in 2:4 and the double "now" vv. 8.10). The *sign* reveals the *glory* of Jesus (v.11) but only to the one who has faith and is a disciple.

CHURCH DOCUMENTS

Pope Paul VI classes the celebration of this memorial as one of the

> kinds of commemorations connected with local devotions which have acquired a wider popularity and interest. (MC 8)

The reason is clear and has been well enunciated by Pope John XXIII in the radio message for the close of the Lourdes centenary year:

> Thousands indeed of Christians of every condition and race have come to Lourdes, united in the same faith and in the same love for the heavenly Mother. Are they not like representatives of the immense catholic family and witnesses of the human community that longs for fraternity and peace? Blessed be Our Lady who, in drawing us to her sanctuary in the Pyrenees, shows the world this astonishing spectacle of universality and love. And if, besides these public manifesta-

---

[13]*In John* 2, lect.l (Marietti ed. 358). See also Schnackenburg, op.cit. (n. 2) 338.

[14]Schnackenburg, op.cit. (n. 2) 337.

tions, we evoke the silent work of grace, our gratitude grows all the more: how many in darkness received light at Lourdes! How many tepid or hardened hearts have got the grace to return to God! How many unsteady wills have received the strength to persevere! In the silence of wordless prayer, or in the midst of eucharistic or marian acclamations, generous people have received the joy of a more generous gift of themselves. The sick received, if not always a cure, at least resignation and serenity in offering their sufferings, whilst the dying learned there to make peacefully the sacrifice of their lives. How wonderful in the eyes of God is this secret history engraved on peoples' hearts; a history of the victory of God, 'who has rescued us from the ruling force of darkness and transferred us to the kingdom of the Son that he loves' (Col 1:13-14).[15]

REFLECTION

The fact that the Latin Church is invited to celebrate a memorial, albeit an optional one, directly connected with an apparition raises some questions. There have been apparitions, or more likely supposed visions of Mary, associated with other feasts, but these latter have a value and status independent of any such apparition, i.e. Our Lady of the Rosary, Our Lady of Mount Carmel, the Dedication of Saint Mary Major. When we honour Mary as Our Lady of a place, we are implicitly saying that we wish to reverence her as she is honoured in that place, or that we wish to receive favours such as she is seen to bestow there.

Before we ask about the significance of Lourdes in the life of the Church it is necessary to dwell on the whole issue of apparitions and visions.[16] We can describe an apparition as the visible

---

[15]*AAS* 51 (1959) 144-148 at 144-145. In similar vein is the letter *Cum annus* of Pope Benedict XV in *AAS* 11 (1919) 37.

[16]See K. Rahner, *Visions and Prophecies.* "Quaetiones Disputatae 10" (Freiburg: Herder—London: Burns and Oates, 1963); R. Laurentin, "Apparizioni," *NDizM* 125-137; J. Aumann, "Visions," *New Catholic Encyclopedia* 14:717; S. De Fiores, "Veggente," in S.

manifestation of a being whose appearance at that place and at that time is quite unusual and inexplicable according to the normal order of things.[17] Associated with apparitions there is usually a "message" for which it is difficult to find an appropriate descriptive term. In recent times the "message" has usually been called a "private revelation," but this manner of speaking is open to some serious objections. On the one hand the message is scarcely "private"—it is well known and in many cases can have a prophetic character for the whole Church. One has only to think of the calls to conversion, to penance and to prayer (especially for sinners) associated with Lourdes and Fatima. On the other hand to call a message a "revelation" can cause confusion with the central revelation of the christian faith, a revelation which closed with the end of the apostolic age. R. Laurentin suggests that we speak of the "foundational" revelation which is the basis of our faith, and "particular" revelations which have occurred since the time of the primitive Church. Indeed if we examine the contents of particular revelations we can note that they tend to be more practical than speculative, a point made by St. Thomas,[18] and later taken up by Pope John XXIII: "they are not to proclaim a new doctrine of faith, but to direct human actions."[19] Again particular revelations are concerned more with hope and charity than with faith.

There is a process of discernment needed in the case of apparitions. Though in recent times, beginning with Guadalupe (1531), some apparitions have been approved either directly or indirectly by Church authorities, several hundred alleged apparitions have never been accepted. Some of these latter were obviously false such as the "visionaries" in Necedah (USA), who left the Church, or Palmar di Troya which at best is schismatic and at worst

De Fiores and T. Goffi, eds., *Nuovo dizionario di spiritualità* (Turin: Ed. Paoline, 1985) 1662-1677.

[17]See Laurentin, "Apparizioni" (n. 16) 126ff to which this section is much indebted.

[18]*Summa theologiae* 2a2ae, q.174, a.6 ad 3.

[19]Radio message at conclusion of Lourdes centenary, *AAS* 51 (1959) 147

heretical. Approbation is usually the prerogative of the local bishop. After investigating all the circumstances he can, if he is satisfied, allow worship at the place.

The classical theological position on apparitions is that of Benedict XIV in a work on beatification which he wrote a few years before becoming pope. He stated clearly that even when an approbation of visions or apparitions is given, the assent of catholic faith is not demanded, and for a good reason one can withhold consent, the assent in any case being human.[20] This technical language needs some examination.

The point at issue is the obligation to believe, and hence the kind of belief that particular revelations demand. Faith is an assent, a yes, to God who speaks, promises or commands. We make an act of faith in God because he is absolute truth and because he has revealed his will or his mystery to us. The reason for faith is the veracity of God, who, in the words of the earlier catechisms "cannot either deceive nor be deceived." We have to make an act of faith in what is revealed in the scripture, or solemnly proposed by the Church as belonging to divine revelation.[21] Particular revelations do not make such peremptory demands. Firstly, it is only by an act of human faith that we believe that a particular revelation has taken place. Secondly, there cannot be a revelation that is strictly speaking "new": a message from a genuine apparition will focus our attention only on what has already been revealed.[22] One could say, however, that to disbelieve in the fact of apparitions at Lourdes and Fatima would be quite temerarious, since both apparitions—Fatima to a lesser degree—have received significant papal support and are widely accepted by the faithful who have a deep spiritual instinct in matters of faith and morals (Vatican II, LG 12). Nonetheless one

---

[20]See *De servorum Dei beatificatione* 2:32, 11; 3:53, 15, and K. Rahner, op.cit. (n. 16) 82-84.

[21]See F.A. Sullivan, *Magisterium. Teaching Authority in the Church* (Dublin: Gill and Macmillan—New York Mahwah, NJ: Paulist, 1983) 61; Rahner, op.cit. 82-83.

[22]Rahner, op.cit. (n. 16) 25-26, 105-106.

would not be outside catholic faith or outside the Church if one rejected some, or even all, of the apparitions which have received approval. Furthermore, one should note the caution of K. Rahner in the matter: he is particularly insistent that even when an apparition has been approved, there can be several facets of "messages" that are open to suspicion or even rejection.

> Much more will a critical attitude be permissible towards the details of a vision which, as a whole, is recognised as genuine.[23]

Finally there is a question of attitudes to apparitions. We can be wrong in being deaf to evangelical calls to penance and prayer that are being given to the Church through some apparition: such calls are not welcome to our sinful condition. But there is another extreme of being focused excessively on visions and apparitions. The calm sober warning of K. Rahner is still apposite for our time, even though written over twenty years ago:

> Where private revelations (for example of new devotions) are taken as disclosing a spiritual trick, a method for acquiring holiness at little cost or changing the way of the Cross into pure joy, or where the entire spiritual life is reduced to revolving round one revelation (however genuine in itself), whose content, in comparison with the whole wide world of Christian truth by which we should live, is bound to be meagre—we can conclude that even genuine revelations have certainly been misunderstood and misapplied.... Lovers of revelations and apparitions should not forget either (as often happens) that Christ appears to us most surely in the poor and suffering. In the Sacrament and in the grace of the Holy Ghost, offered to every Christian, we have God's real presence. The Cross is true mercy, and charity the highest of all gifts. If we do not recognize the

---

[23]Ibid. 83. Note too Rahner's frequent disquiet in this book about some of the details of the Fatima apparitions as reported by various authors.

hand that chastises us as God's merciful and healing hand, we shall not find him in 'revelations' either.[24]

When then we come to consider the meaning of Lourdes for the Church today, we should look at the apparitions and at Bernadette herself, as well as at what is happening there continually in our time. As to the first, the message is not in any way innovative: prayer, especially for the conversion of sinners, penance, and in the direction given by recent popes, prayer for peace. Bernadette followed this call. As R. Laurentin remarks, she profoundly, heroically, and painfully interiorized the evangelical message of Lourdes for the rest of her life.[25] Pope John XXIII speaks of Bernadette's withdrawal from the world, even from Lourdes itself and concludes:

> Lourdes is still a call to penance and to that charity that enables us to detach ourselves from riches and teaches us how to share with those poorer than ourselves. We take up this message now, at a time when millions are aware— unfortunately at times with a violent response—of the scandalous contrast between the wealth of some and the insufficient livelihood of others.[26]

Lourdes is a place of pilgrimage. A pilgrimage is a journey to a holy place, and the actual journey takes on a sacred character. Pilgrimages are known in most religions that have holy places.[27] In our days of easy travel, with food and drink served on comfortable airliners on the way to Lourdes, the spirit of pilgrimage is

[24]Ibid. 84-85.

[25]See "Apparizioni" NDizM 128.

[26]Radio message, 18 February 1959, AAS 51 (1959) 148.

[27]See S.M. Polan, M.C. McCarthy and E.R. Labande, "Pilgrimages," New Catholic Encyclopedia 11:362-372. For comparative religion see B.N. Aziz, "Personal Dimensions of the Sacred Journey: What the Pilgrims Say," Religious Studies 23 (1987) 247-261. E. Turner et al., "Pilgrimage," Encyclopedia of Religion, II: 327-354; J.B. Chethimattam, "Religions and Pilgrimages," Jeevadhara 12 (1982) 341-357.

hard to sustain. Perhaps a spiritual preparation before departure is particularly necessary today.

At Lourdes we are struck by the spring that bubbled up when in obedience to Our Lady's command Bernadette scratched the ground. Her words, "Go drink and wash in the fountain," are still obeyed today, and water from Lourdes is treasured by very many catholics all over the world. This water is one of the elements which are associated with Lourdes as a shrine of healing. It is useful to make a distinction between curing and healing.[28] There have been quite a number of cures at Lourdes, only a small number of which have passed the criteria of the very stringent International Medical Commission and the final judgement of the bishop. A cure is the restoration of health. We can use the word "healing" in a wider sense as covering what Jesus promised, "I came that they may have life and have it to the full" (Jn 10:10). Many, perhaps even the majority, of people who come to Lourdes are healed: they come into a greater fullness of life. The areas in which healing may occur are physical, psychological, and spiritual. A characteristic of healing is inner peace. With healing people find new strength, new hope, new courage, even when the situation to which they return has not changed. That is, they are healed, but not cured.

Of particular importance at Lourdes, as in other marian shrines, is the Eucharist.[29] It is notable that many of the cures at Lourdes do not take place in the healing baths, but during the procession of the Blessed Sacrament. As at the wedding in Cana, Mary still points to her Son. Her shrines are places where he is honoured, where he receives pilgrims who want to enter into deeper discipleship. At Lourdes and at other shrines we are alerted to the healing power of the sacraments, especially the Eucharist during which we pray, "Say but the word and I shall be healed." The

---

[28]See C. O'Donnell, *Life in the Spirit and Mary* Wilmington: Glazier—Dublin: Dominican Publications, 1981) 110-113.

[29]See A. Cabes, "La pastorale liturgique à Lourdes," *La Maison-Dieu* 170 (1987) 102-118.

signs and wonders at Lourdes are not only the relatively small number of cures, but the courage of the sick, the care of the poor, the love of relatives and friends for the sick and handicapped, the united prayer and praise of God that arises from individuals, each one carrying his or her own burden of sorrow or pain.

PRAYER OF THE FAITHFUL

Let us pray to our heavenly Father that the message of Lourdes may be a comfort for all his people.

- We pray that the Lourdes call for penance may be heeded throughout the Church.
- We pray for the healing of the nations through reconciliation, peace and love.
- We pray that those who have recourse to the Virgin conceived without sin may experience her motherly care.
- We pray for those who travel to Lourdes, for those who organize pilgrimages, for the people of the town itself: that they may all know the healing grace of Christ.
- We pray for the sick throughout the world: that they may receive healing and come to fullness of life and inner peace no matter what their illness may be.
  Heavenly Father, we thank you for the revelation of your Son, Jesus, born of the Immaculate Virgin; hear these prayers which we confidently make with her intercession and in the name of Jesus, your Son and our Lord.

ADDITIONAL READING

I. de la Potterie, "Mary and the Mystery of Cana," *Theology Digest* 29 (1981) 40-42.

A. Feuillet, *Johannine Studies* (New York: Alba, 1964) 17-37.

M. Gourgues, "Marie, la 'temme' et la 'mère' en gean" *Nov velle revne théologique* 108 (1986) 174-191.

J.A. Grassi, "The Role of Jesus' Mother in John's Gospel. A Reappraisal," *Catholic Biblical Quarterly* 48 (1986) 67-80.

A. Serra, *Maria a Cana e presso la croce.* (Rome: Centro Mater Ecclesiae, 1985) 9-78.

P. Triple, *God and the Rhetoric of Sexuality* (Philadelphia: Fortress, 1978) 66-68 on Is 66:10-14.

3. J.M. Alonso, B. Billet, B. Bobrinskoy, R. Laurentin and M. Oraison, *Vraies et fausses apparitions dans l'Eglise* (Paris: Lethielleux—Montreal: Bellarmin, 1973).

C.B. Daly, "The Meaning of Lourdes" in K. McNamara, ed., *Mother of the Redeemer* (Dublin: Gill, 1959) 251-285.

R.D. Lawler, "Divine Faith, Private Revelation, Popular Devotion," *Marian Studies* 38 (1984) 100-110.

R. Laurentin, *Bernadette of Lourdes. A Life Based on Authenticated Documents* (London: Darton, Longman & Todd, 1979).

L. Volken, *Le rivelazioni nella Chiesa* (Rome: Ed. Paoline, 1963). *Vivre l'Eucharistie avec Marie* (Paris: Cahiers Mariales—Desclée de Brovwer, 1981). *Etudes Mariales* 36-37 (1979-80) 1-147—on Mary and Eucharist.

THE ANNUNCIATION OF THE LORD
(Solemnity—25 March)

LITURGICAL HISTORY

The Annunciation is clearly tied to the feast nine months later of the birth of the Lord, 25 December. Originally there was a celebration of the Annunciation on the 4th Sunday in Advent, dating from the fourth,[1] or fifth[2] century. The feast of the Annunciation is found in the sixth century in the East, but the first certain evidence for a celebration on 25 March is in the following century, though there are sermons on the Annunciation from the

[1]See Roschini 4:69.

[2]M.M. Pedico, *La Domenica mariana prenatilizia* (Rovigo: Centro Mariano SMR, 1979) especially 26-28.

time of Peter Chrysologus (d. about 450).

The Syro-Sicilian Pope Sergius (687-701) laid down that there be a procession from St. Hadrian's in the Roman Forum to St. Mary Major for this feast as well as for the Birthday, and Assumption of Mary—a procession similar to the one decreed for the Presentation (2 February). There were various names for the feast from early times: "Annunciation of the Angel to the Blessed Virgin Mary," "Annunciation of Christ," "Conception of Christ." It quickly took on the character of a marian feast. In the recent liturgical reform, however, the feast was given back its ancient name, "Annunciation of the Lord."

THEMES

The solemnity has as its main focus the Incarnation: God became man to save us. The Son of God came into this world in obedience (entrance antiphon). The prayers of the Mass and the preface all stress the title of Virgin for Mary. We celebrate the first beginnings of the church (prayer over gifts), the possibility of salvation for all peoples (preface) and we look forward in hope to the fuller realization of our salvation (opening and post-communion prayers).

> The Holy Spirit will come upon you and the power of the most High will overshadow you. (Evening Prayer 1)
> God loved the world so much that he sent his own Son in a nature like ours. (Morning Prayer)
> I am the servant of the Lord: let it be done to me as you have said. (Evening Prayer 2)
> The Mother of God heard expressions she did not understand when the Archangel said to her the words of the Annunciation. She accepted the greeting with faith and conceived You, O God who exist before eternity. Wherefore we sing to you with joy: O God who were incarnate of her and yet suffered no change, bestow peace and your great mercy upon the world. (*Byzantine Daily Worship* 660)

SCRIPTURE READINGS

a) Isaiah 7:10-14

In a time of national peril King Achaz wants to engage himself in political alliances. He is instead told to trust in the Lord, to adopt a policy of faith in God. The Lord addresses him through Isaiah, *Ask Yahweh your God for a sign.* But because he does not want to obey the Lord he refuses with feigned piety, *I will not ask. I will not put Yahweh to the test* (see Dt 6:16—"Do not put Yahweh your God to the test as you tested him at Massah"). A sign is nonetheless given to him the *birth* of a *son,* whose mother *will call him Immanuel,* a name which means God-with-us. This text in Isaiah does not clearly point to the birth of Christ, and the immediate purport may be the promise of a son to Achaz. But the Hebrew word *'almah* (a young woman) was translated as *parthenos* (a virgin) in the Greek LXX translation. Though the Jews did not consider Is 7:14 to be messianic, Matthew clearly sees a fulfilment of this text in the virginal conception of Jesus (see Mt 1:23).[3] In the solemnity of the Annunciation a key idea is that through Mary's yes God-is-with-us.

The *response* prepares for the next reading: "Here I am, O Lord, to do your will,"

b) Hebrews 10:4-10

In this text we are at the heart of the kenotic redemption ("kenotic" from *kenosis*—emptying—in Ph 2:7). It is through the sacrificial obedience and the self-emptying of the Son of God that we are saved. The imperfect priesthood of the Old Testament is contrasted with the perfect priesthood of Christ. The sacrifices of the Old Testament were *incapable of taking away sins.* So Jesus is envisaged as coming into the world saying, *Here I am! I am coming*

---

[3]See *Mary NT* 91-92; Brown 143-153; H. Cazelles, "La Septante d'Is 7, 14" in A.M. Triacca and A. Pistoia, eds., *La Mère de Jèsus-Christ et la communion des saints dans la liturgie. "Conférences* Saint-Serge 1985" (Rome: CLV, 1986) 45-54.

to do your will (see Ps 40:6-8). We are *made holy by the offering of the body of Jesus Christ made once and for all.*

c) Luke 1:26-38

The gospel tells the story of the Annunciation. Luke models the narrative on Old Testament announcement stories in which there are several common features: the visionary is addressed by name; the visionary is described and told not to fear; the woman is to give birth; a name is given and its meaning; the future accomplishments of the child are foretold (see Gen 16:7-12—Ishmael; Gen 17:1-18: 15—Isaac; Jdg 13:3-21—Samson). More immediately the Annunciation to Mary is parallel to the one given to Zechariah (Lk 1:11-21).[4]

But there are some important differences. The angel does not at first call Mary by her name, but addresses her as *you who enjoy God's favour. The Lord is with you.* It is as it were her truest identity to have been deeply blessed by God. She is also told, *Rejoice.* The Greek word here is used in several places in the Old Testament with messianic connotations.[5] The angel then goes on to tell Mary that she is to *conceive* and *bear a son* who is to be named *Jesus.* God's message comes to Mary as she is, a Hebrew young woman. It is thus couched in Old Testament terms: *he will be Son of the Most High*; he will be given *the throne of his ancestor David; he will rule over the house of Jacob forever and his reign will have no end.* After the infancy narratives Luke will abandon this Old Testament language and begin to present Christ in terms of lowliness.

Scarcely any scholar today would claim that we have a verbatim transcript of the dialogue between Mary and the angel. Even assuming that we have a fairly accurate account of the thrust of the encounter, we still could not assume that Mary would have understood her role as that of being Mother of God. Mary's faith

[4]See *Mary NT* 112-115; Brown 155-158.

[5]See Zeph 3:14; Jl 2:21; Zech 9:9 all with *chaire* (rejoice) as in Lk 1:28. For interpretations suggestive of a deliberate evocation of these texts by Luke see McHugh 37-48; Laurentin 67-68, but note also reservations of *Mary NT* 128-134; Brown 321-325.

and understanding of her Son and of both their roles would grow only gradually—Easter and Pentecost would have been important stages in the development of her understanding. We must at all times make a distinction between what Mary knew at different stages of her life and what the evangelist knew in the light of the Paschal Mystery, Pentecost and the fruit of five decades of reflection by the Church prior to the composition of his gospel about the year 80 A.D.

Mary's response to the angel, *But how can this come about, since I have no knowledge of man?*, has been the subject of many differing interpretations.[6] As late as 1974 the Italian translation of the Bible from the Bishops' Conference carried a note to the effect that a vow or intention of virginity is indicated by the question. Few scholars would go that far today.[7] The vast majority simply deny a vow or resolution to preserve virginity, as for example in the *New Jerusalem Bible*. The tradition about some decision with regard to virginity on the part of Mary is quite ancient, going back at least to St. Gregory of Nyssa.[8] Hence it is not surprising to find scholars who would wish to take cognizance of some desire or preference for virginity.[9] In this line perhaps the most satisfactory account is that of Karl Rahner who sees a resolution to remain a virgin as implicit:

> ...she possessed the whole dignity of the will to virginity,
> in the unconditional surrender of her whole self in obedience
> and faith to the will of God, even if within the mental

---

[6]For survey see McHugh 173-199; Brown 303-309.

[7]A notable exception would be Laurentin 189. See too J. Galot who defends an intention of remaining a virgin, for otherwise Mary would not have always been virginal in her heart, *Dieu et la Femme. Marie dans l'oeuvre du salut* (Louvain: Ed. Sintal, n.d.) 143-156.

[8]Sermon from 386 a.d., *In diem natalem Christi*, PG 46:1140/*EnMar* 512. In the West see Augustine, *De sancta virginitate*, PL 40:398/*EnMar* 890.

[9]Thus I. de la Potterie, "L'annuncio a Maria (Lc 1, 26-38)" in *La Madre del Signore*. "Parola spirito e vita. Quaderni di lettura biblica 6" (Bologna: Centro Dehoniano, 1986) 55-73 at 68-69.

perspectives of the Old Testament, she may not, we may suppose, have explicitly realized before the angel's message, that this will of God, to which she was entirely submissive, signified for her perpetual virginity.... Her will to virginity is in a true sense fully comprised in the readiness of the blessed Virgin to submit absolutely and unreservedly always and everywhere to the decrees of God's holy will in whatever form; it is implicit in her freedom and her love as she said: Behold the handmaid of the Lord.[10]

There are other ways of looking at Mary's question that do not bring up the question of an intention of virginity on the part of Mary. J. McHugh suggests that Luke has put this question on Mary's lips because he knows that Mary would remain a virgin:

Luke is asserting *not* that Mary at the moment before the Incarnation had already made a resolution to remain a virgin forever, but that she had in fact been *destined* to remain a virgin all her life. In short, Luke (writing probably between A.D. 70 and 80) is here implicitly affirming that Mary had *in fact* remained a virgin all her life.[11] (italics of author)

R. Brown sees the question as a literary device to move on to another stage of revelation, that is, a specification of how the birth is to take place.[12]

Perhaps the most satisfactory explanation of the question is also a very simple one. Since Luke, along with Matthew, asserts a virginal conception, it is more natural to see Mary's question as a simple inquiry about how the birth of the Messiah is to come about. Since she is a virgin, but engaged to be married to Joseph, she is asking what she is to do: is the child to be fathered by

[10]*Mary Mother of the Lord. Theological Meditations* (Freiburg: Herder—Edinburgh/London: Nelson, 1963) 66-67.

[11]From an essay in the forthcoming, J. Hyland, ed., *Mary and the Church Today. Papers of the National Marian Congress 1984* (Athlone, Ireland: Marist Brothers—Dublin Veritas, 1988). The idea is also developed in McHugh 193-199.

[12]See Brown 307-309.

Joseph, or has God some other plan? Hence unlike Zechariah's doubting question (Lk 1:18) Mary is portrayed as already assenting to God's will, *But how can this come about?* The reply is that *the Holy Spirit will come upon* her, *and the power of the Most High will cover* her *with its shadow.* The conception will therefore be virginal.

Mary is also told, *nothing is impossible to God.* This saying is found in several places in the scripture where there would appear to be insurmountable difficulties—Sarah's age and barrenness (Gen 18:14; see Rm 4:21), the threat to Jerusalem from the Babylonians (Jer 32:27; see too Zech 8:6), the mystery of God's power and wisdom (Jb 42:2), the difficulty for the rich to enter the kingdom (Mt 19:26). Mary is thus given an assurance of God's power to fulfil his own plans. Her reply is the perfect act of faith, *You see before you the Lord's servant, let it happen to me as you have said.* The Greek word translated here as "servant" is more properly "slave"; Mary stands before the Lord as one who has surrendered her rights in total submission. Nor is this submission forced or grudging for the Greek uses the optative mood, which signifies not passive acquiescence but a deep desire, so that we might get the flavour of her reply by rendering it as: "Oh, yes, let it happen to me as you said." Mary's obedience to the Lord reflects the total obedience of her Son in coming into the world (2nd reading). Her *fiat* (Latin: let it be done) to God is perfect.

CHURCH DOCUMENTS

In his exhortation *Marialis cultus* Pope Paul VI develops the idea of the Annunciation as a joint feast of the Lord and Mary:

> For the solemnity of the Incarnation of the Word, in the Roman calendar the ancient title—the Annunciation of the Lord—has been deliberately restored, but the feast was and is a joint one of Christ and of the blessed Virgin: of the Word, who becomes 'Son of Mary' (Mk 6:3), and of the Virgin who becomes Mother of God. With regard to Christ, the East and the West, in the inexhaustible riches of their

liturgies, celebrate this Solemnity as the commemoration of the salvific 'fiat' of the Incarnate Word, who, entering the world, said: 'God, here I am! I am coming to obey your will' (cf. Heb 10:7; Ps 39:8-9). They commemorate it as the beginning of the redemption and of the indissoluble and wedded union of the divine nature with the human nature in the one Person of the Word. With regard to Mary, these liturgies celebrate it as a feast of the New Eve, the obedient and faithful virgin, who with her generous 'fiat' (cf. Lk 1:38) became through the working of the Holy Spirit the Mother of God, but also the true Mother of the living, and by receiving into her womb the one Mediator (cf. 1 Tm 2:5), became the true Ark of the covenant and true Temple of God. These liturgies celebrate it as a culminating moment in the salvific dialogue between God and man, and as a commemoration of the Blessed Virgin's free consent and cooperation in the plan of redemption. (MC 6)

The Pope is here developing ideas found in Vatican II (*Church* LG 56). Further ideas from the same passage in the Council are drawn out by Pope John Paul II (RM 13):

Indeed, at the Annunciation Mary entrusted herself to God completely, with the 'full submission of intellect and will,' manifesting 'the obedience of faith to him who spoke to her through his messenger' (Vatican II, *Revelation* 5). She responded, therefore, with all her human and feminine 'I', and this response of faith included both perfect cooperation with 'the grace of God that precedes and assists' and perfect openness to the action of the Holy Spirit, who 'constantly brings faith to completion by his gifts' (ibid., cf. LG 56).

REFLECTION

In recent years a lot of difficulties have clustered around the central ideas of this feast. We shall deal with some of them in later chapters, but here we take up the complex issue of the virginity of Mary. At the outset one source of difficulty can easily be eliminated: some people confuse the virginal conception (of Jesus) and the Immaculate Conception (of Mary). The real problems can be addressed through a graduated series of questions.

Firstly, did Luke speak of a virginal conception? Matthew clearly did (see Mt 1:18-25). The Lutheran-Roman Catholic study group concluded:

> The majority of the task force was persuaded that Luke really assumed and intended to describe a virginal conception, even though he did not make this point so clearly as did Matthew.[13]

Secondly, granted that Luke speaks of a virginal conception, can we deduce from his text that he is also asserting the *fact* of a virginal conception? This question differs substantially from the first. Luke may have spoken of a virginal conception in order to present another truth, but may not have taught that there was historically a virginal conception. This mode of teaching is technically called a theologoumenon, a word used in differing senses, but which here could be called an expression of theology in narrative form.[14]

In reply to the question we can note that there are those who quite simply deny the fact of virginal conception, e.g. L. Evely[15] and H. Küng[16] the latter being censured for the view by the Sacred Congregation for the Doctrine of the Faith. This position

---

[13]*Mary NT* 120.

[14]See S. de Fiores, "Vergine" *NDizM* 1422. Note that we are not using the term in the more generalized sense: "Theologoumenon. This term may be used to designate a theological doctrine that is not directly taught by the Church's magisterium and thus does not authoritatively demand our consent, but is of such a nature that it sheds light on the connection among other explicit doctrines of the Church and for this reason is commendable." K. Rahner and H. Vorgrimler, *Concise Theological Dictionary* (London: Burns and Oates—New York: Herder, 1965)

[15]*The Gospels without Myth* (Garden City, NY: Doubleday, 1971) 80-82.

[16]*On Being a Christian* (London: Collins—Garden City, NY: Doubleday, 1977) 453-457.

would seem to be in clear conflict with the faith of the Church. Unacceptable too is any attempt to leave the matter open, thus allowing for the possibility of Joseph's being the biological father of Jesus, as for example in the first edition of the so-called *Dutch Catechism*.[17]

Quite different is the conclusion of scholars such as R. Brown who assert that by the tools of historical-critical exegesis a virginal conception cannot be proved in the scriptures. Such a position lies within the boundaries of catholic faith, even though it may be unwise and insufficiently grounded. It is important to see clearly the exact point that is being made by such scholars. Thus R. Brown:

> My judgement, in conclusion, is that the totality of the *scientifically controllable* evidence leaves an unresolved problem.[18] (author's italics)

Similar is the view of the Lutheran-Roman Catholic task force:

> What we did agree upon, with some difference of emphasis among us, was the 'possibility and even probability of a pre-Gospel acceptance of the virginal conception.' In other words ... we traced the virginal conception to *Stage Two* (the formation of traditions about the events as they were interpreted through the eyes of faith), but recognized the inability of a modern scientific approach to trace it to Stage One, the stage of historicity—an inability that in no way constitutes a negation of historicity.[19]

---

[17]*A New Catechism* (New York: Herder—London: Burns and Oates, 1967) pp. 74-75 of 1st edition which was seen as leaving open the possibility of Joseph's being the biological father of Jesus. A revised edition at the behest of Rome and the Dutch bishops removed the ambiguity. For discussion of the whole issue see McHugh 459-461; C. Pozo, *Maria en la obra de la salvación*. "Historia Salutis" (Madrid: BAC, 1974) 265-284.

[18]*The Virginal Conception and Bodily Resurrection of Jesus* (New York: Paulist, 1973) 1-68 at 66-67. See also Brown 298-309 esp. 300-303.

[19]*Mary NT* 124-125 with 9-12 on stages of composition.

These scholars are not denying the virginal conception itself, but are asserting that by critical exegetical methods it cannot be proved.

There are also exegetes who are quite convinced that Luke is teaching here a biological fact, namely, that Joseph was not the father of Jesus, and that Mary conceived by the power of the Holy Spirit.[20] Their position seems more probable, and the argument of J. McHugh convincing:

> If Isaiah had never predicted a virginal conception, and if no Jew has ever suspected that he had done so, there would have been no point in making up such a story, for it would prove nothing to the Jews. . . . There is, I think, one argument which tells directly against accepting this view (a theologoumenon affirming only that Jesus' sonship was unique). If there is one thing certain from the Old Testament, it is that the Israelites most firmly believed that there would come a great deliverer, an anointed king, a 'Messiah,' and that he would be *of the seed of David* (see 2 Sm 7:12; Ps 132:11.17; Is 11:1-3 etc.); and no future research is likely to overturn this statement. And if there is one thing certain from the New Testament, it is that the early Christians most firmly believed that Jesus of Nazareth was this promised Messiah; it was the principal name they gave to him—*Jesus the Christ*. Now if those early Christians wanted to make up, for catechetical purposes, stories about his origin and birth, the obvious thing was to make up stories proving how he was truly descended, through his human father, from the seed of David. The last thing they would have been likely to think up was a tale that he had no human father at all, for that would be conclusive proof that he was *not* truly of the line of David, and therefore *not* the Messiah. The only factor which could possibly have induced them to affirm that he was conceived of a virgin mother was a firm conviction that everything had really so happened. And therefore we see, in Matt. 1:18-25, the emphasis on the fact that Joseph took Jesus

[20]From forthcoming *Mary and the Church Today* (n. 11 above).

as his own son: what the evangelist is there saying is that, *in spite of* the virginal conception, Jesus was still truly of the line of David, because he was legally adopted by Joseph. In short it seems to me inconceivable that the early Christians would have made up *this* particular story denying Jesus any human paternity unless they had been solidly convinced that the fact was so.[20] (author's italics)

One might allude to two other scriptural arguments that are in wide circulation. There is a reading in the prologue to John's gospel that indicates a virginal conception. The *New Jerusalem Bible* notes that there are strong arguments for reading "who was born not from human stock..." (Jn 1:13). In this case the text would refer to the divine origin of Jesus. But the strong arguments are not from the Greek manuscript tradition, but rather from patristic evidence. On the whole, French and Italian exegetes are more open to the singular reading,[21] but English speaking and German exegetes do not find the case convincing.[22]

More strongly based perhaps is the observation that Matthew and Luke both use the Greek word *gennaō* (meaning to generate) about human births, for instance that of John the Baptist, whilst they use the verb *tiktō* (to bear) or a passive of *gennaō* (was generated) about Jesus.[23] The vocabulary thus indicates a special origin of Jesus, and is supportive of a virginal conception.

And so we come to a third question. How can the Church profess as of faith a truth which reputable scholars like R. Brown

[21]e.g. French Jerusalem Bible; Laurentin 480-481; A. Serra, "Vergine," *NDizM* 1445-1448; J. Galot, *Etre né de Dieu. Jean 1:13.* "Analecta Biblica 37" (Rome: Pont. Instit. Biblicum, 1969). See also recent exposition M. Vellanickal, "*Who was born ... of God.* A Text-critical Study of John 1:13" in *La vie de la Parole, Études offertes à Pierre Grelot* (Paris: Desclée, 1987) 211-228; McHugh 255-268; I. de la Potterie, "Il parto verginale del Verbo incarnato: 'Non ex sanguinibus ... sed ex Deo natus est' (Gv 1:13)" *Marianum* 43 (1983) 127-174.

[22]e.g. Brown 520; *Mary NT* 181-182.

[23]See A. Vincent Cernuda, "El paralelismo *de ghenno y tikto* en Luc 1-2," *Biblica* 55 (1974) 260-264 and "La diálctica *ghenno—tikto*," *Biblica* 55 (1974) 408-417; Serra following Cernuda *NDizM* 1429-1431.

are not convinced they can establish in the scripture? The same problem arises even more acutely in the case of the Immaculate Conception and Assumption. But the scientific method of modern exegesis does not exhaust the meaning of scripture. The Church advances in her understanding of revelation not only through careful attention to scientific method, but also through prayerful pondering, mystical illumination, the charisms of the Holy Spirit. The results of these understandings of scripture should never contradict scientific exegesis, but they will go considerably beyond it.[24] We would then answer the third question by saying that the Church's Spirit-guided reflection on the texts of Matthew and Luke (and other texts, such as the whole prologue of John's gospel) led to a certainty of divine faith that the conception of Jesus was in fact virginal. Hence the creeds could assert that Jesus was born from the Virgin Mary.[25]

We continue an exposition of the question of Mary's virginity, even though it takes us a bit beyond the themes of the Solemnity of the Annunciation. Thus we ask fourthly, is it the faith of the Church that Mary was ever virgin? The first use of the expression "Ever Virgin" (*aeiparthenos*) in a council was at Constantinople II (553),[26] after which it became commonplace, and can be said to reflect the faith of the Church. When we examine the word "ever" we can see that there are three phases of Mary's virginity: before, during and after the birth of Christ (*ante partum, in partu* and *post partum*). Though long traditional,[27] the exact expression

[24]See C. O'Donnell, "Mary in Theology and Devotion Today," *Doctrine and Life* 37 (1987) 443-456 at 449-451; on Immaculate Conception and Assumption see F.A. Sullivan, *Magisterium. Teaching Authority in the Catholic Church* (New York: Paulist—Dublin: Gill and Macmillan, 1983) 17, 22, 105, 130.

[25]See DS 10-30

[26]See DS 422/TCC 255

[27]E.g. Leo 1 (d.461) "A virgin she conceived, a virgin she gave birth, a virgin she remained" *Sermon* 22, 2—PL 54:195/*EnMar* 1330. Often taken in a marian sense are indications in the Lateran Council of 649, even though it is clear that the council was speaking more about Christ than Mary, see M. Hurley, *"Born Incorruptibly*: The Third Canon of the Lateran Council (A.D. 649)," *Heythrop Journal* 2 (1961) 216-236. Council text in DS 503/TCC 269.

that Mary was virgin *before, during* and *after* the birth of Christ comes into solemn teaching only in 1555 with the Constitution, *Cum quorumdam,* of Pius IV.[28] We have already seen the faith of the Church to be that Mary was ever virgin; it now remains to examine her virginity after and during the birth of Christ.

Hence our fifth question, who are the brothers and sisters of the Lord? That is, we are asking about Mary's virginity *post partum* (after the birth). There are several texts that speak about the brothers and sisters of the Lord, e.g.

> This is the carpenter, surely, the son of Mary, the brother of James and Joset and Jude and Simon? His sisters, too, are they not here with us? (Mk 6:3; see also Mk 3:20-25; Lk 8:19-21; Mt 12:46-50; Acts 1:12-13; Jn 2:12.)

Before examining the various interpretations of such passages we should see what the conclusions are that modern exegesis arrives at, for example the Lutheran-Roman Catholic study group which agreed on the following points:

> 1) The continued virginity of Mary after the birth of Christ is not a question directly raised by the New Testament.
> 2) Once it was raised in subsequent Church history, it was that question which focused attention on the exact relationship of the "brothers" (and "sisters") to Jesus.
> 3) Once that attention has been focused, it cannot be said that the New Testament identifies them *without doubt* as blood brothers and sisters and hence as children of Mary.
> 4) The solution favoured by scholars will in part depend on the authority they allot to later church insights.[29]

Scientific study of the New Testament, therefore, would seem to leave the question open.

---

[28]See DS 1880/TCC 322.

[29]*Mary NT* 92. See too G.A. Fitzmeyer, *A Christological Catechism New Testament Answers* (Ramsey, NY: Paulist, 1982) 71-73.

There are four interpretations of these passages.[30] The majority of the reformed traditions follow the view of Helvidius (about 382): they were blood brothers and sisters of Jesus and children of Mary. There is, however, a problem with this view. We have seen James and Josef as "brothers" of the Lord (Mk 6:3 quoted above). It is most unlikely that their mother, a "Mary" in Mk 15:40 and 16:1, is Mary the mother of Jesus.

A second interpretation is the one favoured by the Orthodox Churches which follow the *Protoevangelium of James* which dates from about 200 A.D. and possibly earlier.[31] In this view the "brothers and sisters" are children of Joseph by a former marriage. It is remarkable that at such an early date there was an attempt to explain the texts in a way that did not impugn the virginity of Mary. The weakness of this position is that it has no foundation in the gospels.

A third explanation is the one proposed by Jerome against Helvidius: "brothers and sisters" in the scriptures can admit of wide interpretation to include even cousins. Jerome suggests in support of his view that the Mary of Jn 19:25 was a sister of Mary the Mother of Jesus; but it is rather unlikely to have two blood sisters with the same name. There is furthermore the fact that there was a Greek word for "cousin," used elsewhere in the New Testament.

The most satisfactory interpretation remains that of J. McHugh who can make perfect sense of all the passages by a simple hypothesis that Mary the mother of James and Joset (in some texts Jose or Joseph) was a sister of Joseph. In this case the children would be Jesus' first cousins, but living in a close family situation that would justify their being called "brothers and sisters" of Jesus.

One text of the New Testament that cannot be used to indicate that Mary had other children is Luke 2:6—"she gave birth to her

[30]See McHugh 200-254; more briefly in the forthcoming volume above (n. 11).

[31]*Protoevangelium* 9, 2 in E. Hennecke, edited by W. Schneemelcher, *New Testament Apocrypha* 2 vols. (London: SCM, 1963) 1:379. For Orthodox see T. Ware, *The Orthodox Church* (Harmondsworth-New York: Penguin, revised ed. 1983) 262. On Apocrypha see O'Carroll, *Theotokos* 37-44.

first-born." The title "first-born" refers to the rights and the dignity of the child. There is an Egyptian grave inscription from the time that speaks of Arsinoe who died giving birth to her first-born. Clearly she could have had no other children.[32]

We come finally to our sixth question about Mary's virginity and ask: what does the virgin birth (*in partu*) mean? Just as Immaculate Conception and virginal conception are often confused in ordinary speech, so too are virgin birth and virginal conception. We have already dealt with this last, so we are asking about the actual birth of Jesus at Bethlehem. If Mary is confessed in the creeds as "Ever Virgin," she was a virgin at the birth of Christ. We are asking therefore about the mode of Jesus' birth, and more specifically, if it was a miraculous birth, or in some way extraordinary.

The words of the texts of Luke and Matthew, "she gave birth to a son" (Lk 2:7; Mt 1:25) imply at first sight a normal birth. Likewise, as we noted in dealing with 2 February, Luke would hardly have used the Old Testament "opening the womb" (Lk 2:23) if he suspected that the birth of Jesus were other than normal. But from the late second century we find assertions in the apocrypha that the birth was miraculous. These texts are explicit, and detailed, some of them having present a midwife at Bethlehem to testify that Mary's body was unchanged by the arrival of Jesus.[33] It should be noted that the origin of some of these accounts is docetic, that is, from a heresy that denied a true body to Jesus. Hence his birth would in no way change Mary's body.

Belief in a miraculous birth of Jesus is very well attested in the liturgy and theology of the East.[34] There are also many statements about a miraculous birth in the Fathers of the Church, but we do not find unanimity about what is involved in Mary's vir-

---

[32]Brown 398.

[33]*Protoevangelium of James* 19.1—text in E. Hennecke et al (n. 31 above) 384-385.

[34]See J. Ledit, *Marie dans la liturgie de Byzance* "Théologie historique 39" (Paris: Beauchesne, 1976) 174-176.

ginal birth.[35] One could say that in the Fathers we have a mixture of theology, aesthetics and inadequate physiology. (After all the female ovum was discovered only in 1835). The Fathers' idea of what was proper and fitting for Mary and Jesus is exceedingly limited by their knowledge of the process of birth. However, it must be said that a miraculous birth has been a common belief amongst catholics for centuries, and is found today in major theologians such as H. Urs von Balthasar:

> How her womb opened and closed again we do not know, and it is superfluous to speculate about an event which for God was child's play, something much less important than the original overshadowing by the Holy Spirit.[36]

But belief in a miraculous birth is not demanded by the Catholic faith. The birth of Jesus as a birth could have been quite normal.[37] Indeed, if we talk to mothers, especially to those who have had a natural birth and later a caesarean birth, we will learn that the latter is felt somehow to be incomplete or unsatisfactory. A birth that could be paralleled with the appearance of Jesus through closed doors after the resurrection (see Jn 20:19) does not harmonize well with the simple scriptural statement that "she gave birth to a son."

It is not sufficient however to say that the virgin birth is reducible to a statement that Mary who conceived virginally gave birth to Jesus in the normal way. We would have to exclude anything that would imply concupiscence or corruption. Normal changes in her body would not be a "corruption." What we are asserting is that there cannot in the case of the birth at Bethlehem

---

[35]See K. Rahner, "*Virginitas in partu.* A Contribution to the Development of Dogma and Tradition," *Theological Investigations.* vol. 4 (London: Darton, Longman and Todd, 1966) 134–162.

[36]*Mary for Today* (Slough: St. Paul, 1987) 23. See also A. Serra, *NDizM* 1148–1449.

[37]See J. Galot, *Dieu et la Femme* (n. 7 above) 156–175 who defends this view. As a theologian very much in favour with the Sacred Congregation for the Doctrine of the Faith, his view can be safely held.

be anything that is not fitting for one who is without sin. But the question still remains as to whether the birth of Jesus was a painless birth. In Genesis 3:15 we find the pain of childbirth as a punishment for sin. We cannot see Mary as being punished for sin, but it does not follow that her parturition was painless. What is natural about giving birth can safely be ascribed to the birth of Jesus. We can conclude with J. Galot:

> Finally the painful birth manifests the solidarity of Mary's condition with that of other mothers, and at the same time the solidarity of Jesus with other infants. Far from being a source of privileges that would go the way of exemption from suffering, the mystery of the Incarnation assures the greatest possible sharing in the human condition. If Christ was made like us in all things but sin, especially in trials, we can understand that according to the divine plan Mary in her maternity must have been like all other women, and brought forth her child in suffering. In this way she is very close to each human maternity.[38]

There is one final matter to be discussed which arises in the context of the Annunciation, the use of the word "spouse" about Mary.[39] It is easy to allow the words "spouse" or "bride" to slip from our lips until we realize that a foundation for both words is marriage. We would not be comfortable with any expression that might seem to suggest that Mary is the wife of God or of any of the divine Persons, even if qualified as "spiritual wifehood." One need not therefore be surprised to find that some theologians are distinctly cool, if not even hostile, to the notion of Mary as bride.[40] But the expression "spouse" is quite persistent in tradition, especially in the Eastern liturgies, and it has been used in

[38]Ibid 175.

[39]For brief overview of matter see M. O'Carroll, *Theotokos* 333-334.

[40]See J. Crehan, "Maria Paredros," *Theological Studies* 16 (1955) 414-423. See too the theologians mentioned in D. Flanagan, "The Image of the Bride in the Earlier Marian Tradition," *Irish Theological Quarterly* 27 (1960) 110-124 at 114.

recent times by Pope John Paul II (for example twice discreetly in RM 39.43). We should then examine its usage and try to grasp its meaning. The term is not biblical as applied to Mary. Indeed Luke is very careful to avoid anything suggesting a *hieros gamos* (marriage with a god) in the Annunciation story.[41] He chooses instead biblical language, which can be seen as evoking the over-shadowing of the Ark by the cloud (see Ex 40:35).

Modern interest in the concept "spouse" becomes quite marked in the great German theologian, M.J. Scheeben (1835-1888). His major contribution to mariology was to look for a unifying idea which could give a coherent vision to all mariology. He put forth "bridal motherhood" as such a basic principle.[42] But though all later mariologists would accept his idea of a basic principle, very few would follow his particular choice of one.

When we examine the earlier tradition, we find a multiple usage of bridal language about Mary. Sometimes she is called bride without further specification, as in the *Akathistos Hymn*: "Hail bride without bridegroom." Here her true marriage to Joseph is not being denied; she loves God with an undivided heart, and she loves Joseph in God. An associated idea, very frequent in Eastern liturgies is Mary as *Theonymphos* (bride of God). J. Ledit summarizes the findings of the Eastern liturgies:

> When the three Persons of the Trinity are named in the same verse, the Virgin Mary is the Spouse of the Father, the Mother of the Son, the receptacle in which dwells the Spirit who adorned her with virtues and graces. This division must not be taken in an exclusive sense. We will note many texts in which Mary is called spouse of the Son and at least one in which she is called Spouse of the Holy Spirit. She is called *Theonymphos*, spouse of God, but when the three Persons are named, one is rather drawn to say that she is the spouse of

---

[41]Brown 290.

[42]*Mariology* 2 vols. (St. Louis—London: Herder, 1951) 1:187-218. See M.-J. Nicolas, "Le concept de maternité sponsale dans la théologie mariale de Scheeben," *DiVinitas* 32 (1988) 351-359.

the Father because she and he meet one another in the same
Son, who is Son of each of them.[43]

In the West too we find bridal imagery. Mary is said to be spouse
of the Father in Latin patrology and especially in the French
school of spirituality.[44] But more frequent in the West is the idea
of her being spouse of Christ, especially in the context of Psalms
19:5 and 45:11. The idea here is Mary's faithful companionship
with her Son in his redemptive mission. Extremely rare in the
East, the notion of spouse of the Spirit is very common in the
West. The tendency here is to speak of Mary as daughter of the
Father, Mother of the Son and spouse of the Spirit. A particularly
bold expression is that of St. Louis Grignon de Montfort:

> God the Holy Ghost being barren in God, that is producing
> no other Divine Person, became fruitful in Mary, whom He
> espoused. It was with her and in her that He produced His
> masterpiece, God made man....[45]

We have to be very circumspect in using bridal images about the
Persons of the Trinity and Mary. Yet the very attempt to be
theologically exact in using such language has the advantage of
alerting us to the profound relationship of Mary to each of the
Persons of the Trinity. The Father and she have the same Son,
even though she is his mother only according to his human nature.
Mary is the first and most perfect member of the Church (see
Vatican II: *Liturgy* 103). Christ sacrificed himself so that the
Church would be his glorious bride, holy and faultless (see Eph
5:25-27). In Mary the Church has already responded perfectly to
her spouse, Christ Jesus.[46] Mary is overshadowed by the Holy

---

[43]Op.cit. (n. 34) 188.

[44]See A. Amato "Dio Padre," *NDizM* 478-479; J.M. Alonso, "Trinità, *NDizM*
1410-1412.

[45]*Treatise on the True Devotion to the Blessed Virgin.* (Fourth Montfortian Edition. Translated and published by the Fathers of the Company of Mary, England, 1957) n. 20.

[46]See H. Urs von Balthasar, "Die marianische Prägung der Kirche" in W. Beinert,

Spirit: it is his power that made her holy; it was by his power that she conceived. There is a close and deep relationship between the Holy Spirit and Mary, though it is not helpful to speak with L. Boff about a hypostatic union.[47]

The symbol of marriage is not immediately behind all of these uses, but rather the Old Testament notion of spouse:[48] God loves with a faithful love, and the people are to respond to this love. In calling Mary "spouse" we are recognizing the unique love of God for her, and the singularity of her response. The depth and beauty of this mutual love and response are highlighted by the warm and rich symbol of spouse.

We have dealt at length with the question of Mary's virginity and spousal calling. But one hears today two responses: such a doctrine demeans marriage and sexuality; the issue has no relevance for being a committed christian in our world. The first objection can only be handled by accepting as a unique fact the Incarnation, the deep mystery of God becoming man. God who created sexuality knows that it is good and holy. Yet he chose another way, a virginal conception, for the Son. Our only appropriate attitude is wonder and awe. Instead of setting off one of God's actions (creation of sexuality and blessing of marriage) against another (Mary is Ever Virgin), we would do better to pause humbly before the mystery. The body of Mary was a sacred vessel in which God became man. This utterly singular event is not a statement about marriage. Mary and Joseph evidently decided that their marriage should be virginal after the Annunciation and Bethlehem. If we ponder, we may come into a sense of a rightness, of holiness about such a decision.

The second objection is always surfacing in theology. Here we

ed., *Mhe* (Freiburg-Basel-Wien: Herder, 1977) 263-279 at 274-279.

[47]L. Boff, *The Maternal Face of God. The Feminine and Its Religious Expression* (San Francisco-London: Harper and Row, 1987). His language about hypostatic union between the Spirit and Mary has not been well received; e.g. J.-M. Hennaux in *Nouvelle Revue Théologique* 109 (1987) 884-895; *Maria e lo Spirito Santo* (Rome: Marianum—Bologna: Ed. Dehoniane, 1984), A. Amato 65-75, D. Fernández 303-323.

[48]See M.-L. Lacan, "Spouse," *DBT* 576-579.

answer it best perhaps by saying that God has revealed truths to us. Such revelation is his gift. If we become grateful recipients of his word, our commitment to his kingdom can be even greater; we will be allowing ourselves to be drawn into his plans and purposes; we will break out of the narrow limits of our own system of values and world of ideas. God's gift of his truth is good for us.

PRAYER OF THE FAITHFUL

We come to our Father knowing that we can rely on the prayers of his daughter and our Mother Mary Ever Virgin.

- Mary knew God's favour: may the Church and all is members learn to grow in thanksgiving to God for all his gifts.
- Mary was told that nothing is impossible to God: may the great power of God overcome injustice, hatred and conflict in our society and in the world community.
- Mary said a yes to God which was total: may our lives be patterned on Mary's obedient faith.
- Mary was overshadowed by the Holy Spirit: may we be open to a deepening of the grace of the sacrament of confirmation and so know the power of the Holy Spirit in our lives.
- Mary was servant of the Lord: may we be servants of God and of one another.

  Father in heaven, you chose Mary from all eternity to be Mother of your Son, and you chose us as your sons and daughters in him. May our hearts be ever open to the working of your Spirit, so that we may be more perfect disciples of your Son, our Lord Jesus Christ. Amen.

ADDITIONAL READING

D. Bertetto, "L'azione propria dello Spirito Santo in Maria," *Marianum* 41 (1979) 400-444.

A. Clark, The Virgin Birth: A Theological Reappraisal" *Theological Studies* 34 (1973) 576-593.

J.F. Craghan, "The Gospel Witness to Mary's *ante partum* Virginity," *Marian Studies* 21 (1970) 28-68.

De Fiores 436-451.

G. Gironés, "Respuesta a Schoonenberg sobre la virginidad de Maria," *Ephemerides mariologicae* 23 (1973) 121-128.

I de la Inmacolada, "La unción de Maria por el Espiritu Santo," *Ephemerides Mariologicae* 34 (1984) 11-40.

F.M. Jelly, "Mary's Virginity in the Symbols and Councils," *Marian Studies* 21 (1970) 69-93.

F.M. Jelly, "Virgin Birth," *A New Dictionary of Theology* eds. J.A. Komonchak, M. Collins, D.A. Lane (Wilmington: Glazier—Dublin: Gill and Macmillan, 1987, pp. 1077-81.

R. Masterson, "Mary's Virginity in Secular Culture," *Marian Studies* 20 (1969) 89-111.

M. Miguens, *The Virgin Birth. An Evaluation of the Scriptural Evidence* (Boston: St. Paul, 1981[2]).

A.C. Piepkorn, "The Virgin Birth Controversy. A Lutheran's Reaction," *Marian Studies* 24 (1973) 25-65.

K. Rahner, "Mary's Virginity," *Theological Investigations*, vol 19 (London: Darton, Longman and Todd, 1984) 218-231.

H.W. Richardson, "Theological Reflections on the Virgin Birth," *Marian Studies* 24 (1973) 66-82.

Roschini 3:338-438.

A. Schmemann, "Mary and the Holy Spirit," *Marian Studies* 23 (1972) 69–78.

W.B. Smith, "The Theology of the Virginity *in partu* and its Consequences for the Church's Teaching on Chastity," *Marian Studies* 31 (1980) 99–110.

A.B. Vaughan, "Interpreting the Ordinary Magisterium on Mary's Virginity," *Marian Studies* 22 (1971) 75–90.

H. Urs von Balthasar, "Maria und der Geist," *Geist und Leber* 53 (1983) 173–177, *Maria e lo Spirito Santo* (Rome: Marianum— Bologna: Ed. Dehoniane, 1984).

THE VISITATION OF THE BLESSED VIRGIN MARY
(Feast—31 May)

LITURGICAL HISTORY

Though it is a relatively modern feast, scholars are by no means unanimous about the origin and reasons for the dates given to the feast of the Visitation. From the sixth century the gospel story of the Visitation was read on the Friday after the third Sunday of Advent, but this was not a Visitation feast. The idea that the feast was established at a Franciscan chapter in 1263 meets with scholarly approval[1] and dissent.[2]

---

[1] E.g. M. O'Carroll *Theotokos* "Liturgy" 221; H.J. Schulz, *Mhe* 154; B. Kleinheyer *HBdMK* 428

[2] E.g. D. Sartor, "Visitazione" *NDizM* 1476

We are on sure ground in pointing to the influence of the Archbishop of Prague, John Jenstein, who had the feast approved in the Synod of Prague (1386). His motive for establishing the feast, not only in his diocese but more widely in the Church, was intercession for unity of the Church, a unity splintered at the time by the antipope Clement VII at Avignon who was in conflict with Urban VII of Rome. Urban prepared for the feast's introduction by declaring a Jubilee Year in 1390, but he died before it was actually established. His successor, Boniface IX, antedated approval to the reign of his predecessor (1389).

The reasons for the first dating of the feast are unknown. There is little scholarly support nowadays for seeing a July date as a deliberate attempt to parallel the great eastern feast of Blakhernae (Deposition of Mary's Garment) celebrated on 2 July. Bishop Jenstein wanted the feast to be celebrated on 28 April for three reasons: it would always be outside the Lenten season; it would be in Paschal time; it would be after the Annunciation (25 March). In the revised calendar the feast is celebrated on 31 May, thus after the Annunciation and before the Birthday of John the Baptist (24 June).

THEMES

In response to the prompting of the Holy Spirit Mary set out on a mission of charity (opening prayer). Mary's love for God is the spirit in which we come before God (prayer over gifts). Like John the Baptist we are to recognize with joy the presence of Christ. The feast is clearly about the Lucan narrative; other elements of the liturgical celebration revolve around this text.

> When Elizabeth heard the greeting of Mary she cried out with joy and said, 'Why should I be honoured with a visit from the mother of my Lord?' (Morning Prayer)
> "All generations will call me blessed, because God has had regard for his servant in her lowliness. Alleluia. (Evening Prayer)

SCRIPTURE READINGS

There are two possibilities for the first reading at Mass. Depending on the one chosen, different aspects of the feast will be emphasized.

a) Zephaniah 3:14-18

The prophecy comes from a time of religious and social disintegration (640-609 B.C. in the reign of Josiah). The prophet warns of impending judgement and ends with a message of hope which is the text for this feast. Jerusalem, the *Daughter of Zion* is told: *shout aloud* and *exult with all your heart*, because *Yahweh is king among you*; he is *the warrior-Saviour* who will *rejoice over you with happy song*; he will *renew you by his love*.

The reading is chosen for its emphasis on joy, which thus points to the rejoicing of the Visitation itself. More significant though is the theme of the presence of God: he will visit his people. Mary bearing Jesus in her womb is a new Ark of the Covenant, wherein God dwells with his people. The further idea of dancing looks to John the Baptist who, in his mother's womb, leapt with joy at Mary's greeting. In addition we can compare 2 Samuel 6:1-11 with this text and with the Visitation narrative and see foundations for the use of the title Ark of the Covenant for Mary: as Mary brought Jesus and thus blessing on the house of Elizabeth, so too the Ark blessed the house of Obed-Edom.

b) Romans 12:9-16b

The first eleven chapters of Romans are doctrinal, and the concluding four are largely moral exhortation. A choice of this reading instead of Zeph 3:14-18 is a decision to reflect on Mary's solicitude and practical charity. The passage gives the dispositions and attitudes that are to characterize the disciples of Jesus. We can see each of them reflected in Mary: sincere *love without pretence; deep affection* leading to *expression; in the service of the Lord* working *with conscientiousness and an eager spirit;* sharing with those *in need;*

looking *for opportunities to be hospitable; rejoice with others when they rejoice.* These aspects of Christian charity emerge in a consideration of the Visitation narrative.

The *response* celebrates God's presence: "Great in your midst is the Holy One of Israel."

c) Luke 1:39-56

We postpone until 15 August a fuller treatment of the Magnificat and concentrate on the meeting of the two women. The text is a rich tapestry of Old Testament themes and symbols. *Mary set out at that time and went as quickly as she could into the hill country to a town in Judah.* Luke implies swiftness in setting out which may be attributed to Mary's desire to go to Elizabeth and share with her the joy of two pregnancies and to her eargerness to help her elderly (see Lk 1:18) cousin. Luke does not give the name of the *town*, but he is specific about its location; it is in the *hill country* of *Judah*, that is, an area surrounding Jerusalem. We are reminded of Isaiah 52:7: "How beautiful on the *mountains* are the feet of the *messenger* announcing *peace*, of the messenger of *good news* who proclaims *salvation* and says to Zion, 'your God is king.' Again, we know that Luke structures his entire Gospel in terms of Jesus' ascent to Jerusalem (see 9:51.53; 17:11; 19:28...). Already in his mother's womb he is ascending towards the place of his death and glorification.

Mary *greeted Elizabeth.* We are not told that there is anything special about the greeting: the Greek could signify either a verbal greeting or an embrace. Its effect is dramatic. *The child leapt in Elizabeth's womb and she herself was filled with the Holy Spirit.* Mary, who is bearing Jesus, is an instrument of blessing both for Elizabeth and for her unborn child. It is through Mary's greeting that the prophecy of the angel is fulfilled: "from his mother's womb he will be filled with the Holy Spirit" (Lk 1:15). Elizabeth gives a *loud cry*: the word, used frequently in the psalms, can have almost a liturgical overtone; at the very least it indicates that Elizabeth recognizes the presence of the Lord. Elizabeth proclaims that *of all women* Mary *is most blessed,* and *blessed* too is her child. She then states that it is an honour to have *a visit from the mother of her Lord.* The main protagonists in the scene seem to be the two women, but it is their children who are the reason for the blessings pronounced and received.

Some scholars see in Elizabeth's praise an echo of the praise of Judith by the high priest: "May you be blessed, my daughter, by God Most High, beyond all women on earth; and blessed be the Lord God" (Jdt 13:18). . . . Judith, who set her people free by killing Holofernes, would thus be an image of Mary chosen to have an important role in the divine plan that would set humanity free (see Lk 24:21).[3] Again exegetes point out that there are other parallels in the Old Testament for Elizabeth's blessing.[4] We should not therefore insist too strongly on the resemblance of Judith and Mary, though it is suggested that the pondering of the event in the early Church could have caused the parallel to surface so that it could have been a quasi liturgical blessing formula.[5]

Elizabeth confirms the effect of Mary's greeting: *the child in my womb leapt for joy.* But then she goes on to focus more clearly on Mary's greatness: *blessed is she who believed that the promise made her by the Lord would be fulfilled.* The two blessings of Elizabeth are not identical: the first (v. 42) is praise of God for what he had done in Mary; the second (v. 45) declares Mary to be blessed or fortunate because of her faith.[6] We find a similar transition from praise of Mary's motherhood (Lk 11:27) to a praise of her faith (Lk 11:28) later in the gospel in the incident of the woman in the crowd praising Mary only to hear from Jesus where his mother's true greatness lay, namely in hearing the word of God and keeping it.

On the Magnificat we might be content to note here only its key affirmation: *the Almighty has done great things for me. Holy is his*

---

[3]E.g. Laurentin 199-200.

[4]See Brown 344.

[5]E.g. McHugh 69-72.

[6]Verse 42 has *eulogēmenē* but v. 45 has *makaria*; for the difference see Brown 332.

name. Mary acknowledges the wonderful thing that has happened to her, but she immediately praises God for it.

The gospel message ends with the observation, *Mary stayed with her some three months and then went home*. Some presume that Mary returned home just before the birth of John the Baptist, or a month beforehand if we take the biblical notion of pregnancy as lasting for ten lunar months.[7] From a literary viewpoint it is convenient to have Mary off the scene before the narration of the birth of John. In Mary's situation one can suggest her need to return home and to meet Joseph in order to discuss with him all the events that had happened.

CHURCH DOCUMENTS

Vatican II in its Constitution on the Church states (LG 57):

> This union of the mother with the Son in the work of salvation is made manifest from the time of Christ's virginal conception up to his death; first when Mary, arising in haste to go to visit Elizabeth, is greeted by her as blessed because of her belief in the promise of salvation and the precursor leaped with joy in the womb of his mother (cf. Lk 1:41-45).

Pope Paul VI observes that, of the "celebrations that commemorate salvific events in which the Blessed Virgin was closely associated with her Son,"

> the liturgy (of the Visitation) recalls the Blessed Virgin carrying her Son within her and visiting Elizabeth to offer charitable assistance and to proclaim the mercy of God. (MC 7)

[7]See Brown 264. 338. 345-346.

In his recent encyclical Pope John Paul II writes:

> Moved with charity, therefore, Mary goes to the house of
> her kinswoman.... While every word of Elizabeth's is filled
> with meaning, her final words would seem to have a *funda-
> mental importance*: 'And blessed is she who believed that there
> would be a fulfilment of what had been spoken to her from
> the Lord (Lk 1:45). These words can be linked with the title
> 'full of grace' of the angel's greeting. Both of these texts
> reveal an essential Mariological content, namely the truth
> about Mary who has become really present in the mystery of
> Christ precisely because she 'has believed,' The *fullness of
> grace* announced by the angel means the gift of God himself.
> *Mary's faith*, proclaimed by Elizabeth indicated how the
> Virgin of Nazareth *responded to this gift*. (RM 12—italics in
> original)

REFLECTION

It would be out of keeping with the entire thrust of Luke 1-2 to
consider the Visitation as a family event between Elizabeth and
Mary. It must rather be seen in terms of salvation history—
Elizabeth a model of the Old Testament (see Lk 1:6) meets the
New Testament in Mary's faith in the mystery of her own destiny.
But it is even more than the meeting of two women at the
intersection of the two Testaments. What is most significant is
the meeting of their unborn children. John, who leaps in his
mother's womb, is already anticipating his future role of proclaiming the Messiah.

There has been a lot of discussion about whether Mary is being
presented as the Ark of the Covenant in the Annunciation scene
(Lk 1:35 reflecting Ex 40:35).[8] The question comes up again about

[8]In favour Laurentin 69-73 and McHugh 56-63; against Brown 327-328 and *Mary NT*
132 and 134. See further A. Serra, "Aspetti mariologici della pneumatologia di Lc 1,
35a," *Maria e lo Spirito Santo.* "Atti del 40 Simposio Mariologico Internazionale" (Rome:
Marianum—Bologna: Ed. Dehoniane, 1984) 133-200.

the visitation narrative, this time in connection with the transfer of the Ark to Jerusalem (2 Sm 6:1-11). There are several words and ideas in the LXX or Greek version of the Old Testament that suggest expressions in Luke's account: Mary arose—a village in Judah—hill country—the mother of the Lord visiting—joy—blessing of the house—three months.[9] The equivalence is resisted by many exegetes.[10] We can say that whether Luke intended to present Mary as a new Ark of the Covenant is disputed. But the question of what Luke intended (called the "literal meaning") is not the only one that can be asked about the text. We can ask if "Ark of the Covenant" as in the Litany of Loreto is a helpful way of understanding Mary and her role as portrayed by Luke. Here we go beyond, but do not contradict the meaning as established by sound exegesis.

If we look at what the Old Testament says about the Ark of the Covenant,[11] we can see clearly that the Ark was a symbol of God's presence by his action (e.g. Nb 10:33-35) and by his word (e.g. 1 Sm 3; Dt 31:26-27) in his salvation of the people. The Ark accompanied them from Sinai and was later brought by David to Jerusalem as a common religious symbol uniting Israel and Juda. It was a sign of God's power to save his people (See Jos 3:1-17; 6:8.13). God's definitive presence to his people is Jesus, God-with-us. In going to Elizabeth Mary effects a divine visit. Hence the event may be understood in terms of the Ark, even though Luke may well not have intended to assert this in his text.

The narrative of the Visitation is one from which Christian reflection may look to Mary as model of the apostolate of the Church.[12] She brings Jesus and a blessing on the house of Zechariah. The experience of the primitive Church was that the power of the Lord was the highest gift it had to offer. Peter says

[9]See Laurentin 73-77; McHugh more guarded 62-63.

[10]E.g. Brown 344-345.

[11]See A. Ridouard, "Ark of the Covenant" DBT 30-31.

[12]On apostolate see further, J.J. McQuale, "Mary and the Apostolate," *Marian Studies* 22 (1971) 54-74.

to the lame man: "I have neither silver nor gold, but I will give you what I have: in the name of Jesus Christ the Nazarene, walk!" (Acts 3:6). To bring Jesus will always be the supreme norm of any genuine apostolate; the Church's mission is to show him as wisdom and power in each situation of human need.

Further, the liturgy invites us in the post-communion prayer to recognize the presence of Christ in our midst in the Eucharist. Such recognition may be of his presence at Mass or where the Blessed Sacrament is reserved. One is reminded of the realism of the greeting to a priest on a sick call in the Irish language, *fáilte róimh* (you—plural—are welcome). But the presence of Christ is to be discovered not only in the Eucharist: he is met in others, and he asks us to serve him in others. Mary's service of Elizabeth by her visit remains also a model for the Christian who would wish to meet Christ in daily life.

Though Luke does not give very much indication about the feelings of the two women, except to underline the joyous, faith and Spirit-filled character of their meeting, we can nonetheless ponder the attitudes of the two cousins. Mary believed in the word of the Lord. It was a special consolation for her to have her faith (Lk 1:38. 45) confirmed by the sign of her cousin's pregnancy (see Lk 1:36). We can easily understand the mutual comfort given and received by the two expectant mothers as they discussed motherhood and the mysterious future destinies of their sons in the light of their knowledge of their people's history. They can barely glimpse the divine plan. Luke is careful to point out to us on several occasions that Mary was troubled, astonished, or unable to grasp the divine plan as it unfolded (see Lk 1:29.4; 2:33.48.50).

We must remember that except for the Annunciation, Mary like us had to walk by faith. Faith is darkness and light: it is dark because we cannot fully grasp divine truth; it is light since faith brings us to truths that we cannot otherwise know. Mary walked in the light of faith; God told her enough about his plan for her to make each new step. At the time of the Reformation and at Vatican I (1870) there were in circulation ideas about faith which denied the intellectual side of this virtue. The Church's response was to assert strongly that faith is intellectual. One consequence was a tendency to see faith almost exclusively as intellectual. A redress came about by the middle of this century and in Vatican II a much richer idea of faith was put forward. Faith is not only intellectual, that is belief: it is also trust and action. Pope John Paul gives a fine picture of Mary's faith in his marian encyclical:

> To believe means to abandon oneself to the truth of the word of the living God, knowing and humbly recognising 'how unsearchable are his judgements and how inscrutable his ways' (Rm 11:33). Mary, who by the eternal will of the Most High stands, one may say, at the very center of those 'inscrutable judgements' of God, conforms herself to them in the dim light of faith, accepting fully and with a ready heart everything that is decreed in the divine plan. (RM 14)

In short, faith is to say Amen (so be it) to the word, the command and the promises of God.

The Pope also compares the faith of Abraham and Mary: "Abraham's faith constitutes the beginning of the Old Covenant; Mary's faith at the Annunciation inaugurates the New Covenant." When there seemed to be no hope, Abraham, "our father in faith" (Eucharistic Prayer 1), "hoped and believed that he would become the father of many nations in fulfilment of the promise" (see Rm 4:18); Mary allowed the hope of her people for a Messiah to be embodied in her total yes to God. We have already seen that the assurance that "nothing is impossible to God" was given to both Abraham and Mary (see Gen 18:14; Lk 1:37). Luke explicitly recalls the promise made to Abraham (see Lk 1:55 and Gen 13:14–16; 22:17-18). Both are praised for their faith (Lk 1:45; Gen 15:6). Both are asked to sacrifice their sons and each ascended a hill of sacrifice. But whereas Abraham was spared the actual death of his son (see Gen 22:12), Mary was to see her Son die (see Jn 19:25-30). Again, Abraham "obeyed the call to set out for a country which was an inheritance given to him and his descendants, and he set out without knowing where he was going" (Hb 11:8); Mary embarked on "a pilgrimage of faith" (LG 58) that would lead her to Calvary and the Upper Room at Pentecost. In Mary and in Abraham faith and obedience merge in a total yes to God.

We should note another characteristic of Mary's faith, one that is common also to ours. It is mediated, that is, God speaks to us through others. We come to know God, to know his saving plans through people (parents, teachers, preachers, etc.) in the Christian community. Revelation is not made directly to us. Except for the quite singular experience of the Annunciation, Mary came to a knowledge of God's will through others: Joseph is told in a dream that his marriage with Mary is to go ahead (see Mt 1:18-25); Elizabeth tells her of the blessing which resulted from her visit (see Lk 1:43-44); the shepherds tell her about the angelic proclamation (see Lk 2:15-19); Joseph is guided again by dreams about how to care for the Holy Family (see Mt 2:13.19.22); Simeon and Anna give her prophecies about the future destiny of her Son (see Lk 2:28-38); Jesus himself instructs her about the higher priority of his Father's will (see Lk 2:49); again, he teaches her and his family about the precedence of hearing the word of God, and doing it, over family bonds (see Lk 8:21 and parallels); Jesus gives her a new role from the cross (see Jn 19:25-28a); she hears Peter guiding the early Church in the days preceding Pentecost (see Acts 1:14-26). Mary had then to walk by faith, learning God's ways from others, especially the revelation she received from Jesus, and she had to ponder in her heart the various events of the divine plan (see Lk 2:19.51).

The faith of Mary which is praised by Elizabeth, brings her to the dignity of being Mother of the Lord and to the still greater blessedness of being a true disciple.[13] We can easily have a wrong idea about Mary's faith, thinking that because of her Immaculate Conception and her sinlessness faith would have been easier for her than for us. The contrary is true. It would have been more difficult for Mary to believe than for the apostles. They had only

[13]See C. O'Donnell, "Mary the True Disciple" in P. Rogers, ed., *Sowing the Word* (Dublin: Dominican Publications, 1983) 230-237.

a very rudimentary understanding of Jesus' Messiahship. Mary was told about all the future glory of her Son: he would be a great king with a reign that would never end (see Lk 1:32-33). She herself looked back with thanksgiving and forward in hope to God's mighty deeds in routing the arrogant and pulling down princes (see Magnificat). The very strength of her faith in the Annunciation promises would have made it infinitely more difficult for her to see her Son rejected at Nazareth (see Lk 4:22-30) and at Jerusalem by the religious authorities of her people. The faith of the apostles was so frail that they could abandon it and run away at the passion; Mary who had hoped for so much for her Son walked with him to Calvary. The darkness that overwhelmed the soul of Jesus—"My God, my God why have you forsaken me"— would not leave Mary untouched either. Just as her deep faith in the messianic promises made the prophecy of Simeon so difficult to grasp (see Lk 2:33-35), the angel's message about the royal dignity of her Son made the inscription on the cross, "This is the King of the Jews" (Lk 23:38), the supreme test of her faith. Pope John Paul II observed that the expression "blessed is she who believed" is a kind of key that unlocks the innermost reality of Mary (RM 19). An awareness that this faith was difficult, involving deep struggling, gives us an insight into Mary's life and further evidence of her likeness to us, sharing fully in the human condition, but without sin.

PRAYER OF THE FAITHFUL

We come before our Father who blessed Mary with a spirit of obedient faith and who wishes us to pattern our lives on her discipleship of Jesus.

- Mary went with haste to Elizabeth: may the Church always be eager in response to the promptings of the Holy Spirit.
- Mary's greeting was a blessing for Elizabeth and for her unborn Son: may words of healing and peace be spoken by political leaders throughout the world.

- Mary was blessed above all for her faith: may all Christians come to recognize with joy the biblical message about the Mother of Jesus.
- Mary celebrated God's work in her: may we too learn to rejoice at the wonder of our being and at the gifts of God which we and others have received.
Heavenly Father, may we come to you in a fullness of truth and holiness. May what we have received from you be of service to others, so that your name may be glorified. We make this prayer relying on the intercession of Mary, and in the name of your Son, our Lord Jesus Christ. Amen.

ADDITIONAL READING

P.J. Bearsley, "Mary the Perfect Disciple: A Paradigm for Mariology," *Theological Studies* 41 (1980) 461–504.

W.P. Dewan, "Mary's Faith as Response to God's Graciousness," *Marian Studies* 16 (1965) 75–93.

H. Urs von Balthasar, *The Threefold Garland. The World's Salvation in Mary's Prayer* (San Francisco: Ignatius Press, 1982) 35–41.

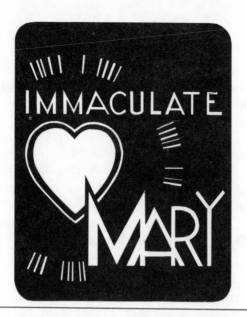

THE IMMACULATE HEART
OF MARY
(Optional Memorial—Saturday following the Second Sunday after Pentecost)

LITURGICAL HISTORY

St. John Eudes (1601-1680) was called by both Leo XIII and Pius X the "father, teacher and first apostle" of devotion to the hearts of Jesus and Mary.[1] Two decades before celebrating the Heart of Jesus, he was already observing with his followers 8 February as a feast of the Heart of Mary (1643). Five years later there was a public celebration in the diocese of Autun. Pius VI allowed Palermo to have the feast, and Pius VII further extended it to any diocese or congregation requesting it, but the liturgical text was to be that of Our Lady of the Snow (5 August), with

---

[1]See D. Sartor, "Cuore Immacolato" *NDizM* 453-455.

some modifications. In the 1914 reform of the Missal, the Mass of the Heart of Mary was transferred to an appendix "to be used in certain places." In 1942, the year in which he consecrated the world to the Immaculate Heart of Mary, Pius XII raised the feast to the rank of a double and assigned it to the 22 August, the octave day of the Assumption. In the 1969 reform it was reduced to the status of an optional memorial and it was given the more suitable date of the day following the feast of the Sacred Heart, that is, the Saturday after the second Sunday after Pentecost.[2]

THEMES

There is a special entry verse in the Mass of the memorial: "My heart rejoices in your saving power. I will sing to the Lord for his goodness to me" (Ps 13:6). The opening prayer reminds us that God prepared the heart of Mary as a fitting home for the Holy Spirit, and asks that we may become a temple of his glory. The other prayers of the Mass ask that, as we honour Mary, we may come to receive divine help. Central then are the themes of joy and of the Lord's dwelling in the heart of Mary.

My heart and my soul ring out their joy to God, the living God. (Morning Prayer)
My heart rejoices in the Lord, the Almighty who works marvels for me. (Evening Prayer)

SCRIPTURAL READINGS

a) Isaiah 61:9-11

The first reading is from the Book of Consolation in Isaiah. It takes up the theme of rejoicing which is very dominant in this

[2]On theology and history see J.M. Alonso, "Cuore Immacolato," *NDizM* 443-453; M. O'Carroll, *Theotokos* "Heart of Mary" 166-168, "St. John Eudes" 201-202.

part of Isaiah which has so many promises of restoration. *I exult for joy in the Lord, my soul* (heart) *rejoices in my God.* The reason for this joy is God's salvation, his message of hope. The passage invites us to be in harmony with God's saving work, with his joy in his gifts to us. But this being atuned to God cannot come about without reflection. We need to ponder if we are to see Mary and ourselves *adorned with jewels*, if we are to rejoice in the justice and praise which he makes *spring up*. The image of the *bridegroom* and *bride* is a discreet evocation of Mary as bride, a theme we have treated in the context of the Annunciation.

The *response* echoes the mood of rejoicing: "My heart exults in the Lord my Saviour."

b) Luke 2:41-52

Twice Luke reminds us that Mary pondered in her heart: the first occasion is at Bethlehem (2:19), the other is in his narrative concerning the loss of Jesus at the age of twelve (2:51). *Each year,* we are told, Mary and Joseph *used to go to Jerusalem for the Passover.* Luke is at pains to point out several times that Jesus' parents were obedient to the Old Testament Law (see 2:22-24; 2:41) and to the civil law (see 2:1-5). Indeed he is careful to show that Jesus was declared by civilians—Pilate, the good thief and the centurion—to have been innocent (see 23:11-15.41.47). He also pointed out that Jesus fulfilled the Old Testament (see 24:26-27)

On this occasion Jesus *stayed behind in Jerusalem.* When Mary and Joseph *failed to find him* after *a day's journey*, they then *went back to Jerusalem looking for him everywhere.* After *three days* they found him. We have already noted that the *third day* (Jn 2:1) is a decisive time (see 2 February): it is often in both Testaments a time of grace and favour—Sinai (Ex 19:11), restoration (Hos 6:2-3) and the resurrection, itself symbolized by Jonah's three days (see Jon 1:17 with Mt 12:40). The *third day* is just one of the passion motifs that can be detected in the account of the loss of Jesus.

Luke shows us the human reactions of Mary and Joseph: they were *worried* at his loss; *they were overcome* when they saw him. His reply to Mary's reproachful, *My child, why have you done this to us?* indicates that something unusual has happened. The reply of Jesus points to a higher priority than family bonds, *Why were you looking for me? Did you not know I must be in my Father's house?* Luke notes carefully, *But they did not understand what he meant.* At one level there is an abrupt transition from the normal usage at Nazareth, *your Father and I* to the *Father* of the *Temple.* A new relationship will be established in which Jesus will until Calvary divorce himself from his mother. The supreme norm of his life will be the will of the Father, as it must also be Mary's (see Lk 8:19-21; 11:27-28). But the break is not to occur at this point; for the moment *he goes down to Nazareth and lives under their authority.*

Mary stored up all these things in her heart. The Hebrew idiom that lies behind this statement uses the word "things" in the sense of *dabhar*: what is spoken or something done. Mary has both events and words to ponder. She does not grasp what has happened— surely Jesus could have given some indication.... Only careful meditation and time would reveal to Mary the meaning of the incident.

She certainly could not have understood that the event could have been a prophetic foreshadowing of the Paschal Mystery. Just as the prophets did symbolic actions to highlight the word of God, so we can see the loss of Jesus as pointing to events in his passion, death and resurrection:

> There are eight themes in the narrative that will be found again in the last pages of Luke's gospel. The incident takes place in *Jerusalem* (2:41.43.45), which is central also in the account of Jesus' death and resurrection. Indeed, the whole Gospel of Luke is written as a journey up to Jerusalem (9:51.53; 13:22; 17:11). Jesus is found in the *Temple* (2:46); the Temple figures in the passion narrative, for Jesus is charged with speaking against it, and Luke's Gospel ends where it began—in the Temple (1:8; 24:53). It is *passover* time; Jesus dies at passover time (22:1). There is a loss for *three days* (2:46); Jesus' own predictions of his passion stressed three days (9:22), and the resurrection is on the third day (24:7.

21.46). There is the theme of *accomplishment/fulfilment* (2:43); the Scriptures must be fulfilled (24:44). Jesus *must* (Greek *dei*) be in his Father's house; in the passion and resurrection accounts there is a great emphasis on the need for the Scriptures to be fulfilled and for the Father's will to be accomplished (with *dei*—22:37; 24:7.26.44). Mary and Joseph *do not understand* (2:50); incomprehension is a characteristic of the resurrection passages (24:11.25.41.45). The boy Jesus is *sought* (2:45); Jesus is sought after his burial (24:5.23-24).[3]

After Pentecost Mary's pondering, and the pondering of the early Church, would come into a deeper understanding of the symbolic loss of Jesus at the age of twelve.

CHURCH DOCUMENTS

In his exhortation *Marialis cultus* Pope Paul VI instances the celebration of the Immaculate Heart of the Blessed Virgin as expressing "tendencies that have emerged in contemporary devotion" (MC 8). Pope John Paul II in his first encyclical *Redemptor hominis* develops the theme of Mary's heart as being completely united with her Son:

> We can say that the mystery of the Redemption took shape beneath the heart of the Virgin of Nazareth when she pronounced her 'fiat.' From then on, under the special influence of the Holy Spirit, this heart, the heart of both a virgin and a mother, has always followed the work of her Son and has gone out to all those whom Christ has embraced and continues to embrace with inexhaustible love. For that reason her heart must have the inexhaustibility of a mother.[4]

---

[3]C. O'Donnell, *Life in the Spirit and Mary* (Wilmington: Glazier—Dublin: Dominican Publications, 1981) 72 with dependence on R. Laurentin, *Jésus au Temple: Mystère de Pâques et foi de Marie en Luc 2, 48-50* (Paris: Gabalda, 1966).

[4]*AAS* 71 (1979) 322-323—English tr. London: Catholic Truth Society, paragraph n. 22.

REFLECTION

Many people will not feel neutral towards either contemplation or celebration of the Immaculate Heart of Mary. People tend to be either deeply attracted to, or completely untouched by this devotion. It has in recent years suffered the same fate as devotion to the Sacred Heart of Jesus, and for much the same kinds of reasons: people can feel that devotion to these hearts is not very relevant to the urgent needs of the Church; the active spiritualities of our time experience difficulty in finding a place for devotions which paradoxically appear to be both too sentimental and too theoretical; these same active spiritualities seem to find that the devotion to the Hearts of Jesus and Mary demands excessive passivity. People are furthermore put off by theologically suspect presentations of reparation and by various "promises" associated with these devotions. Finally, there is the undoubted problem of bad taste both in devotional writing and in artistic representations.

Though in a sense devotion to the Immaculate Heart of Mary can be regarded as a rather recent development, it has deep roots in the Middle Ages,[5] and in the Latin Fathers. What we shall see shortly in examining the scriptural teaching on the heart, is already found in the well-known saying of Augustine that Mary conceived in her mind before she conceived in her womb, that she was a disciple even before she was a mother,[6] and in Ambrose's calling on us to imitate the heart of Mary: "she was a virgin and humble of heart" and "as Mary did, do also in your heart."[7]

We find what might be called the classical exposition of devotion to the Heart of Mary in two passages from St. John Eudes:

> Although at times 'heart' stands for the whole interior life of man, if especially signifies love. Therefore when we honour

[5]Alonso, art. cit. (n. 2) 446-447.

[6]See *Sermo* 191, 1—PL 38:1014/*EnMar* 868; *Sermo* 215, 4—PL 38:1074/*EnMar* 863; *Serm. Denis* 25, 4—Pl 46:935/*EnMar* 967.

[7]*De virginibus* 2, 7 PL 16:220; see *De instit. virginis* PL 16:345.

the Heart of Mary, we have in mind not merely a given mystery, action or quality, nor even the most worthy person of the Virgin, but the source and origin of the value and holiness of these things, namely, her love and charity.[8]

This admirable heart is the exemplar and model of our hearts, and perfection consists in our hearts' becoming living images of the Heart of Mary ... And just as she has borne, and will continue to bear, her Son Jesus in her heart, she also bore and will always bear, in her Heart the members of Jesus as children of hers that she loves, and continually offers to God as fruit of her maternal Heart.[9]

Though we can trace the tradition associated with the Heart of Mary, it is more important to see its scriptural foundation. In the Old Testament and in the New the word "heart" (*leb, lēbāb, kardia*) is at the root of the moral and religious relationship with God. The heart is considered to be at the centre of psychological, moral and religious life; it is the place where our good and bad dispositions are formed. In modern language we would use terms like "conscience," "interiority," "deepest recesses of the person" for the biblical word "heart." Hence we can understand that we need the new heart promised in Ezekiel (see 11:19-20), since our heart, our inner being, is fickle and torturous (see Jer 17:9). In a very dense passage Paul speaks of the need for a new creation:

> It is God who said, 'Let light shine out of darkness' that has shone into our hearts to enlighten them with the knowledge of God's glory, the glory on the face of Christ. (2 Cor 4:6)

Here he is clearly echoing Genesis 1:2, in which we see the initial chaos given order by the creative word, "Let light shine out of darkness." The depths of our heart, the whole shadow of Jungian psychology, stands in need of a newly creating word from God.

---

[8]*La dévotion au très saint Coeur et au très saint nom de la bienheureuse Vierge Marie. Oeuvres complètes* 12 vols. (Paris 1905-1909) 8:431.

[9]*Le coeur admirable de la très sacrée Mère de Dieu* ibid. 6:148.

Only then we can come into "knowledge," which in the bible is not purely intellectual, nor mere information, but an existential relationship with God, who is known, loved and obeyed (see Eph 3:14-19; Ph 3:8—"the surpassing knowledge of Christ.")

It is only by becoming aware of the rich symbolism of the heart in scripture that we avoid overemphasis on the physical organ, and more importantly that we get beyond shallow sentimental notions about the heart. When we look at our own hearts, we see that what we need is not a feeling but conversion. To contemplate Mary's heart is to walk a personal path of deepened self-knowledge and change of heart. Mary's heart, the whole of her being, her most profound inner attitudes were centred on God. She can teach us how to make God welcome in our lives, how to be nourished by his word, how to hunger and thirst for him.[10]

Mary's heart was a temple of the Holy Spirit, and a temple for the Eternal Son of God. In the Old Testament the Temple was where God dwelt and where he was to be worshipped authentically. Both of these aspects of the Temple find expression in the life of Mary. In that true devotion to Mary which is imitation, we have to allow our own hearts, the core of our being, to be a dwelling place for God, and centre of true worship.

Contemplation of the Heart of Mary brings us into the heart of the Church. The astonishingly fertile insight into the petrine and the marian aspects of the Church proposed by H. Urs von Balthasar[11] is now becoming more diffused in writing on Mary, but not yet sufficiently in ecclesiology or theology of the Church. It is the marian element that shows us what the Church essentially

---

[10]This paragraph owes much to D. Sartor, *NDizM* 455.

[11]See "The Marian Principle" in *Elucidations* (London: SPCK, 1975) 64-72; *Mary for Today* (Slough: St. Paul, 1988); *The Threefold Garland* (San Francisco: Ignatius, 1982); "Mary-Church-Office" in *A Short Primer for Unsettled Laymen* (San Francisco: Ignatius, 1985) 88-96. More Technical are *The Glory of the Lord. A Theological Aesthetics. Vol. 1:Seeing the Form* (San Francisco, Ignatius—Glasgow: T. & T. Clark, 1982) 362-365; "Die marianische Prägung der Kirche" in W. Beinert, ed., *Maria heute ehren* (Freiburg-Basel-Vienna: Herder, 1977) 264-279. See further, C. Smith, "Mary in the Theology of Hans Urs von Balthasar" in A. Stacpoole, ed., *Mary and the Churches* (Dublin: Columba, 1987) 132-148.

is; the petrine or institutional element has meaning only in being a service of the marian dimension. It is well known that von Balthasar is opposed to the suggestion of women's ordination. But to hear him speak about the marian dimension (in reply to a question about ordination!) is to realize that however urgent and indeed painful this contemporary issue may be, it is still quite secondary compared with what the Church is really about. The encounter with God in prayer and in self-sacrificing love for others is our echo of the bridal relationship which is already perfect between Christ and Mary. The still much needed renewal of the Church will involve the petrine element serving the marian response of God's people; the power that belongs to the petrine element of the Church is not the power to dominate, but a power of the Spirit that becomes effective only to the extent that the institutional ministers of the Church can empty themselves of everything that is redolent of the power cherished by the world (see Mt 20:24-28). The Church will be marian to the extent that it can respond with, or rather resound with, the annunciation yes of Mary. If at some future date women are indeed admitted to ministerial priesthood, the petrine dimension will not thereby obtain any increased importance; the marian dimension will still be the essential characteristic of the whole Church. The heart of the Church must always seek to resemble the heart of Mary.

Since the Reformation and the Enlightenment the petrine (*animus* of Jung, *yang* of Chinese philosophy, the masculine) has been dominant over the marian (*anima* of Jung, the *yin* of the Chinese, the feminine). The Church overemphasized what is rational and aggressive and did not give sufficient attention to what is intuitive and receptive. One of the consequences was that the devotional side of christian life tended towards immature sentimentality rather than towards mature expressions of affectivity in the area of faith.

Important though it be, it is not easy to speak with accuracy of the marian element of the Church. On the one hand we have to pay attention to feminist writers who are acutely sensitive to any distortion of the feminine role; on the other hand it is easy to fall into a position that would logically lead to Christ's being the model for men, and Mary the model for women, whereas both Christ and Mary are models for each man and woman.

It is now widely accepted that both masculine and feminine traits are to be found in each man and woman. In a particular individual one will of course dominate though a balanced male or female personality will fully harmonize both characteristics. Christ is the reflection of the Father's glory, and bears the imprint of the Father's own being. But the infinite Father has in Christ's humanity a created, and hence limited, image. The Incarnation is a limiting factor: Christ was born in a particular place and time, into one sex, into one limited human nature. Though he clearly shows feminine characteristics appropriate to a male, he does not fully express the feminine glory of the infinite God. Though Mary displays male characteristics, she can express in a created way other aspects of God's glory through her very femininity. Here we are not asserting anything more than the infinite images of the infinite God. Poets, musicians, martyrs, athletes, unselfish and wise politicians, craftsmen—to name but a few categories of those specially gifted—can show us other reflections of God's glory in ways that are not so obvious in either Christ or Mary.

What we have been saying about psychological traits, though true, has but a rather restricted value.[12] One problem is obvious: the gospels are not the kind of literary documents that can enable us to develop a detailed psychology of either Christ or Mary. But more particularly the perspective of St. Paul invites us to theologize not so much about the mysteries of the earthly Jesus as about the Risen One. And the mystery of Mary is best sounded not in the actual events of her life, but in her relationship to the Trinity.

Christ shows us the way to the Father (see Jn 14:6-7); only he redeems (see I Tm 2:5); he is the only gate of the sheepfold (see Jn 10:7-9). We must follow him (see Mk 8:34), but we have been

---

[12]See M. O'Carroll, *Theotokos*, "Personality of Mary" 385-386.

given a model of true discipleship.[13] In Mary we see a true daughter of the Father, totally dedicated to the Son, open to, and graced by, the Holy Spirit. If we can trace in our lives the Trinitarian lines of her discipleship, we too will grow in being disciples.

As yet the Church is perfect only in its Head, Jesus Christ, and in Mary the true disciple. There is already in them a fulfilment of the text of Eph 5:26-27:

> Christ loved the Church and sacrificed himself for her to make her holy by washing her in cleansing water with a form of words, so that when he took the Church to himself she would be glorious, with no speck or wrinkle or anything like that, but holy and faultless.

Mary's yes at the Annunciation was the beginning of a full spousal relationship between God and humanity. Mary conceived the human nature which would in time give birth to the Church on Calvary. In patristic terms the New Eve gave the New Adam his body. From that body in blood and water (see Jn 19:34) came the Church from the side of the New Adam as he slept on the cross (see Gen 2:22). The Church as Eve will the perfect companion for the New Adam; but his espousal is consummated as yet only in the perfect yes of the Immaculate Virgin already assumed into glory. The earthly Church, burdened by sin, not least the sin of its petrine ministers, struggles to become "holy and faultless" as it is being continually washed clean by the water of baptism and the blood of the Eucharist.

We have already observed that the heart of Mary is also to be the heart of the Church. We have also stressed the marian and feminine principle in the Church. We would wish also to emphasize Mary's receptivity. It might generally be agreed that receptivity is a feminine characteristic, provided only that one makes

[13]See C. O'Donnell, "Mary the True Disciple" in P. Rogers, ed., *Sowing the Word* (Dublin: Dominican Publications, 1983) 230-237.

two very important qualifications: firstly, that the feminine role is not seen exclusively as receptive; secondly, that there is recognized as also belonging to receptivity an integrated male personality. Mary is above all the receptive Virgin.[14] Everything that is most significant in what are called the marian dogmas are mysteries of God's gifts to her: the Immaculate Conception is pure gift; the perpetual virginity is again gift; the divine maternity is from the power of the Holy Spirit upon the Virgin who merely said a yes to its accomplishment; the Assumption is again total gift. To use the term dear to the Reformation tradition, we can say that Mary is the most perfect exemplar of *gratia sola*, pure unmerited grace. This marian receptivity is at the heart also of the Church. The Church is primarily receptive: it is being continually constructed through grace. All its activities are no more than a response to what God has already called and empowered it to do. Just as Mary was a true disciple, so too must the Church walk in discipleship. Receptivity does not mean passivity; it demands activity, but activity based on what has been received.

One might be tempted to think that our rather long excursus on the marian principle in the Church, following largely on the thought of von Balthasar, is excessively theoretical. The opposite is the truth. Our search for a marian principle in the Church has enormous practical consequences, as two final quotations from the Swiss theologian will make clear. The imbalance of the male principle has meant that the Church has

> to a large extent put off its mystical characteristics, it has become a Church of permanent conversations, organisations, advisory commissions, congresses, synods, commissions, academies, parties, pressure groups, functions, structures and restructurings, sociological experiments, statistics, that is to say, more than ever a male Church, if perhaps one should not say a sexless entity....[15]

[14]Idem. "Mary the Receptive Virgin" in *Life in the Spirit and Mary* (Wilmington: Glazier—Dublin: Dominican Publications, 1981) 26–43.

[15]*Elucidations* (n. 11) 70.

And again,

> Christianity threatens imperceptibly to become inhuman.
> The Church becomes functionalistic, soulless, a hectic enter-
> prise without any point of rest, estranged from its true nature
> by the planner. And because, in this masculine world, all
> that we have is one ideology replacing another, everything
> becomes polemical, critical, bitter, humourless, and ulti-
> mately boring, and people in their masses run away from
> such a Church.[16]

One final point should be made about the feast of the Immaculate Heart of Mary. And indeed it is a comment that could be
made in each chapter of this book. In the Church we have
religious congregations, many of them called after one of the
titles of Mary. The Church needs to learn from these congregations. Their marian charism will be a lived experience of special
dedication to one aspect of Mary's response to God. Thus, Père
Jean Gailhac, founder of the Religious of the Sacred Heart of
Mary wrote:

> You are daughters of the Sacred Heart of Mary, of that
> heart which so closely cooperated in the work of redemption.
> This title alone indicates what your devotedness should be,
> with what zeal you should cooperate in the work of calling
> others to holiness for the glory of God. Everything in you
> must speak of holiness; your whole life must draw others to
> God.

Here we have one reflection on the Heart of Mary, and there are
many other different visions to be found in the constitutions and
writings of religious institutes. We can all learn from them. But
there is also a converse: in sharing their own charism with the
Church, the religious in question will themselves penetrate more

[16]Ibid. 72.

deeply their marian charism.[17] The charism of an institute is discovered not only by historical research into the origins of a congregation and by reflection within its communities, but also through having their charism mirrored back to them from other members of the Church. The very numerous congregations dedicated to the Heart of Mary have spiritual insights that could enrich the Church, and in turn be still more life-giving for their own members.

PRAYER OF THE FAITHFUL

We turn to our heavenly Father and make our prayers to him as we rely on the intercession of Mary his beloved daughter.

- The Heart of Mary was a temple of the Holy Spirit: may the Church always be mindful of the grace and gifts it received.
- Mary rejoiced in God's love: may the world learn that true rejoicing which is to be found in following the ways of God.
- Mary pondered in her Heart: may we learn more and more to come before God in silent praise and wonder.
- Mary said from her Heart a complete yes to God: may we reflect her complete openness in childlike trust.
- Mary's heart has been the source of inspiration for many religious congregations of women and men: may they all be renewed and strengthened so that the Church may benefit from the gifts they have received.
  Heavenly Father, by the power of the Spirit you made holy the Heart of Mary. May all of us be touched by this same Spirit, and so come into more perfect discipleship of Jesus, your Son and our Lord. Amen.

---

[17]See C. O'Donnell, "Religious Community as Apostolic Resource," *Religious Life Review* 24 (1985) 307-316 at 313-315.

ADDITIONAL READING

J.F. Murphy, "The Immaculate Heart" in Carol 3:168–178.

Pius XII, Acts of Consecration, Office and Mass, *AAS* 37 (1945) 44–52.

Pius XII *"Singulis annis"* Letter to Cardinal Maglione, 15 April 1943. *AAS* 35 (1943) 103–105.

P. Trible, *God and the Rhetoric of Sexuality* (Philadelphia: Fortress, 1978).

H. Urs von Balthasar, *The Threefold Garland* (San Francisco: Ignatius, 1982) 59–68.

OUR LADY OF MOUNT CARMEL
(Optional Memorial—16 July)

LITURGICAL HISTORY[1]

Mount Carmel in the Holy Land is not so much a peak as a mountain range about 25 km long. Hermits settled on it near the Fountain of Elijah in the late 12th century.[2] We know that they had an oratory dedicated to Our Lady in the midst of their cells.

---

[1]See A.M. Forcadell, *Commemoratio solemnis Beatae Mariae Virginis de Monte Carmelo. Historia et liturgia.* (Rome: Generalates of O. Carm. and O.D.C., 1951); L. Saggi, "Santa Maria del Monte Carmelo" in L. Saggi, ed., *Santi del Carmelo.* (Rome: Institutum Carmelitanum, 1972) 109-135; V. Macca, "Carmelo" *NDizM* 312-316.

[2]See J. Smet, *The Carmelites. A History of the Brothers of Our Lady of Mount Carmel. Vol. 1—Ca. 1200 Until the Council of Trent* (Rome: Carmelite Institute, 1975) 9.

Perhaps even then, but certainly by the middle of the following century, the hermits were known as the "Brothers of Our Lady of Mount Carmel."[3] As early as 1252 papal documents used the title in relation to the hermits by then known in Europe as friars.[4] In the 14th century a Solemn Commemoration of the Blessed Virgin was celebrated on 17 July, a day chosen apparently to remember the closing date of the Council of Lyons (17 July 1274), which narrowly allowed the Order to continue in existence. It was called the "Solemn Commemoration" to highlight its importance over and against the normal Carmelite commemoration on each Saturday. The feast was later transferred to the previous day in the late 15th century. By the end of the Middle Ages the wearing of the Brown Scapular led to a diffusion of devotion to Our Lady of Mount Carmel and the feast was extended to the universal Church in 1726. It survives as an optional memorial in the recent reform of the liturgical calendar.

THEMES

The intercession of the Virgin Mary helps us, and her protection assists us, to reach the holy mountain, who is Christ (prayer of the Mass from the Latin text. The English translation is considerably weaker).

> I sought wisdom openly in my prayer; it has come to flower
> like early grapes. (Morning Prayer)
> Mary treasured the word of God and pondered it in her
> heart. (Evening Prayer)

SCRIPTURE READING

In the Carmelite Order the readings concern the prophet Elijah

[3]Ibid. 9, 24-27.
[4]Ibid. 9.

(I Kgs 19:42-45) and Mary at the foot of the cross (Jn 19:25-27). The Roman lectionary which is followed here offers the same readings as for the Presentation of the Virgin, 21 November.

a) Zechariah 2:14-17

The first part of Zechariah can be dated 520-519 b.c. The prophet is concerned with rebuilding the Temple and especially with the moral restoration of the people. Jerusalem, the *daughter of Zion* is to *rejoice*, for now *I am coming to live among you—Yahweh declares*. This coming of the Lord is associated with the fact that *many nations will be converted*. The Lord who blesses demands a response of faith and conversion. *Yahweh will take possession of Judah*, that is, he will defend it.

As we pray to Mary, we always seek God's power and defence through her intercession. We are reminded too of the contemplative tradition of Carmel by the words, *let all people be silent before Yahweh*. The primary meaning of this command is that the people must listen to God who is about to speak; contemplation requires a profound listening in silent worship.

The *response* to this reading is, "The Almighty works marvels for me. Holy is his name."

b) Matthew 12:46-50

The immediate sense of this passage is that the one *who does the will of the Father* is blessed. This obedient faith is more significant even than family bonds in natural kinship with Jesus.

But the text can also invite us to consider new bonds with Jesus through discipleship. Jesus stretches out *his hand towards his disciples* and says: *Here are my mother and my brothers. Anyone who does the will of my Father in heaven is my brother and sister and mother.* When we do the will of the Father, we become more and more his children, hence we enter into a deeper relationship of brother and sister to Jesus his Son. Furthermore, our obedient faith in doing the will of the Father allows us to bring forth Jesus in our home, our environment and our lives. Hence we are symbolically his mother, for we give him life and existence in a new way, in yet another place. The parallel passage in Luke 8:19-21, as a reinterpretation of the same logion used by Matthew, shows Mary as Luke's model of believer and disciple.

CHURCH DOCUMENTS

Pope Paul VI wrote in *Marialis cultus:*

> Then there are others (feasts), originally celebrated by particular religious families but which today, by reason of the popularity they have gained, can truly be considered ecclesial, e.g. 16 July, Our Lady of Mount Carmel. (MC 8)

On the seventh centenary of the Brown Scapular, Pope Pius XII wrote:

> There is no one who is not aware how greatly a love for the Blessed Mother of God contributes to the enlivening of the Catholic faith and to the raising of moral standards. These effects are especially secured by means of those devotions which more than others are seen to enlighten the mind with heavenly doctrine and to excite souls to the practice of the Christian life. In the first rank of the most favoured of these devotions that of the holy Carmelite scapular must be praised as a devotion which, adapted to the minds of all by its very simplicity, has become so universally widespread among the faithful and shown many salutary fruits ... the holy scapular, which may be called the habit or garment of Mary, is a sign and a pledge of the protection of the Mother of God. . . . May those (associated with the Carmelite Order) see in this keepsake of the Virgin herself a mirror of humility and purity; may they read in the very simplicity of the garment a concise lesson in modesty and simplicity. Above all may they behold in this same garment, which they wear day and night, the eloquently expressive symbol of their prayers for divine assistance; finally may it be to them a sign of their

consecration to the most Sacred Heart of the Immaculate Virgin.[5]

REFLECTION

The various titles of Mary in the liturgy and in piety usually emphasize some aspect of her relationship to God or to us, or they refer to some place or religious institute. In these two last cases we have to expand the title if we are to grasp its full meaning. Thus "Our Lady of Lourdes" indicates "Our Lady as manifested at, and honoured in, Lourdes." Similarly, "Our Lady of Mount Carmel" means "Mary as she is honoured in the Carmelite Order." Carmelite marian insights are rich and complex. We can conveniently divide them into three overlapping stages, all of which combine to form a particular pattern of devotion.[6]

Mary is first seen as Patron. The chapel of the original hermits on Carmel was, as we have seen, dedicated to her. The Carmelite *Rule* specified that this church was to be in the middle of the cells of the hermits. It was thus a focal point for the daily Mass (which was rather unusual at the time of the *Rule*). In the reflection of the Carmelite Order on Mary in the 13th and 14th centuries we find many statements to the effect that the Order was founded in honour of Our Lady. The historical inexactitude of this claim does not take away from the spiritual attitude that also lay behind the hermits' choice of Mary as dedicatee of the chapel on Mount Carmel. When the Order came to Europe one of the favourite titles for its churches was the Annunciation.[7] Given the feudal overtones of "the service of Jesus Christ" (*obsequium Jesu Christi*)— a key notion of the *Rule*—it is easy to see how the idea of Mary as Patron grew. The annual (as well as the weekly) Commemoration of Our Lady celebrated a descending action of Mary towards the

[5]*Neminem profecto*, 11 February 1950. *AAS* 42 (1950) 390.

[6]See Saggi art. cit (n. 1) 109-110; E.R. Carroll, "The Marian Theology of Arnold Bostius, O.Carm. (1445-1499)" *Carmelus* 9 (1962) 197-236, especially 212-216.

[7]See Saggi, art. cit. (n. 1) 114-116 and n. 22. For the idea of Mary as the "Lady of the Place" see Smet, op.cit. (n. 2) 65-66.

Carmelites, namely protection, and an ascending action of Carmelites towards Mary, that is, thanksgiving and service. Along with the title of "Patron of Carmelites" there arose at the same period the title of "Mother of Carmelites."

The second stage of marian devotion in Carmel was an emphasis on the Most Pure Virgin in the 14th and 15th centuries. What is stressed is not so much the chastity of Mary as rather her purity of heart which excluded all sin and involved a total dedication to God.[8] One can therefore understand the attraction of the mystery of the Annunciation and why churches were dedicated under this title.[9]

This cult of Mary as Virgin is attested by the fact that when the Carmelites were adapting the Roman Missal in 1584, they replaced *Sancta Maria* each time with *Beata Virgo*. In this same period Carmelites were to the fore in defence of the Immaculate Conception.[10]

A devotion to Mary as the Most Pure Virgin also harmonized well with the contemplative ideal of the Order, which was given clear definition by a pseudonymous work, *The Institutes of the First Monks,* ascribed to John the forty-fourth bishop of Jerusalem, but appearing only in 1370:

> In regard to that life we may distinguish two aims, the one of which we may attain to, with the help of God's grace, by our own efforts and by virtuous living. This is to offer God a heart holy and pure from all actual stain of sin.... The second aim of this life is something that can be bestowed upon us only by God's bounty, namely to taste in our hearts and experience in our minds, not only after death but even during this mortal life, something of the power of the divine presence, and the bliss of heavenly glory.[11]

[8]V. Hoppenbrouwers, "Virgo purissima et vita spiritualis Carmeli," *Carmelus* 1 (1954) 255-277, esp. 268-272; idem., *Devotio mariana in ordine fratrum BVM de Monte Carmelo a medio saeculi xvi usque ad finem saeculi xix* (Rome: Carmelite Institute, 1960) 240.

[9]See Saggi, op. cit. (n. 1) 128-129.

[10]See ibid. 125-127; Smet, op. cit. (n. 1) 65-67.

[11]Tr. B. Edwards (privately published at Boars Hill Oxford, 1969) ch. 2, pages 3-4.

The inspiration of this text, and its allied spirituality, led Carmelites to keep reflecting on Mary as model for its contemplative life.

Alongside this second stage of seeing Mary as the Most Pure Virgin, there was a development of the idea of Mary as "sister." The inspiration for such a title may well be the medieval penchant for a profusion of titles. But it was also in keeping with the official name of the Order, "Brothers of the Most Blessed Virgin Mary of Mount Carmel," a name which was attacked but which the Order fought vigorously to retain.[12] The title "sister" is found in the writings of the Fathers.[13] It was taken up by Pope Paul VI in his closing address at the end of the third session of Vatican II:

> Like ourselves, she too is a daughter of Adam, and hence our
> sister according to our shared human nature.[14]

Mary is the ideal child of the heavenly Father, his "beloved daughter" (LG 53), since she above all others has been guided by the Holy Spirit (see Rom 8:14). Moreover, Carmelites living in the spiritual tradition of the celibate Elijah, felt intuitively a bond with Mary the first of virgins among women.[15] Furthermore, the idea of Mary as "sister" in Carmelite devotion gathers together a number of points:[16] in God's providence the name of the Order was *Brothers* of the Most Blessed Virgin Mary of Mount Carmel; the Order is dedicated to her, so that it becomes, as it were, her house in which people receive the gift of divine intimacy; Elijah was the first celibate among males; Mary was first in rank among women; the Carmelite contemplative vocation, "pondering the

[12]See Smet, op. cit. (n. 2) 25-26.

[13]See V. Macca, "Sorella," *NDizM* 1323-1327 at 1323.

[14]*AAS* 56 (1964) 1016. See further discourse of 8 December 1969 and 11 October 1963, *AAS* 55 (1963) 874.

[15]See Saggi, art. cit. (n. 1) 123-124 and Macca, art. cit. (n. 13) 1325.

[16]For what follows see Macca, art.cit. (n. 13) 1326; less positive is Hoppenbrouwers, *Devotio mariana* (n. 8) 250-252.

law of the Lord" (*Rule* 7), resembles Mary's own vocation for the greater part of her life; as servant/handmaid of the Lord, she becomes the model of true discipleship, of the service (*obsequium*) of Jesus Christ which lies at the heart of the *Rule*. These points are of relevance not only to professed members of the Carmelite Order (First, Second and Third), but to all who are touched by Carmelite devotion to Mary by wearing the Brown Scapular, to which we now turn.

The third way in which Mary is honoured in the Carmelite family is through the Brown Scapular. It becomes dominant from the 16th century, though the first (Patron) and the second (Most Pure Virgin) are also present giving their own shape to Carmelite devotion expressed in the Scapular. There are a number of problems about the origin of the Scapular devotion: the evidence for a vision of Mary to St. Simon (Stock?) is late, nearly two hundred years after the attributed event; the historical character of the evidence is not fully satisfactory;[17] the narrative can be paralleled in other Orders, even to the point of Mary's giving a garment.[18] The conclusion of J. Smet is judicious: "the possibility of a basis in fact for the story cannot be entirely ruled out."[19]

But the Scapular devotion does not rest on the authenticity or otherwise of the vision. The basic idea of the Scapular is that of a symbol of Mary's protection. A garment as such a symbol is found elsewhere in christian tradition, most notably in the Eastern icon tradition in the Madonna of the Mantle. Along with the notion of Mary's protection, the Scapular (itself a symbol of the Carmelite habit) includes the idea of consecration to Mary. Consecration is most properly an act done by God, so that when we say we consecrate ourselves to God and to Mary, we are principally stating that we freely want God's will, the Lordship of Jesus, to be manifested in our lives. The wearing of the scapular is a sign that we want the values lived out by Mary to be evident

[17]See Saggi (n. 1) 130-132.

[18]E.g. M. O'Carroll, *Theotokos* "Caesar of Heisterbach" 93-94.

[19]Op. cit. (n. 2) 27.

in our actions and dispositions. Such a declaration has been officially approved by the Church in making the Scapular a sacramental and in the past enriching its wearing with many indulgences.

It is commonplace to refer to a present-day crisis of symbolism. The Scapular has declined notably in the past three decades, even though many continue to wear it. In order that it may be a meaningful symbol there is need of a "meditative reconstruction"—to use E. Voeglin's phrase. It will remain, or become, meaningful only to the extent that people become aware reflectively of its basic inspiration: Mary's protection and the response of consecration, imitation and service.

We need not delay over the issue of the so-called "Sabbatine Privilege." Its origins are spurious,[20] but it expresses confidence in the power of Mary's intercession at the time of death and later in the purification and healing which is Purgatory. It would be far from wise to speak of a deliverance from Purgatory on the Saturday after death. But the "conditions" ascribed to this "privilege" can be preached with confidence, not on the basis of a vision or "promise" but in terms of the New Testament which inculcates strongly all three conditions: prayer, chastity according to one's state in life, and penance.

PRAYER OF THE FAITHFUL
(from the Carmelite liturgy)

As we honour the Holy Mother of God under whose patronage we live, let us pray with confidence to Christ our Lord:

- You said, "Blessed are the poor in spirit, for theirs is the kingdom of heaven"; may we stand with Mary among the poor and humble of the Lord, so that you may be our only wealth.

[20]See L. Saggi, *La "Bolla Sabbatina": ambiente, testo tempo* (Rome: Carmelite Institute, 1967).

- You said, "Blessed are the pure in heart, for they shall see God"; in following the Immaculate Virgin may we come to love that purity of heart that makes us eager to see the Father's face.
- You said, "Blessed are those who have not seen, and yet believe"; with Mary at our side, may we never cease to trust in the love you have for us as we journey in this night of faith.
- You said, "You ought to pray always and never lose heart"; teach us to pray like Mary, treasuring your word in our hearts and proclaiming it in our lives.
- You said, " A new commandment I give you: love one another as I have loved you"; united in one heart and mind, may we be ready to spend our lives for our brothers and sisters and share with Mary in your work of redemption.
- Dying on the cross, you said to John, and through him to all disciples, "Behold your Mother"; may we always please you by living in the intimate company of the Mother of grace.

Father, your Word filled Mary's heart and inspired all her actions. In your service may our love become like hers and so unite us more closely with the work of redemption. Through Christ our Lord.

ADDITIONAL READING

A. Bandera, "De la devoción mariana a la consagración a Maria," *Estudios Marianos* 51 (1986) 113-141.

La consagración a Maria. Teología—historia—espiritualidad. "Estudios Marianos 51" (Salamanca: Soc. Mariológica Española, 1986).

E. Llamas, "La consagracion a la Virgen Maria. Su valor y su actualidad," *Ephemerides Mariologicae* 31 (1981) 383-388.

R.M. Valabek, *Mary Mother of Carmel. Our Lady and the Saints of Carmel,* "Carmel in the World's Paperbacks." 2 vols. (Rome: Carmelite Institute, 1987--).—An important study of Carmelite marian writers. Vol. 1 deals with 15 writers up to the 17th century.

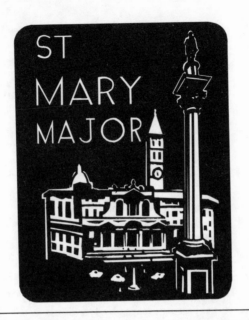

THE DEDICATION OF THE BASILICA
OF
SAINT MARY MAJOR
(Optional Memorial—5 August)

LITURGICAL HISTORY

The legend surrounding this feast goes back to Pope Liberius (d. 366): in a vision to him and to the Patriarch John, Mary asked that a church be built where snow would be found on 5 August, usually a time of oppressive heat in Rome. We are on surer ground when we look to the triumphal arch, and a later basilica, on the Esquiline hill from the time of Pope Sixtus III (d. 440) and begun the year after Mary was declared *Theotokos*, Mother of God, at the Council of Ephesus (431). The church was also known later as St. Mary of the Crib (S. Maria ad praesepe) from the timbers—supposedly of the crib of Bethlehem—which lie under the high altar.

The feast was originally a Roman one, but began to be diffused to other parts of the world from about the 14th century. Its acceptance was rather slow, probably due to the associated snow legend. It was extended to the universal Church by Pius V (d. 1572). The Basilica, if not indeed the oldest, is certainly the most important Church dedicated to the Mother of God in the Western Church. As a patriarchal church it is linked with Antioch.

THEMES

The prayer of the Mass focuses on the need to have our sins forgiven and on the prayers of the Virgin Mary which assist us. The Latin version of the prayer has the idea, missing in the English ICEL translation, that because by our actions we cannot of ourselves please God we rely on the intercession of Mary.

> Holy Mary, Mother of God, ever Virgin: you are the most blessed of all women, and blessed is the fruit of your womb. (Morning Prayer)
> Holy Mary Mother of God, pray for us sinners, now, and at the hour of our death. (Evening Prayer)

SCRIPTURE READING

a) Revelation 21:1-5

The seventh vision of the Apocalypse is that of the *new Jerusalem*. It is *a new heaven and a new earth*. The vision opens with a negative aspect: the *sea*, a symbol of destructive force and chaos, is no longer. The text then moves to positive statements: the *holy city*, the *new Jerusalem* is seen *coming down out of heaven*. It is a wedding scene with Jerusalem *prepared as a bride to meet her husband*. The husband is the Lamb. Then there is a solemn proclamation: *look, here God lives among human beings*. It is a definitive act of God to dwell with his people, making *his home among them*, so that he is

God-with-them. All evil and pain is overcome for he *will wipe away all tears from their eyes*, and there will be an end to *death, mourning, sadness* and *pain*. The *One on the throne* then interprets all that is happening: *Look, I am making the whole of creation new*. This text would seem to have been chosen for the memorial of Mary Major, because of the notion of a temple in which God lives and moves among his people.

The *response* centres on Mary, "You are the highest honour of our race."

b) Luke 11:27-28

This gospel passage parallels in some way the Visitation story. *A woman in the crowd* declares the mother of Jesus to be blessed (*makaria*, the same word as used in the Beatitudes, see Mt 5:1-11; Lk 6:20-22). Elizabeth too praised Mary as Mother of the Lord (see Lk 1:42), with however the word *eulogēmenē*—which expresses praise of God who favoured Mary. Jesus corrects, or rather focuses the woman's praise, *more blessed still*: it is especially *those who hear the word of God and keep it* that are blessed. Elizabeth made the same transition from praise of Mary's motherhood (see Lk 1:42) to praise of her faith (see Lk 1:45—"Blessed is she who believed"). Faith involves both hearing God's word and keeping it. The gospel passage shows, therefore, Mary's true blessedness. As we celebrate her motherhood, we are invited to contemplate her faith.

CHURCH DOCUMENTS

Pope Paul VI gives the characteristic of the kind of celebration we have in the Dedication of Saint Mary Major: "(The calendar) includes other kinds of commemoration which have acquired a wider popularity and interest" (MC 8).

Commenting on the gospel passage Pope John Paul II writes:

These words were an expression of praise of Mary as Jesus' mother according to the flesh ... But to the blessing uttered by that woman upon her who was his mother according to the flesh, Jesus answers in a significant way: 'Blessed rather are those who hear the word of God and keep it' (Lk 11:28). He wishes to divert attention from motherhood understood only as a fleshly bond, in order to direct it towards those mysterious bonds of the spirit which develop from hearing and keeping God's word.... If it is true that 'all generations will call her blessed' (cf. Lk 1:48), then it can be said that the unnamed woman was the first to confirm unwittingly that prophetic phrase of Mary's *Magnificat* and to begin the *Magnificat* of the ages. (RM 20)

REFLECTION

In the liturgy of the dedication of the churches[1] there is a continual interplay between the church as a building of stone, and the church which is a building of the followers of Jesus. The Temple in the Old Testament was the place where God was seen to dwell and to be worshipped. The Temple then found fulfilment and perfect expression in Jesus, the Word made man. In his flesh God truly dwelt (see Jn 1:14) and the Father was worshipped (see Jn 17:4); indeed he called his own body a temple (see Jn 2:20-22).

But the christian community is also a temple. We find in Eph 2:20-22 the idea that Jesus is the cornerstone of the new building: everything knit together in him "grows into a holy temple in the Lord, and you too, in him, are being built up into a dwelling of God in the Spirit." Again, Paul writes to the Corinthians:

Do you not know that you are the temple of God with the Spirit of God dwelling in you?... God's temple is holy, and you are that temple. (I Cor 3:16-17)

---

[1]See P. Jounel, "Dedicazione delle chiese e degli altari," D. Sartori and A.M. Triacca, eds. *Nouvo dizionario di liturgia* (Rome: Ed. Paoline, 1984) 352-367.

The individual christian, and especially the christian community, is where God dwells and where he is worshipped in "spirit and in truth" (see Jn 4:23).

Mary too is a temple of God the Ark of the Covenant, as the Litany of Loreto calls her. We allude again to the idea of Mary as temple in connection with the memorial of the Presentation (21 November). When we commemorate her greatest church in christendom, we are at the same time celebrating the mystery of how she became the first member of the Church and its finest ornament.

But we need to look also at the piety of the Church which has given rise to countless thousands of churches dedicated to Mary and to the many forms of veneration of the Mother of God according to circumstances of time and place, the different sensibilities of peoples, and their different cultural traditions (see MC 24). The marian basilica of St. Mary Major is only the high point of a mentality that has deep and extensive roots. We will never understand marian devotion if we fail to look to the grass-roots of the Church where the Spirit "breathes as he wills" (see Jn 3:8). Vatican II speaks of a "sense of the faith" which has four characteristics: it is aroused and sustained by the Spirit of truth; guided by the Spirit the Church receives the word of God; the Church adheres to this faith; it penetrates the faith more deeply and applies it to daily life (see LG 12).

There is probably no expression of marian theology or devotion that had its first beginning in papal teaching or in the pronouncement of a council. Both theology and devotion grow from within the Church, and at a certain stage receive official approval. A. Agius observed the same about liturgy:

> Marian liturgical recognition was not occasioned by a series of feasts imposed from above: it was the acceptance of popular acclamation exerting pressure from below.... It was the faithful, drawing upon Holy Scripture, who first apprehended the Marian prerogatives: these were elaborated by the Fathers and Scripture Commentators (such as Origen +

254), and then, thirdly, the beliefs found their place in the liturgy.[2]

There is growing interest in recent years in phenomena variously described as "popular piety," "popular religiosity" or "popular faith."[3] In his exhortation on evangelization (*Evangelii nuntiandi*, 1975—abbreviatd EN) Pope Paul VI prefers the term "popular piety" and observes that "it does indicate a certain thirst for God, such as only those who are simple and poor in spirit can experience" (EN 48).

There are many scientific studies of popular piety. But unless they take account of the fact that popular piety is at heart a quest for God from the depths of a people's interiority, these analyses miss the point. Thus we find explanations of popular piety merely in psychological terms (e.g. emotional relief from accumulated frustrations), in a socio-economic or marxist vision (e.g. a counter-culture, an expression of the tensions and hopes of the oppressed), or in purely secular terms (a factor of cultural deprivation, remnant of paganism). At the 1974 Synod of Bishops, Cardinal Pironio gave a useful description of popular piety: "the way in which christianity is incarnated in different cultures and ethnic states, is lived out, and is manifested in the people."[4] There are two ideas here: inculturation of the message and the variety of ways in which it is expressed and lived. It is a translation and an enunciation of the christian message. We have to look, therefore, to the truths and to the prayers, which are contained sometimes imperfectly, in such popular piety.

G. Agostino notes four characteristics of popular piety. It is *spontaneous* and arises from feeling rather than from reason. People

---

[2]"Our Lady in the Early Latin Liturgy," *Marian Studies* 19 (1968) 27-40 at 30.

[3]What follows owes much to G. Agostino, "Pietà populare," *NDizM* 1111-1122. See also J. Castellano, "Religiosità populare e liturgia," *Nuovo dizionario di liturgia* (n. 1 above) 1168-1187; B.M. Bosatra, "Recenti miscellanee Sulla Religiosità populare," *La scuola cattolica* 110 (1982) 65-84, 300-313, 451-472; *Concilium* 186 (1986) 1-135; De Fiores 341-347.

[4]Agostino, art. cit. (n. 3) 1113.

can feel more than they know, and there is a limit to what we know intellectually. Popular piety is deeply intuitive. Secondly, it is *festive* for it goes beyond the monotony of everyday existence to what is imaginative and creative.[5] Hence it is opposed both to the marxist ideology of work and to the cartesian ideology of reason. Thirdly, popular piety does not use conceptual language, but rather symbolic communication. It arises from *a sense of poverty and openness to the transcendent*. Religious experience can reach beyond reason to a true contact with the Wholly Other. Finally, popular piety arises out of *communal memory*. Some event is recalled which gives a reason for a present celebration.

For well over a thousand years Mary has been a powerful symbol and focus for popular piety. Though exaggerations, theological inexactitide, or even superstition, may at times be present, popular piety does have an authentic nucleus in centering on Mary as Mother of God and Mother of the Redeemer. What piety adds is above all a personal "you" that makes Mary alive in the hearts of those who approach her. She is seen as a powerful advocate and merciful mother. Piety senses rather than deduces that in Mary God has given us a gift to relieve our burden and distress. It grasps intuitively that she is a way to approach God— "pray for us sinners, now and at the hour of our death." She is further seen as different to us, for she is the all pure, all holy one. Poetry, prayers, art, liturgical texts, all heap up exuberant expression about her beauty. (I have argued elsewhere that devotion to Mary is strong and healthy only to the extent that three factors are safeguarded and kept in proper harmony: Mary's relation to Christ; her relation to us; and her beauty).[6] But for all her difference from our sinful condition she is not seen as distant. Indeed, the very titles by which she is praised, are a kind of sacramenta-

---

[5]On celebration see F. Dubuyst, "Feast Days and Festive Celebrations," *Concilium* 9/4 (November 1968) 5-9.

[6]See forthcoming "Growth and Decline in Mariology" in J. Hyland, ed., *Mary and the Church Today. Papers of the National Marian Congress 1984* (Athlone, Ireland: Marist Brothers—Dublin: Veritas, 1988).

lizing of the world. She is known as Sorrowful Mother, Mother of Perpetual Succour, Star of the Sea, Lady of the Wayside.... She is invoked as patroness of countries, towns, and private dwellings. She is depicted in the clothes and in the ethnic features of different races. All of these facts suggest that Mary is seen as being present in the history of each people.

Responses to Mary are numerous: prayers, hymns, festivals, pilgrimages, offerings, forms of consecration—all of which are signs of confidence in her help and a living litany of praise and intercession. They allow for the important dimension of feeling in prayer.[7]

Though exaggerations and deviations are to be found in some marian theology, difficulties are more often experienced in popular piety. Pope Paul VI too was aware of the dangers: popular piety can open the way to false forms of religion and may verge on superstition; it can be shallow and not grow into a generous adherence to the faith; it can lead to the establishment of sects and factions (see EN 48). Though pastors must be vigilant, their approach should be sympathetic for there are important values in popular piety:

> it indicates a certain thirst for God ... it can arouse in people a capacity for self-dedication and for the exercise of heroism when there is a question of professing the faith. It gives them a keen sensitivity by virtue of which they can appreciate the ineffable attributes of God: his fatherly compassion, his providence, his benevolence and loving presence. It can develop in the innermost depths of people habits of virtue rarely to be found otherwise in the same degree, such as patience, acceptance of the cross in daily life, detachment, openness to others and a spirit of ready service. (ibid)

---

[7]See D.E. Saliers, "Prayer and Emotion: Shaping and Expressing Christian Life" in J. Gallen, ed., *Christians at Prayer.* "Liturgical Studies" (Notre Dame: University Press, 1977) 46-60.

If such are the possibilities of popular piety, there is clearly much at stake. One can note with some misgiving the fact that devotions of doubtful origin and theology can circulate without adequate response from pastors. Does not Church authority always tend to be more lenient towards right-wing rather than towards left-wing errors? Yet both sin against the truth. Mary is not honoured by false devotions, nor by those which do not lead people to her Son.

It is often asked if devotion to Mary is necessary for Catholics. At times Catholics can feel guilty because of the low affective level of their relationship to Mary, or because they are not drawn to, or are actually repelled by, certain forms of devotion. In such cases the reason may also be psychological, and lie in the quality of a poor relationship with one's natural mother. This situation can be paralleled in those who find difficulty with prayer to the heavenly Father for the same kind of psychological reason, only in this case, their human father. To those with difficulty about devotion to Mary one can say that growth in devotion takes time, and can be started very gently and gradually, perhaps with the prayer ascribed to St. Ignatius: "Jesus show me your Mother; Mary show me your Son."

It is true that theoretically speaking devotion to Mary is not absolutely necessary for a christian. The one mediator with all-sufficient salvation is Christ Jesus (see 1 Tim 2:5). In practice, however, those who can accept God's full plan in which Mary has an important, but secondary role are enriched in a way that others are not. In the words of H. Urs von Balthasar:

> The veneration of Mary is the most sure and the shortest way of concretely approaching Christ. In meditating on the life of Mary in all its phases, we learn what it is to live for Christ and with Christ in daily life in a closeness that does not show any emotional high, but is instead a perfect interior closeness.[8]

[8]"O Vierge, Mère et fille de ton Fils" in J. Ratzinger and H. Urs von Balthasar, *Marie Première Eglise* (Paris: Apostolat des Editions—Montreal: Ed. Paulines, 1981) 65.

To return to the celebration of St. Mary Major. The basilica is one of the focal points of any pilgrimage to Rome. But the austere beauty of the basilica style of architecture, whilst admirably suited to splendid liturgy and perhaps to a Taizé meeting of ten thousand young people, is not however, very favourable for popular piety. Groups saying the rosary are dwarfed by the sheer size of the building. Even the obviously exuberant singing of a southern European or Polish pilgrimage seems a trifle wispy. We celebrate in that church the central mystery of the *Theotokos*, Mother of God, but it is perhaps only in its icon chapel of Mary, or elsewhere on their return home, that people will find their deepest attachment to Mary. There is an urgent task facing the Church to renew devotions, to foster piety that will lead to, and lead from, liturgy in a form that will resonate in people's lives. We need marian devotion that is integral, as demanded by von Balthasar:

> ...all marian piety, if it wishes to be catholic, must never be isolated but must always be inserted and orientated in a christological, and hence trinitarian way, and ecclesially.[9]

PRAYER OF THE FAITHFUL

As we honour Mary, Christ's gift to us, we come in confidence in his name to our Father.

- That the Church may always like Mary hear the word of God and do it.
- That our society may work for justice and peace and for a lessening of mourning, sadness and pain.
- That those who practise unhealthy devotions to Mary may learn to purify their approach to her.
- That we may be guided into a devotion to Mary that is suited to our times and our culture.

[9]Ibid. 62.

• That those who visit the Basilica of Saint Mary Major as pilgrims and tourists may have their hearts uplifted and experience something of the beauty of God's glory.
Father in heaven, you draw us continually to yourself by the guidance of the Holy Spirit. Grant that as we honour Mary by praise and imitation we may become more perfect disciples of your Son, Jesus our Lord and only Saviour. Amen.

ADDITIONAL READING

C. Dehne, "Roman Catholic Popular Devotions" in J. Gallen, ed., *Christians at Prayer.* "Liturgical Studies." (Notre Dame: University Press, 1977) 83-99.

B. Fischer, "Relation entre liturgie et piété populaire après Vatican II," *La Maison-Dieu* 170 (1987) 91-101.

P. O'Dwyer, *Mary. A History of Irish Devotion* (Dublin: Four Courts, 1988).

Equipo Seladoc, ed., *Religiosidad Popular.* "Materiales 13" (Salamanca: Ed. Sigueme, 1976).

Roschini 4:5-18 especially 11-14. The whole of vol. 4 is a history of devotion to Mary.

A. Verwilghen, "La religiosité populaire dans les documents récents du magistère," *Nouvelle revue théologique* 109 (1987) 521-539.

THE ASSUMPTION
OF THE BLESSED VIRGIN MARY
(Solemnity—15 August)

LITURGICAL HISTORY

There are some obscurities with regard to the origins of this feast,[1] although it is certain that it arose in the East, probably in Jerusalem. The Emperor Maurice (582-602) decreed that it be celebrated throughout the Empire. It came to Rome perhaps through Eastern monks fleeing from Persian invasions. Pope Sergius (683-701) laid down a solemn procession for the feast (as well as for the Presentation—2 February—Annunciation and Birthday of Mary). An octave for the feast was decreed by Leo IV (d. 855). In the Middle Ages it was a day for the blessing of

---

[1]See D. Sartor, "Assunta. Celebrazione liturgica," *NDizM* 178-181.

crops and first fruits, especially in Southern Europe. In the revised Missal of 1970 it is the only marian feast to have a vigil. In the christian East it is celebrated with great solemnity, and it is preceded by a fast lasting a fortnight.

THEMES

The two opening prayers of the Mass stress the fact of the bodily assumption of Mary. The role of the Assumption in the divine plan is indicated: she who bore the Son of God would not see decay; we are to follow her example in order to join her in glory. The Assumption is a sign of hope and comfort (preface, prayer over gifts); we can rely on Mary's intercession (prayer after communion). The Assumption is thus related to Christ—decay was not to touch the body which had given him birth, and to the Church—Mary is the beginning and pattern of the Church in its perfection (preface).

> Behold, all generations will call me blessed, for he who is mighty has done great things for me.
> Alleluia (Evening Prayer 1)

> See the beauty of the daugher of Jerusalem, who ascended to heaven like the rising sun at dawn.
> (Morning Prayer)

> Today the Virgin Mary was assumed into heaven; rejoice and be glad, for she will reign for ever with Christ.
> (Evening Prayer II)

> O Pure and most holy Virgin, the choirs of angels in heaven and the race of men on earth sing the praise of your glorious Dormition, for you have become the Mother of the Creator of All, Christ our God. We beg you to intercede constantly for us, for we have placed our hope in you next to God, O most glorious and ever-virgin Mother of God.
> (*Byzantine Daily Worship* 758)

SCRIPTURE READINGS

a) Revelation 11:19; 12:1-6.10

Modern exegetes predominantly favour an interpretation of the difficult twelfth chapter of the Apocalypse as primarily pointing to the divine plan in the Old and New Testaments.[2] There are those however who, to varying degrees, allow for some secondary marian symbolism.[3] Thus T. Vetraci goes judiciously beyond the literal sense of the text:

> Though the woman refers directly to the messianic people, we can know that this messianic people is not an abstract reality or a pure ideal. It has been incarnated in the Church, and most particularly in Mary. We can understand this text of the Apocalypse in the light of our deeper grasp of Mary's position in the Church, its first and fullest member, already sharing in the triumph of the Church.[4]

We hold here that the author is not directly speaking about Mary. He describes the primeval battle of good and evil in which the messianic people and now the Church is always engaged. Victory is, however, assured, and Mary already shares in the total triumph of her Son. The symbolism of the text requires some explanation. The astronomical symbols are from the Old Testament. *Robed*

---

[2]For example *Mary NT* 218-239 at 231-234; J.-L. D'Aragon, "The Apocalypse" in *Jerome Biblical Commentary* (Englewood Cliffs, NJ: Prentice-Hall—London: Chapman, 1968) part 2: 482-483. A.Y. Collins, *The Apocalypse*. "New Testament Message 22" (Wilmington: Glazier—Dublin: Veritas, 1979) 82-88 stresses the Jewish character of the text.

[3]For example see J.-M. Salgade, "Le chapitre XII de l'Apocalypse à la lumière des procédés de composition littéraires de saint Jean" in *Maria in sacra Scriptura*. "Acta congressus mariologici-mariani ... 1965 celebrati" (Rome: Pontifical Marian Academy, 1967) 5:293-360 with good bibliography of ancient and modern writers; McHugh 404-432; M. Thurian, *Mary. Mother of the Lord—Figure of the Church* (London: Faith Press, 1963) 176-183; A. Serra, "Bibbia," *NDizM* 292-301; O. Knoch, *HBdMK* 82-84.

[4]"La donna dell'Apocalisse" in *Parola spirito e vita—Quaderni di lettura biblica. 6.—La Madre del Signore* (Bologna: Ed. Dehoniane, 1986) 152-170 at 169. Not dissimilar is A. Feuillet, *Jésus et sa Mère* (Paris: Gabalda, 1974) 30-47 and 138-139.

with the sun indicates God's care in clothing the *woman* (see Gen 3:21—Adam and Eve; Mt 6:30—the lilies). God clothes her with his glory, which is so frequently symbolized in the Bible by light, hence the *sun*. The woman is *standing on the moon,* which with its waxing and waning is a symbol of change. She is not then controlled by seasons and times, but dominates them. *On her head* is *a crown of twelve stars.* The stars are seen as belonging to the divine area of existence (see Jb 22:12). They are *twelve,* a reference to the full people of Israel often symbolized by the twelve patriarchs. A *crown* is a sign of triumph. But the *woman* belongs also to the New Testament. The passage concerning the *great sign* begins with a reference to the *ark of the covenant* (11:19) that *could be seen.* The immediate meaning here concerns God dwelling with his people. Though it is not the intention of the sacred writer, the liturgy, by the choice of this text, is hinting at the idea that Mary is the new Ark of the Covenant; just as God dwelt in the Ark, so too he dwelt in Mary. (The same point is also implied by the choice of 1 Chron 15:3-4.15-16; 16:1-2 for the Mass of the Vigil of the Solemnity.) *She was pregnant* and *was delivered of a boy child;* the reference here is a veiled one to the resurrection which is described in the New Testament in terms of a reinterpretation of Psalms 2 and 110. The *huge red dragon* indicates the forces of evil that cannot destroy the child. The Church at the time was being severely persecuted, probably under Domitian (81-96). God *prepared a place for her to be looked after* in the *desert.* But we know that the desert is also a place of trial (see Dt 8:2): the Church will be tested there, but not defeated. God takes the *child straight up to his throne;* the allusion here is again to the resurrection. The extract ends with a chant of victory: *Salvation and power and empire for ever have been won by our God, and all authority for his Christ.*

Even this short extract shows that there are statements about the woman that apply more directly to God's people, now the Church, and that there are texts that would easily be seen to have at least a secondary marian significance.

The *response* to this reading is, "On your right stands the queen in gold of Ophir."

b) I Corinthians 15:20-26

The triumph over evil in the first reading is now made specific and is narrowed down to victory over death. *Christ has been raised.* His resurrection is the key to ours, and is indeed such a central truth that without it our faith is in vain (vv. 16-19). He is *the first-fruits of all who have fallen asleep.* The first fruits were offered to God and symbolized the dedication of the whole crop to him (see Dt 26:1-11). Here the idea is rather that the first-fruit is a sign and assurance that the full harvest will follow, that is, our resurrection in glory. St. Paul continues, *all will be brought to life in Christ.* The forces of evil now operating in the world will be overcome, and *the last of the enemies to be done away with is death.* The victory of death is only illusory, for we shall all rise and join Mary who already shares in the full triumph of her Son.

c) Luke 1:39-56

The gospel for the solemnity is the story of the Visitation and it includes the *Magnificat.* We have already seen some aspects of this text in treating of the Visitation (31 May). But there are some features that have their fuller meaning in the Assumption. Elizabeth can see that Mary is *of all women the most blessed,* and she gives as the reason, *blessed is she who believed that the promise made her by the Lord would be fulfilled.* The same point is emphasized by the choice of Luke 11:27-28 for the Mass of the Vigil: true blessedness is in hearing and keeping the word of God. Elizabeth praises Mary, and therefore indirectly celebrates the divine work in her.

Mary's response to Elizabeth's praise and blessing is to *proclaim in her turn the greatness of the Lord.* It is all God's work: *he has looked upon the humiliation of his servant,* and as a consequence Mary can state, *Yes, from now onwards all generations will call me blessed.* The *great things* God has done for Mary are an example of his providence: *faithful love* for *those who fear him;* the *hungry filled;* the *arrogant routed;* the *promise* made to the *ancestors* and to *Abraham* remembered. By the time of the Visitation the *Almighty* had *done great things* for her. The crowning gift is the Assumption. Pope John Paul II remarks about this passage:

> In her exultation Mary confesses that she finds herself in the
> very heart of this fullness of Christ. She is conscious that the
> promise made to the fathers, first of all 'to Abraham and to
> his posterity for ever' is being fulfilled in herself. She is thus
> aware that concentrated within herself as the Mother of
> Christ is the whole salvific economy, in which 'from age to
> age' is manifested he who, as the God of the Covenant,
> 'remembers his mercy.' (RM 36)

We have to make a similar transition from the *Magnificat* as the
song of the Virgin of Nazareth to the *Magnificat* as the song of
Mary in heaven. Only by looking backwards over the life of
Mary do we get the full meaning of the canticle.

CHURCH DOCUMENTS[5]

The key document is of course the proclamation of the dogma
of the Assumption by Pius XII in 1950:

> We pronounce, proclaim and define it to be a divinely
> revealed dogma that the immaculate Mother of God,Mary
> ever Virgin when the course of her earthly life was over,
> was taken up body and soul into the glory of heaven.[6]

The pope asserted that the fact of the Assumption is a dogma. He
used the circumspect clause, "when the course of her earthly life
was over" to leave open the question of Mary's death. The vast
majority of the Fathers of the Church and of theologians believed
that Mary, like her Son, did die,[7] but there was a minority opinion

---

[5]See E.R. Carroll, "Mary in the Documents of the Magisterium" in Carol 1:24–32;
K. Healy, *The Assumption of Mary.* "The Mary Library." (Wilmington: Glazier, 1982)
15–29.

[6]DS 3903/TCC 334c.

[7]See M. O'Carroll, *Theotokos*, "The Death of Mary" 117-118 with bibliography. For

to the contrary. The phrase "body and soul" does not imply any particular anthropology; it means simply, "Mary fully as a person."

In this Apostolic Constitution, *Munificentissimus Deus,* which contained the definition, Pope Pius XII appealed to a long tradition of belief in the Church and to the present faith of the Church. In fact the preliminary questioning of residential bishops revealed that only six out of 1181 hesitated about the revealed character of the Assumption.[8] The story of the tradition about the Assumption is by no means simple, nor as yet fully clear. In the Apostolic Constitution the pope made no reference to the assumption apocrypha, stories about the *transitus Mariae,* Mary's "passing." Their date is earlier than the 5th century to which they had been ascribed, and their origins could be at least 3rd century. Historically they are worthless, but theologically they attest to an early conviction, presented in the form of legend or myth, that Mary's end was miraculous and that she was taken to heaven.

The earliest clear discussion of Mary's death is in Epiphanius (d. 403). He gives the two possibilities—she died or she did not—and he then confesses that he does not know which is true.[9] We have to wait more than a century for the first homilies on the Assumption from Theotoknos of Livia in the 6th century. His homilies were published only in 1955,[10] and so were unavailable to Pius XII. He speaks of Mary's Assumption (*analēpsis,* not Dormition—*koimēsis*). His theological basis for the Assumption is most significant:

patristic evidence see W. J. Burghardt, *The Testimony of the Patristic Age Concerning Mary's Death.* "Woodstock Papers 2" (Westminster, 1957) and in *Marian Studies* 8 (1957) 58-99.

[8]See E.R. Carroll, "Papal Infallibility and the Marian Definitions: Some Considerations," *Carmelus* 26(1979) 213-250 at 231. For summary see Healy, op. cit. (n. 5) 18-20.

[9]See *Pararion* 78, 11—*EnMar* 714 and 78, 24—*EnMar* 720.

[10]See A. Wenger, *L'Assomption de la très sainte Vierge dans la tradition byzantine du VIe au Xe siècle* (Paris: Institut Francais d'Etudes Byzantines, 1955) 96-110 and text 271-291. Summaries in Healy, op. cit. 59-60; Roschini 3:493-494 and more fully G. Söll, *Storia dei dogmi mariani.* "Accademia mariana salesiana 15." (Rome: LAS, 1981) 192-196.

It was fitting that the most-holy body of Mary, the God bearing body, the receptacle of God, which was divinized, incorruptible, illumined by divine grace and full of glory. . . should be entrusted to the earth for a short while and be raised up in glory to heaven, with her soul pleasing to God.[11]

He is following the Greek tradition of grace which is seen as divinizing, and elsewhere he sees a connection between virginity, grace and incorruption. After him came the major homilies of Modestus of Jerusalem, Germanus of Constantinople, and John of Damascus—all cited by Pius XII in defining the Assumption.

Though the feast and doctrine of the Assumption were held quite constantly in the East,[12] there were some hesitations in the West:[13] doubts were expressed by St. Adamnan of Iona (d. 704), by St. Bede (d. 735) and in two spurious letters ascribed to Augustine and Jerome. Paschasius Radbert (d.c. 865)[14] in a work *Cogitis me,* which he ascribed to Jerome, took up an agnostic position about the Assumption. The fact that his work was deeply conscious of Mary's beauty and graces, finding its way even into the Roman Breviary, proved to be somewhat of a hindrance to growth in the acceptance of the Assumption in the West. By the 13th century, however, the doctrine was universally held.

The Second Vatican Council (1962-1965) repeated the words of the definition in 1950, but we can note some theological development. It retains the personal and christological aspects of *Munificentissus Deus,* but adds:

In the most holy Virgin the Church has already reached that perfection whereby she exists without spot or wrinkle." (LG 65)

[11] Wenger, op. cit. (n. 10) 276-278.

[12] See W.J. Burghardt, "Mary in Eastern Patristic Thought," Carol 2:139-153.

[13] See idem, "Mary in Western Patristic Thought," Carol 1:147-154.

[14] See further, M. O'Carroll, *Theotokos,* "Paschasius" 277-279 and "Assumption" 55-58.

Here we see the Assumption being given an ecclesial significance, which is made more specific by the addition of the clause, "the faithful still strive to conquer sin and increase in holiness." The relationship between the Virgin assumed into heaven and the Church is taken up again towards the end of the Constitution on the Church:

> In the meantime the Mother of Jesus in the glory which she possesses in body and soul in heaven is the image and the beginning of the Church as it is to be perfected in the world to come. Likewise she shines forth on earth, until the day of the Lord shall come (cf. 2 Pet 3:10), a sign of certain hope and comfort to the pilgrim People of God. (LG 68)

The Council therefore develops the doctrine by seeing the Assumption both as the beginning and the aim of the Church, as well as seeing this gift to Mary as being of eschatological importance for all members of the Church.

REFLECTION

We have already seen the various words that were used in earlier times, Passing (*transitus*), Dormition (*koimēsis*), and Assumption (*analēpsis*). In English we would distinguish theologically between assumption and *ascension* (normally used only of Christ, though the English liturgical texts sometimes say Mary "ascended") and *resuscitation* (bringing back to life a dead corpse, as in the case of Lazarus). Mary's assumption is glorification: she is in the final state of perfection through the resurrection of the dead. If one were to ask what the meaning of the definition of the Assumption is, the reply of K. Healy is apposite:

> Mary in the fullness of her person is glorified. She has reached her final destiny. Her life on earth is over, her association with Jesus that began with the Incarnation, and her cooperation with him in her subordinate role, has reached

a perfect final stage. Now her association with him continues in heaven.[15]

We do not know what a resurrected body is like, except for some indications in the gospel resurrection narratives and in I Corinthians 15. We find also the image of a grain of wheat (see Jn 12:24) and the seed (see I Cor 15:35-44). Thus if we never saw an oak tree or a carnation, we could never imagine from looking at an acorn or a seedling what the developed tree or flower would be like. There is, nonetheless, continuity: something dies to *become* something more wonderful and beautiful.

The Apostolic Exhortation of Paul VI gives a brief but rich summary of the different aspects of the dogma. It is a gift to Mary as a person, completing her relationship with her Son and bringing this latter to a new stage of perfection:

> It is a feast of her destiny of fullness and blessedness, of the glorification of her immaculate soul and of her virginal body, of her perfect configuration to the Risen Christ. (MC 6)

But the Assumption is not merely a personal privilege for Mary, for the Pope goes on to say:

> (The Assumption is) a feast that sets before the eyes of the Church and of all mankind the image and consoling proof of the fulfilment of their final hope, namely that this full glorification is the destiny of all those whom Christ has made his brothers, having 'flesh and blood in common with them' (Heb 2:14; cf. Gal 4:4).

Mary's Assumption is therefore related to us. L. Scheffczyk indicates in a few phrases what this means: Mary's Assumption is both the anchor of hope and the task and aim of the Church, giving the Church the way it is to follow.[16] As Mary is and where

[15]Op. cit. (n. 5) 27.
[16]See *Mhe* 142.

she is we are to be. Our bodies are to be glorified. As L. Boff
rightly observes, the bodies which are to be glorified are bodies
which some people wrongly worship, and others, equally wrongly
despise.[17]

The *Magnificat* found in the gospel for the Solemnity of the
Assumption is a favourite text for exponents of liberation theology,[18] especially the lines:

> He has used the power of his arm,
> he has routed the arrogant of heart.
> He has pulled down princes from their thrones
> and raised high the lowly.
> He has filled the starving with good things,
> sent the rich away empty.
> He has come to the help of Israel his servant,
> mindful of his faithful love. (Lk 1:51-54).

As M. Thurian observes,

> Mary, the first christian woman, is also the first revolu-
> tionary of the new order. The Church, of which the virgin is
> the type, cannot proclaim the good news of salvation without
> at the same time making the love of God concrete by the
> defence of justice for the poor and the needy.[19]

This passage from the original French book of 1962 is easy to
parallel in later liberation theology. The use of the *Magnificat* in

---

[17]See L. Boff, *The Maternal Face of God. The Feminine and its Religious Expression* (San
Francisco—London: Harper & Row, 1987) 170.

[18]See for example S. Galilea, *Following Jesus* (Maryknoll: Orbis, 1981) 110-119; Boff,
op. cit. (n. 17) 188-203; V. Elizondo, "Mary and the Poor: A Model of Evangelising
Ecumenism," *Concilium* 168 (1983) 59-65. On the text, but not from a liberation
perspective, see W.F. Maestri, *Mary: Model of Justice. Reflections on the Magnificat* (New
York: Alba, 1987).

[19]Op. cit. (n. 3) 93. From the ecumenical perspective one should also note Luther's
famous commentary on the *Magnificat* in *Luther's Work* (St. Louis: Concordia, 1956)
21:295-353.

the social situation of Latin America and elsewhere is legitimate, but demands some caution. It is important to see the infancy gospel of Luke in relation to his whole gospel. A central thesis in a work of J. Massyngbeerde Ford seems unassailable. Though the infancy gospel of Luke has numerous premonitions of the future destiny of the child, its perspective is that of the Royal Messianism of the House of David. It is only as Jesus' ministry develops that we find that the supreme act of kingship will be the cross. Hence the care with which we need to treat the triumphal, indeed military, imagery of the infancy gospel, including the *Magnificat*.[20]

The liberation theologians are right to show us neglected insights into the *Magnificat*. Indeed Pope John Paul II writes in his marian encyclical (n. 37):

> Drawing from Mary's heart, from the depths of her faith expressed in the words of the *Magnificat,* the Church renews ever more effectively in herself the awareness that the truth about God who saves, the truth about God who is the source of every gift, cannot be separated from the manifestation of his love of preference for the poor and humble, that love which, celebrated in the *Magnificat*, is later expressed in the words and works of Jesus. The Church is thus aware—and at the present this awareness is particularly vivid—not only that these two elements of the message contained in the *Magnificat* cannot be separated, but also that there is a duty to safeguard carefully the importance of 'the poor' and of 'the option in favour of the poor' in the word of the living God. These are matters and questions intimately connected with the Christian meaning of freedom and liberation. 'Mary is totally dependent upon God and completely directed towards him, and, at the side of her Son, she is the most perfect image of freedom and of the liberation of humanity and of the universe. It is to her as Mother and Model that the Church must look in order to understand in its completeness the meaning of her own mission.' (S.C. Doctrine of the Faith, *Instruction on Christian Freedom and Liberation*, 1986)

[20]*My Enemy is my Guest. Jesus and Violence* (Maryknoll: Orbis Books, 1985).

Liberation theology shows us the urgency and obligation to work for justice and against oppression, so that something of God's salvation in Christ Jesus may be achieved even in this life through just social structures and the works of peace. But the Assumption is a potent reminder that full salvation, the completion of God's work, lies beyond the grave.[21]

In recent years another issue has surfaced in relation to the Assumption. It can be indicated by a question: is Mary's Assumption a "singular" privilege, as was the Immaculate Conception?[22] The question does not directly affect mariology, which holds simply that Mary is fully in glory. It belongs more to eschatology, the theology of the Last Things. Briefly it can be said that there have been suggestions that for all who die in Christ there is immediate resurrection, and the dead do not have to wait for the *parousia* or Second Coming for their full glorification. D. Flanagan,[23] among others, has argued that the question remains an open one. The Sacred Congregation for the Doctrine of the Faith, despite the fact that its present prefect Cardinal Ratzinger at one time seems to have allowed immediate resurrection of all, has shown its disapproval of the viewpoint.[24]

Finally, we can note some ecumenical perspectives. The Orthodox East is firm in both belief in the fact of the Assumption and in celebrating it liturgically, a few anti-Roman voices in 1950 excepted. The Churches of the Reformation are negative towards the Assumption mainly on the grounds of the silence of scripture about Mary's end. There are some Anglicans who will accept the fact of the Assumption, though they are not willing to call it

---

[21]The point is made, but over-harshly against liberation theologians, by L. Scheffczyk, *Mhe* 141-142.

[22]See G. Montague, "Our Lady and Eschatology," *Marian Studies* 17(1966) 65-85; H.M. McElwain, "Christian Eschatology and the Assumption," *Marian Studies* 18(1967) 84-102.

[23]See D. Flanagan, "Eschatology and the Assumption," *Concilium* 5(1969) 60-65.

[24]See *AAS* 71(1979) 939. On this text and on the issues involved see D. Lane, "Eschatology," *The New Dictionary of Theology* (Wilmington: Glazier—Dublin: Gill and Macmillan, 1987) 329-342, especially 336-338.

dogma.[25] The Final Report of the Anglican-Roman Catholic dialogues (ARCIC) sought agreement on the fact that Mary has already entered into glory. In a footnote it is stated that the two marian dogmas of the Immaculate Conception and Assumption are not concerned with Mary simply as an individual, but as a "sign" of salvation. Thus her entry into glory is a sign that humanity has already begun to share in the fruits of redemption won by her Son. E. Yarnold, a Roman Catholic member of the ARCIC team noted seven points of agreement in the discussions and in the Report:

> 1. Mary's role is not to be so interpreted as to obscure the fact that Jesus Christ is the one mediator between God and man (see I Tm 2:5).
>
> 2. Christian understanding of Mary is inseparably linked with the doctrines of Christ and the Church.
>
> 3. Mary, as Mother of God Incarnate, received a unique vocation.
>
> 4. God prepared her by his grace to be the Mother of the Saviour, by whom she was herself redeemed.
>
> 5. She has already entered into the glory of heaven.
>
> 6. Both Churches honour Mary in the Communion of Saints and observe liturgical feasts in her honour.
>
> 7. Mary is a model of holiness, obedience and faith. She can therefore be regarded as a 'prophetic figure of the Church.'[26]

But along with the areas of agreement, there are also substantive problems that lie not in mariology but in other key areas of theology. Any listing of these will depend a good deal on those

---

[25]E.g. J. Saward, "The Assumption" in A. Stacpoole, ed., *Mary's Place in Christian Dialogue* (Slough: St. Paul, 1982) 108-122.

[26]E. Yarnold, "Mary in the Final ARCIC Report." (Occasional papers of the Ecumenical Society of the Blessed Virgin Mary, January 1985).

involved in a particular discussion, but the issues that emerged in Irish dialogues between the Anglican, Methodist, Presbyterian and Roman Catholic Churches in 1982/3 would not be untypical. In our discussions we identified six underlying problems:

> the relation of Mary to the Person of Jesus Christ;
> one Mediator and human mediation;
> the nature of grace—cooperation with grace;
> the nature of scriptural interpretation;
> the teaching authority of the Church;
> the place of Mary in an integral statement of christian doctrine.

In the context of the Assumption one can make an important observation. One of the least developed areas of theology is that of the Communion of Saints which we profess in the Apostles' Creed. The "Communion" here and in other creeds could be a sharing in either holy persons or holy things. Through the mystery of the Assumption we can look at Jesus and at Mary. The love of the Son for his Mother, and the love of the Mother for the Son are surely not lessened in glory. As Cardinal Suenens remarked in a lecture given in Dublin (June 1982), "Jesus in heaven does not point to Mary and say, 'you see that one over there, she used to be my mother.'" Mary, the true disciple, is still concerned with her Son and with his desire for the salvation of all. At the heart of some protestant difficulties about Mary there is, it would seem to the outsider, a failure to take seriously enough the Communion of Saints, and in particular the human relationship of Son and Mother, a relationship transformed by glory, but a perfection of human bonds, not their total transcendence, much less their destruction. If the Churches of the Reform are frightened by excesses in the Roman Church, they can be asked to look again perhaps at the prophecy in Luke 1:48—"All generations shall call me blessed."

The ecumenical problems besetting mariology and marian devotion are indeed theological, but more profoundly perhaps they are in the area of feeling. The Orthodox and Eastern

Churches have through their highly developed sense of the Communion of Saints, symbolized by their icons, a deeper feeling for Mary than any other Church apart from the Roman one. There is some substantial agreement between Roman and Lutheran scholars about Mary in the New Testament, as the volume of collaborative studies frequently cited on these pages shows. There has been little ecumenical study of the Communion of Saints, except for some papers by R. Laurentin and others to the Ecumenical Society of the Blessed Virgin Mary (founded in 1968). There is even less on the whole area of feeling. One should note a small volume by Canon Allchin, *The Joy of all Creation: An Anglican Meditation on the Place of Mary.*[27] The importance of this study is that it gives us Anglican views on Mary through the eyes of preachers, poets and devout persons. It could point a way forward for ecumenical mariology.

A further area of difficulty is that of invoking the intercession of Mary. As we treat of the matter elsewhere, it is sufficient to note at this point the importance of a sound theology and practice of intercession.[28] Protestants are quite right when they express unease at some marian devotions. But it is not so easy to follow the protestant logic that refuses all intercession of Mary, since all christians pray for one another at some time in their lives, and such intercession for another is not seen as taking from the one mediation of Christ. The catholic view of the intercession of Mary is no more than a higher, more perfect form of what we are accustomed to do for one another.

If we in the Roman Church are to develop our appreciation of the Communion of Saints, our key focus should be on the intercession and sharing which is the Eucharist. In each of the four Eucharistic Prayers we allign ourselves with Mary and the saints:

[27]A. Allchin, *The Joy of all Creation: An Anglican Meditation on the Place of Mary* (London: Darton, Longman & Todd, 1984).

[28]See Healy, op. cit. (n. 5) 92-101. For a Methodist view see G. Wakefield, "Intercession" in A. Stacpoole, ed., op. cit. (n.25) 263-270

In union with the whole Church we honour Mary, the ever Virgin Mother of Jesus Christ our Lord and God ... and all the saints. May their merits and prayers gain us your constant help and protection. (I)

Have mercy on us all; make us worthy to share eternal life with Mary the Mother of God. (II)

May he (the Holy Spirit) enable us to share in the inheritance of your saints, with Mary, the Virgin Mother of God ... and all your saints, on whose constant intercession we rely for help. (III)

Father, in your mercy grant also to us, your children, to enter into our heavenly inheritance in the company of the Virgin Mary, the Mother of God, and your apostles and saints. (IV)

It is then the Communion of Saints that makes the doctrine of the Assumption not just a personal gift to Mary, but a sign of hope and comfort for us on our pilgrim way (see Preface of the Mass of the Assumption).

PRAYER OF THE FAITHFUL

In wonder and praise we turn to our heavenly Father.
- The Assumption is Mary's final glorification: may we come to know her and her Son Jesus in glory.
- The Assumption is the glorification of Mary in body and spirit: may people come to treasure and respect their own and other peoples' bodies which are destined for glory.
- The Assumption is an anchor of hope: may our minds not be limited to what is material in our world.
- The Assumption is God's full acceptance of what is creaturely: may our crops be blessed to provide food for the hungry.
- The Assumption is a sign of God's favour: may he give us a gift of deeper unity among all the followers of Christ.
  Father, in your loving plan the Mother of your Son could suffer

death, but she who brought forth your Son, our Lord Incarnate from herself could not be held back by the bonds of death; grant our prayer which we make relying on her intercession and in the name of Christ, your Son and our Lord. Amen. (based on the 8th century prayer *Veneranda*[29])

[29]Prayer sent by Pope Adrian to Charlemagne between 784 and 790. See O'Carroll, *Theotokos* 57; Roschini 3:506.

ADDITIONAL READING

J. Alfaro, "The Mariology of the Fourth Gospel. Mary and the Struggles for Liberation," *Biblical Theology Bulletin* 10 (1980) 3-16.

P.J. Cahill, "Our Lady's Present Role in the Communion of Saints," *Marian Studies* 18(1967) 31-45.

E.R. Carroll, *Understanding the Mother of Jesus* (Wilmington: Glazier—Dublin: Veritas, 1979) 141-143 has bibliography on Assumption in English.

J. Dupont, "Le *Magnificat* comme discours sur Dieu," *Nouvelle revue théologique* 102 (1980) 321-343.

De Fiores 496-509.

J. Galot, *Dieu et la Femme. Marie dans l'oeuvre du salut* (Louvain: Ed. Sintal, n.d.) 289-331

J. Galot, "Maria e la liberazione dell'umanità," *Civilta cattolica* 131 (1980) 2:218-230.

R.J. Karris, "Mary's *Magnificat* and Recent Study," *Review for Religious* 42 (1983) 903-908.

J.P. Kenny, "The Assumption of Mary: Its Relevance for Us Today," *Clergy Review* 63(1978) 289-294.

M. O'Carroll, "Immaculate Conception and Assumption" in J. Hyland, ed., *Mary and the Church Today. Papers of the National*

Marian Congress 1984 (Athlone: Marist Brothers—Dublin: Veritas, 1988) forthcoming.

K. Rahner, "The Interpretation of the Dogma of the Assumption," *Theololgical Investigations.* vol. 1 (London: Darton, Longman & Todd, 1961) 215-227.

K. Rahner, *Mary Mother of the Lord. Theological Meditations* Edinburgh-London: Nelson, 1962) 83-92.

H. Urs von Balthasar, *The Threefold Garland* (San Francisco: Ignatius, 1982) 127-132.

Articles on *Magnificat* in *Ephemerides mariologicae* 36 (1986).

THE QUEENSHIP OF MARY
(Memorial—22 August)

LITURGICAL HISTORY

From 1900 requests were sent to Rome asking for a feast of the Universal Queenship of Mary. After the institution of the feast of Christ the King (1925), the momentum for a marian feast of queenship increased. In 1933 a cathedral in Port Said was dedicated to Mary Queen of the World. Pius XII wrote an encyclical on Mary's queenship (*Ad coeli Reginam,* 11 October 1954) and later in the marian year he proclaimed a feast of the Queenship of Mary, to be celebrated on 31 May. In the revised calendar it has become a memorial on the octave day of the Assumption, 22 August.

THEMES

Mary has been given to us as Mother and Queen; supported by her intercession our hope is to come to the kingdom of heaven (opening prayer). We rely on the humanity of Christ sacrificed for us (prayer over gifts). The central idea of the celebration is that Christ is our King and Mary is Queen in some subordinate role.

> Hail, O Queen of all the world, ever Virgin Mary. You bore Christ, the Head, the Saviour of all creation. (Morning Prayer)
>
> Blessed are you, O Virgin Mary, because you believed in all the things which were told you by the Lord. You will reign forever with Christ. (Evening Prayer)

SCRIPTURE READINGS

a) Isaiah 9:1-3.5-6

The text is a prophecy to those who are oppressed, *of a country in shadow dark as death.* It probably belongs to the latter part of the eighth century after the Syro-Ephraimitic War and voices the prophet's hope for a genuine Davidid on the throne. There is to be born *a son* and *dominion has been laid upon his shoulders.* He is *Wonder-Counsellor, Mighty God, Eternal-Father* and *Prince of Peace.* His *dominion* is to be extended *in boundless peace.* The Church has always seen this text as being fulfilled in Christ. Mary's Son is therefore a King.

The *response* to this reading is "May the name of the Lord be blessed for evermore."

b) Luke 1:26-38

The Annunciation story has been chosen for this memorial as it gives a prophecy about the kingship of Mary's Son: *He will be great and will be called Son of the Most High.* In the parallel verse we see how he will be great: it is through being a king in the line of David; *the Lord God will give him the throne of his ancestor David; he will rule over the house of Jacob forever and his reign will have no end.*

There is here a development in the notion of the Davidic dynasty. We find frequent Old Testament references to David's line being everlasting. But here we have the promise that it will be eternal in one person, *his reign will have no end.* Mary's yes, *You see before you the Lord's servant,* is her acceptance of the invitation to assume a role in the divine plan involving an everlasting King.

CHURCH DOCUMENTS[1]

Pope Paul VI wrote in *Marialis cultus:*

> The Solemnity of the Assumption is prolonged in the cele-
> bration of the Queenship of the Blessed Virgin Mary, which
> occurs seven days later. On this day we contemplate her
> who, seated beside the King of Ages, shines forth as Queen
> and intercedes as Mother. (MC 6)

Vatican II had earlier stated that Mary

> occupies a place in the Church which is highest after Christ
> and also closest to us; (LG 54)

and

> Finally the Immaculate Virgin, preserved free from all stain
> of original sin, was taken up body and soul when her earthly
> life was over, and exalted by the Lord as Queen over all,
> that she might be the more fully conformed to her Son, the
> Lord of Lords (cf. Apoc 19:16) and conquerer of sin and
> death; (LG 59)

---

[1]See E.R. Carroll, "Mary in the Documents of the Magisterium," Carol 1:45-50.

and

> she is exalted above all the angels and saints. (LG 69)

These recent documents take up in summary form the main magisterial teaching on Mary's Queenship, the encyclical *Ad coeli Reginam* of Pius XII (1954).[2] In it the pope asserts that the foundation for Mary's queenship is abundantly expressed in the ancient documents of the Church, in the books of the sacred liturgy, in the writings of the saints, in devotion and in art (paragraphs 6-25). He then goes on to develop four main themes: she is Queen because she is Mother of God (par. 26); as Christ is King by being redeemer, so also is Mary associated with him, for she is the intimate companion of the Redeemer and the New Eve (par. 27-28); she is Queen by her preeminent perfection (par. 30) and by her power of intercession (par. 31). The pope then gives a warning against overstatement and understatement that is appropriate when one reflects on the royal dignity of Mary and at other times as well:

> At the same time, in this, as in other marian matters, theologians and preachers should take care scrupulously to avoid certain aberrations, so as not to be betrayed into one or other of two mistakes. They should, on the one hand, be on their guard against unfounded opinions and exaggerated expressions. On the other hand, they should beware of a too constricted attitude of mind in face of the singular, sublime, not to say almost divine, dignity which the Angelic Doctor, St. Thomas Aquinas teaches us to ascribe to the Mother of God 'by virtue of the infinite good which is God' (*Summa theologiae* 1a, q.25, a.6 ad 4)

He then directs the attention of theologians and preachers to the teaching authority of the Church, established by Christ "for the purpose of elucidating and explaining what is only obscurely and

[2]*AAS* 46(1954) 625-640. English tr. London: CTS 1958. Key extracts in DS 3913-3917.

implicitly contained in the deposit of faith" (par. 32-33). The encyclical ends with an exhortation to honour Mary, and to imitate her, and to consider her as the Queen of the Persecuted and the Queen of Peace (par. 34-38).

REFLECTION

Though we may not always deeply reflect on it, the idea of Mary as Queen is taken for granted in catholic piety: the fifth glorious mystery of the Rosary (16th century); the Hail Holy Queen (*Salve Regina,* 11th century), the Easter antiphon, Queen of heaven rejoice alleluia (*Regina coeli* 12th—13th century), the hymn "Hail holy Queen" (not only the modern one but *Ave Regina coelorum* of the 12th century).[3] All of these, as well as more modern prayers are reminders of Mary's queenship. It is interesting to note that four of the six papal additions to the Litany of Loreto as used in the universal Church are invocations to Mary as Queen: Gregory XVI and Pius IX—Queen conceived without original sin; Leo XIII—Queen of the Most Holy Rosary; Benedict XV— Queen of Peace; Pius XII—Queen assumed into heaven.[4]

The title Queen could arise only out of cultures which knew empresses and queens. It is not surprising then that the title was first used in the East. In the lyrical prayers ascribed to St. Ephrem (d. 373) she is called Lady (feminine of "Lord") and Queen, more splendid than the cherubim and more glorious than the seraphim; she is Mother and after the Mediator, she is Mediatrix.[5] The Byzantine liturgy does not have a feast of Mary as Queen, but its hymns abound with regal titles: she is Empress (*basilissa* or *basilis*), Queen or Princess (*anassa*), Universal Queen (*pantanassa*) and Sovereign Lady (*Kyria*).[6] In the West both in the germanic peoples

[3]See E. Lodi, "Preghiera mariana," *NDizM* 1137-1147 at 1143-1145.

[4]See G. Besutti, "Litanie," *NDizM* 759-767 at 764-765.

[5]See *Orat. ad Dei Matrem EnMar* 340-348; 351; *Serm. EnMar* 350.

[6]See J. Ledit, *Marie dans la liturgie de Byzance.* "Théologie historique 39" (Paris: Beauchesne, 1976) 241-252.

and in the Holy Roman Empire there was a sense of royalty which was easily transferred to Mary.[7]

In our time however the dominant political ideology is democracy. Where we find kings and queens as in Belgium, Britain, etc. they are constitutional monarchs. We have, therefore, to make a special effort where regal terms are involved. For we cannot ignore them, since they occur everywhere in the bible.

In the New Testament the title of King was appropriate (see Lk 1:49). But Jesus himself showed some reserve about it. It is passed by without special comment when Nathanael uses it (see Jn 1:49). He accepted the title with reservations when questioned by Pilate (see Jn 18:33-37), and he refused to become a popular king after the miracle of the loaves (see Jn 6:15). More common in the New Testament is the equivalent concept of Lord (from a divine title in the Old Testament). He is Lord through humble service (see Mt. 20:24-28), and especially in his humiliation and death after which he is proclaimed Lord (see Ph 2:11). All four evangelists note the statement affixed to the cross "King of the Jews." He is definitively Lord through the resurrection: victorious over all his enemies (see Hb 1:13): every ruler, authority and power (see 1 Cor 15:24), sin (see Hb 9:13-14), the devil (see Hb 2:14) and finally death (see 1 Cor 15:26).

From the New Eve theology of the 2nd century there is a constant tradition that Mary was closely associated with her Son's saving work. Blessed most especially because she believed (see Lk 1:45; 11:27-28), she gave herself totally to God's plan. Indeed there are echoes of the hymn of the humiliation and exaltation of Jesus (Ph 2:5-11) in St. Luke's infancy narrative.[8] Mary is then a

---

[7]See L. Scheffczyk, *Mhe* 191.

[8]"It is worth remarking that the great hymn of redemption in Philippians 2:5-11 finds echoes in the first chapter of St. Luke's gospel. Jesus took the form of a slave (Greek *doulos;* Ph 2;7), Mary describes herself as a slave (Greek *doulē* Lk 1:38). Jesus humbled himself (Ph 2:8); Mary describes her state as one of humiliation (Lk 1:48). God exalted Jesus (Ph 2:9); the humble are exalted (Lk 1:52). Every knee shall bend . . . confess Jesus is Lord (Ph 2:11); all generations will call Mary blessed (Lk 1:48). The similarity of Greek expressions throughout seems to suggest deliberate borrowing by Luke to

close associate with Jesus who is King and Lord. But we can examine more closely the bible to try to understand why tradition can call Mary a Queen.

In mariological circles, but significantly not so much in exegetical ones, there is a lot of interest in the Old Testament notion of the Queen-Mother (*gebîrah*). The mother of the king was a person of great influence in the semitic world. Indeed the role of Mary at Cana was not unlike the kind of influence exercised by the Queen-Mother in the Old Testament.[9]

We are perhaps on surer ground when we examine the regal notions in the New Testament as used about the followers of Jesus. In 2 Timothy we find what is probably an ancient christian hymn:

> If we have died with him,
> then we shall live with him.
> If we persevere,
> then we shall reign with him. (2 Tm 2:11-12).

We have also the words of Jesus to Peter who asked what reward would be given to those who left all and followed him:

> In truth I tell you, when everything is made new again, and the Son of man is seated on his throne of glory, you yourselves will sit on twelve thrones to judge the twelve tribes of Israel. (Mt 19:28)

Again, at the Last Supper Jesus said to the apostles:

> You are the men who have stood by me faithfully in my trials; and now I confer a kingdom on you; you will eat and

illustrate the mystery of poverty being exalted in both Son and mother." C. O'Donnell, *Life in the Spirit and Mary* (Wilmington: Glazier—Dublin: Dominican Publications, 1981) 45. One can at least point to a common tradition to which Paul and Luke had access.

[9]See on *gebîrah* A. Serra, "Regina," *NDizM* 1189-1197 at 1191-93. R. de Vaux, *Ancient Israel. Its Life and Institutions* (London: Darton, Longman, Todd, 1961) 117-119.

drink at my table in my kingdom, and you will sit on thrones
to judge the twelve tribes of Israel. (Lk 22:28-30)

Finally in the Apocalypse we read:

> If any of you hears me calling and opens the door, I will
> come in to share a meal at that person's side. Anyone who
> proves victorious I will allow to share my throne, just as I
> have myself overcome and taken my seat with my Father on
> his throne. (Rev 3:20-21).

Mary is portrayed in the New Testament and contemplated in
christian tradition as the one who faithfully followed Jesus,
persevered in trials and opened her heart to God—thus fulfiling
all the conditions for attaining royal status cited in the texts we
have just quoted. She is therefore blessed with heavenly royal
dignity. God's free response to her fidelity was to make her
Queen. And we believe that she is incomparably greater than all
the others who are kings and queens in heaven.

Another way in which we can approach the Queenship of
Mary is through the text on the kingly office of the laity in
Vatican II. The Constitution on the Church (LG 36) gives as the
hall-marks of the royal dignity of the baptized: sharing in Christ's
kingdom; conquering sin; serving Christ in others to bring them
to him; reigning by serving; concerned with the spread of the
kingdom. All of these are fulfilled in Mary.

What we have been saying is summarized very well in Pope
John Paul's encyclical on Mary:

> Connected with this exaltation of the noble 'Daughter of
> Sion' (LG 55) through her Assumption into heaven is the
> mystery of her eternal glory. For the Mother of Christ is
> glorified as 'Queen of the Universe.' She who at the Annun-
> ciation called herself the 'handmaid of the Lord' remained
> throughout her life faithful to what this name expresses. In
> this she confirmed that she was a true 'disciple' of Christ,
> who strongly emphasized that his mission was one of service:

the Son of Man 'came not to be served but to serve, and to give his life as a ransom for many' (Mt 20:28). In this way Mary became the first of those who 'serving Christ also in others with humility and patience lead their brothers and sisters to that King whom to serve is to reign' (LG 36), and she fully obtained that 'state of royal freedom' proper to Christ's disciples: to serve means to reign! (RM 41)

S. De Fiores has put forward a limited but useful notion of Mary as "Leader."[10] It is useful in that it can give us in modern terms much of what we understand by the notion of Queen. It is limited in that it will not suffice for a complete statement of Mary's dignity and role. De Fiores notes various qualities that the sociologists ascribe to leaders: they incarnate values and ideals, they have dynamism, they have propulsive and stimulating power. We can see Jesus then as King, and Mary as Leader: she inspires recognition of her human, religious, and spiritual values: people have an affective attachment to her; she demands a radical reorientation and focusing of their lives. But it is by accepting Mary as "Leader" that we come into more perfect discipleship not of her, but of her Son.

Finally, it may be remarked that contemplation of Mary as Queen not only directs our thoughts on her Son, but also encourages us to look to our own royal dignity as baptized followers of the one King and Lord.

PRAYER OF THE FAITHFUL

In heaven we have a Mother who is Queen; we come therefore to our heavenly Father assured of her intercession.

- That the kingdom of Christ be spread in the Church and in the world through works of truth, service and love.
- That nations may strive for justice and peace.

[10]See "Regina," *NDizM* 1197-1203 at 1201-1202.

- That we may be converted from pride to humility, from arrogance to service.
- That we may imitate the humble virtues of Mary, the servant of the Lord.
- That we may rejoice in our royal priesthood as the baptized and know Mary's love, care and leadership in our lives.
  Father in heaven you give us your good gifts, and especially your Son, Jesus. Send your Spirit upon us that we may walk in his paths and follow the example of Mary our Mother and Queen to the glory of life with you; for you are Lord for ever and ever. Amen.

ADDITIONAL READING

M. O'Carroll, "Queenship, Mary's," *Theotokos* 301–302.

Roschini 2:345–515.

F.M. Schmidt, "The Universal Queenship of Mary," Carol 2:493–549.

G. Söll, *Storia dei dogmi mariani.* "Accademia mariana salesiana 15" (Rome: LAS, 1981), 383–386.

H. Urs von Balthasar, *The Threefold Garland* (San Francisco: Ignatius, 1982) 133–139.

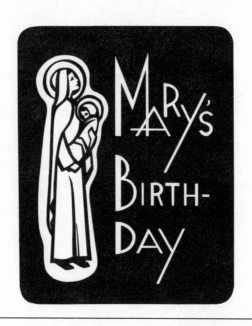

THE BIRTHDAY
OF THE BLESSED VIRGIN MARY
(Feast—8 September)

LITURGICAL HISTORY

The feast of Mary's birthday probably originated in Jerusalem about the 6th century.[1] But from about the 5th century we have evidence of a church dedicated to St. Anne north of the Temple in Jerusalem. Sophronius, Patriarch of Jerusalem asserted in 603 a.d. that it marked the birthplace of Mary. The choice of a September day came about from the fact that in Constantinople the year began on 1 September—as it still does in the Eastern Church. The 8 September would later fix the date for the Immaculate Conception as 8 December, that is nine months

---

[1] See G. Mealo, "Natività di Maria," *NDizM* 1012-1017 at 1013.

earlier. The feast of the birthday was introduced in Rome towards the 7th century and it was well enough established for inclusion with the other· three marian celebrations for which the Syro-Sicilian Pope Sergius I (687-701) laid down a procession (*litania*) from the Roman Forum to St. Mary Major.

THEMES

The English translation of the prayers of the Mass for the feast changes the meaning quite substantially. In the Latin text we are invited to see Mary's birth as the dawn of our salvation (opening prayer and prayer after communion). The Church on this day asks for an increase of peace (not "lasting peace" of the English translation). We place our trust in the Son born of Mary. His birth "did not diminish but sanctified her integrity" (prayer over gifts); the reference is to Mary's virginity at the birth of Christ, and should not have been rendered as follows: "The birth of Christ ... increased the Virgin Mother's love." The themes of dawn and light are very much to the fore in the Office of the feast.

> When the sacred Virgin was born then the whole world was filled with light (Morning Prayer)
>
> Today is the birthday of the holy Virgin Mary whose life illumined all the Churches. (Midday Prayer)
>
> Today is the birthday of the holy Virgin Mary. God looked on her beauty and came to visit her in her lowliness. (Evening Prayer)
>
> Come, all you faithful, let us hasten to the Virgin: for long before her conception in the womb, the one who was to be born of the stem of Jesse was destined to be the Mother of God. The one who is the treasury of virginity, the flowering Rod of Aaron, the object of the prophecies, the child of Joachim and Anne, is born today and the world is renewed

in her. Through her birth, she floods the Church with her splendor. O holy Temple, Vessel of the Godhead, Model of virgins and Strength of kings: in you the wondrous union of the two natures of Christ was realized. We worship Him and glorify your most pure birth, and we magnify you. (*Byzantine Daily Worship 441-442*)

SCRIPTURE READINGS

There are two possibilities from which to choose a first reading.

a) Micah 5:1-4

This is a messianic prophecy which is probably from the 8th century before Christ, but which may have received some editorial revision about the time of the exile (587-538). The prophet has been castigating Israel and foretelling doom. Then the tone changes to one of light. There is a prophecy to Ephrathah, originally a clan that had settled near Bethlehem, and later a name for this town. The prophet is thinking of the Davidic origins of Bethlehem and he sees *a future ruler of Israel*. God will protect his people *until she who is in labour gives birth*. The reference here is to the mother of the Messiah, and the prophet may be thinking of the birth of Immanuel (see Is 7:14). This Davidic ruler *will shepherd* God's people and *they will be secure*. Finally, *he himself will be peace*.

The choice of this prophecy for the birthday of Mary suggests that the fullness of time came with the birth of Mary: it is already the dawn of the messianic age.

b) Romans 8:28-30

This passage evokes the eternal plan of God, what *he decided beforehand; that is, for those who love him* he *turns everything to their good*. The divine purpose is that people are *to be moulded into the pattern of his Son, so that he should be the eldest of many brothers*. The idea of first-born, the *eldest* implies the dignity of the Son. Elsewhere we are told that we are to be transferred to the kingdom of his beloved Son, for he is the beginning, the first-born from the dead (see Col 1:14.18). The divine plan is then made more explicit in the text for the feast: he *destined*, he *called*, he *justified*, and *brought into glory*. Thus in the divine plan we have the context for celebrating Mary's birth.

The *response* is: "I exult for joy in the Lord."

c) Matthew 1:1-16.18-23

R.E. Brown aptly remarks, "To the modern reader there are few things in the bible less meaningful than the frequent lists of descendants and ancestors."[2] The fact that the Lectionary allows the shortening of the gospel text by the omission of vv. 1-16 makes it rather unlikely that the full text will frequently be used. It would be a pity to ignore these verses, but the whole purpose of the genealogy needs some explanation.

The genealogies of Matthew (1:1-17) and Luke (3:23-28) differ quite substantially, Neither is concerned with giving a list of forebears in a biological sense. Matthew sets out his purpose in the first verse of his gospel: *the genealogy of Jesus Christ, son of David, son of Abraham*. He wants to show Jesus' Davidic heritage through his adoption by Joseph, and to demonstrate to his gentile christian audience that Jesus was a son of Abraham in whom "all nations will bless themselves" (Gen 22:18). Luke places his genealogy at the baptism of Jesus, when he was declared from heaven to be the Son (see 3:22) . He traces the ancestry backwards to Adam, "the son of God" (3:38)

Matthew's genealogy, the one used in the feast, is an elaborate invention of three groups of fourteen generations. One of the most attractive answers to the question, "why fourteen?," is the suggestion that the number is chosen as it is the number of waxing and waning days of the moon. Hence human history waxed to the time of David, waned during the Babylonian captivity, and then

[2]Brown 64.

there followed a decisive waxing to the time of Jesus.[3]

For our purpose perhaps the most significant aspect of the list of ancestors is the naming of four women. Each of these had somewhat irregular unions, but were instrumental in God's plans: Tamar (see Gen 38) ensured the dynasty of Judah (see Gen 49:10), Rahab the prostitute made it possible for the people to enter the promised land (see Josh 2); Ruth followed her mother-in-law to Israel and gave birth to David's grandfather Obed (see Ruth 2-4); Bathsheba, an adulteress, was mother of Solomon (see 2 Sm 11; 12:24). All were also probably foreigners as well as women chosen for God's plans.[4] We can perhaps also see a comparison of Mary with these women, for to Jewish eyes it was irregular to have a conception during the time of betrothal. We take up this point in more detail later in this chapter.

But one could reasonably ask why this genealogy of *Joseph* should be used for the feast of the Birthday of *Mary*. The reason is that it shows how Mary is to fit into the divine plan: it will be as Joseph's wife and as overshadowed by the Holy Spirit. Mary's birth and role are thus seen in the perspective of salvation history.

The text of Matthew 1:18-25 which forms the second part of the gospel for the feast has been the source of innumerable difficulties and not a little embarrassment among commentators and preachers. An explanation is possible if we grasp the fact that Joseph *being an upright man* did not want to appear to be the father of the wonder child. He wanted too *to spare Mary disgrace* and so *decided to divorce her informally.* There is no reason to suppose that Mary and Joseph did not discuss the matter, and that Mary kept secret from Joseph the divine origin of her pregnancy. The angel addresses Joseph formally, *Joseph son of David,* not as we would expect from 1:16, "son of Jacob." Joseph's scruples about acting as the child's father are removed: *Do not be afraid to take Mary home as your wife.* She is to *give birth*, and Joseph *must name* the child *Jesus.*

[3]Brown 80, n. 39 shows some interest in this explanation put forward by C. Kaplan in 1930.

[4]See Brown 71-73; Laurentin 399-401; A. Serra, "Bibbia," *NDizM* 231-311 at 239-240.

To name a child is an acknowledgement of paternity. Joseph then is to adopt Jesus who thus enters into the Davidic line. Legal adoption for the Hebrews was not less strong than biological generation.[5] At the end of the passage we are told that Joseph *named him Jesus.*

The whole gospel, genealogy and the annunciation to Joseph, firmly establishes the significance of Mary, and so gives us reason to rejoice liturgically at her birth. With her birth God's plan moves to a definitive stage, the "completion of time is at hand" (Gal 4:4).

CHURCH DOCUMENTS

In *Marialis cultus* (n. 7) Pope Paul VI writes that there are

> celebrations that commemorate salvific events in which the Blessed Virgin was closely associated with her Son. Such are the feasts of the Nativity of Our Lady (8 September), the hope of the entire world and the dawn of salvation...

REFLECTION

The scriptures do not give us any account of the birth of Mary. But pious reflection was not long in constructing a narrative, the apocryphal *Protoevangelium of James,* to be dated now sometime prior to 200 A.D. O. Cullmann remarks that "the whole work is written for the glorification of Mary."[6] Though never regarded as canonical, indeed it was condemned in the West during the 5th century, the work nonetheless had enormous importance in the

---

[5]On Hebrew legal paternity see Brown 139.

[6]See O. Cullmann in E. Hennecke, edited by W. Schneemelcher, *New Testament Apocrypha.* 2 vols. (London: SCM, 1963), "The Infancy Gospels" I:363-417 at 373. For dating see M. O'Carroll, *Theotokos* 39-40.

development of piety, liturgy and christian art, most particularly in the East.

Although as we remarked in another context, the apocrypha have no historical value, they do have a theological importance which lies behind what they assert in narrative fables. In the case of the birth of Mary we find an account of infertile parents, Joachim a rich just man, and his wife Anna or Anne. At the opening of the narrative both are depicted as lamenting their childless state. In answer to Anne's lament there is a divine intervention:

> And behold an angel of the Lord came to her and said: 'Anna, Anna, the Lord has heard your prayer. You shall conceive and bear, and your offspring will be spoken of in the whole world.' And Anna said, 'As the Lord my God lives, if I bear a child, whether male or female, I will bring it as a gift to the Lord my God, and it shall serve him all the days of its life.' (*Protoevangelium* 4.1)[7]

Joachim too received a message that his prayer was heard (ibid. 4:2)

Quite obviously this passage is modelled on the infertile wives of the patriarchs, Abraham, Isaac and Jacob. In their case God's promise of descendants for Abraham (see Gen 15:1-6) meets with an impossible human obstruction. His special intervention showed that it was God who was making his own promises come true. The blessing of fruitfulness for Sarah (Gen 21:1-7), Rebekah (Gen 25:19-21) and Rachel (Gen 30:22-24) meant that God's plans became operative, but only by his power. In the case of Mary's parents there is infertility too, but God's plans will not be thwarted. They have a child, Mary. The author of the *Protoevangelium* sees in Mary a child who is crucial for God's plans. As in the case of the patriarchs, God himself sees to the fulfilment of his promises to his people. This story of the birth of Mary lies

---

[7]Hennecke-Schneemelcher (n. 6) 376.

behind and is explicitly used in the Byzantine liturgy:

> Today Anne the barren one claps her hands for joy, the earth is bathed in light, kings sing their happiness, priests enjoy all blessings, and the whole universe rejoices: for the Queen and immaculate Bride of the Father comes forth from the stem of Jesse. Behold; no woman will ever again bear child in sorrow or anxiety, for joy has come forth in abundance and life has filled the world. Joachim's offerings shall no more be rejected, for the tears of Anne have now been turned into joy. And now Anne can say: 'Rejoice with me, all you chosen ones of Israel, for the Lord has given me the palace of his divine and living glory, to be a place of joy and happiness for the whole universe and for the salvation of our souls. (*Byzantine Daily Worship* 441)

There are several interesting elements in this liturgical reflection. It is clearly based on the *Protoevangelium of James,* as the reference to the refusal of Joachim's gift, makes clear. Because he had produced no offspring for Israel, his gift at the Temple had been refused (*Protoevangelium* 1, 1-3). Indeed it is only from this apocrypha that we first learn the names of Mary's parents. Again, it is assumed that Mary was of the tribe of David ("stem of Jesse" who was David's father). But modern scholars confess their inability to determine Mary's tribe.[8] More significant is the cosmic rejoicing that is evoked by the passage: salvation is now really at hand in the birth of Mary.

But quite apart from the fancies of the apocrypha we can make some quite important observations about Mary in the context of celebrating her birthday. The Church mostly celebrates saints' feasts on the day of their death, that is their birth into eternal life. In three cases birthdays are celebrated: we honour the birth of Jesus, of Mary and of John the Baptist for we know that their whole lives were significant in the working out of God's designs. Since Mary's role in salvation history emerges in part as we

[8]See Brown 287-288; Laurentin 403-404.

celebrate each of her feasts, we might do well to reflect on her humanity in this feast of her birth. There is a danger that as we think of her Immaculate Conception, her unique holiness, we can so concentrate on her uniqueness that we overlook her humanness. Just as we delight to share birthdays with our relatives and friends, so as we celebrate Mary's birth we are being invited to know Mary better and to develop more deeply a bond of friendship and affection for her.

To think of Mary as a small baby, as a young mother, as a widow who has lost her only Son, can help people to meet in Mary not a distant remote figure of surpassing holiness, but one who like her Son was "put to the test in exactly the same way as ourselves, as apart from sin" (see Hb 4:15). A further help in this line of reflection is the short verse in Matthew's gospel belonging to the account of his visit to Nazareth. The people of his own town do not want to accept Jesus and his teaching, so they reply, "Is not Mary his mother?" (13:55). These few words can lead us right to the heart of the mystery of the Incarnation, a mystery of weakness and poverty. The Son of God so emptied himself (see Ph 2:7) that no one suspected his divine origins. Mary too despite her sinlessness, and her divine election to be Mother of God, seemed so ordinary that her neighbours could use as an argument against accepting Jesus the fact that they knew so well Mary his mother. The life in Nazareth was totally veiled, and to outsiders utterly normal. The marian encyclical of Pope John Paul II gives some rich insights into this hidden life:

> During the years of Jesus' hidden life in the house of Nazareth, Mary's life too is 'hid with Christ in God' (cf. Col 3:3) through faith ... Mary is in contact with the truth about her Son only in faith and through faith! She is therefore blessed, because 'she has believed,' and continues to believe day after day amidst all the trials and adversities of Jesus' infancy and then during the years of the hidden life at Nazareth, where he 'was obedient to them' (Lk 2:51). ... The Mother of that Son, therefore, mindful of what had been told her at the Annunciation and in subsequent events,

bears within herself the radical 'newness' of faith: the beginning of the Gospel, the joyful Good News. However, it is not difficult to see in that beginning a particular heaviness of heart, linked with a sort of 'night of faith'—to use the words of Saint John of the Cross (*Ascent of Mount Carmel* 2:3, 4-6)—a kind of 'veil' through which one has to draw near to the Invisible One and to live in intimacy with the mystery. And this is the way that Mary, for many years, lived in intimacy with the mystery of her Son, and went forward in her pilgrimage of faith... (RM 17)

Far from being remote, therefore, Mary shared fully in our human condition, especially in walking by faith. She grew up as a girl until eventually she was promised in marriage to Joseph. It is only from the *Protoevangelium of James* that we get the idea of Joseph's being an old man; quite clearly the idea of the author is to have him so old that Mary's virginity would be safeguarded (9, 1-2).

The normal age for marriage was about twelve or thirteen. It began with betrothal or consent. This act was more than what we know as engagement: the woman was already called wife, and sexual intercourse with another was considered adultery. Between the couples it was frowned on in some places and strictly forbidden in others. The couple came to live together about a year later. It is clear from the accounts of Matthew and Luke that the conception of Jesus took place before Mary and Joseph began to live together (see Lk 1:56—after three months she went home; Mt 1:18—before they came to live together). The birth of Jesus was therefore too soon after the completion of the marriage of Mary and Joseph, and would have been irregular in Jewish eyes. Some stigma would have been attached to Mary and Joseph as a result. Mary would thus have appeared not only ordinary in the eyes of those in Nazareth, but indeed less than a wholehearted observer of the law.

We should not follow the approach of the apocryphal gospels and try to glean information about Mary's life that God has not in fact chosen to reveal to us. It is far more fruitful to try to understand what he has given us for example in the text of Matthew 13:55, a picture of Mary as quite ordinary and certainly not in very high esteem in the eyes of her neighbours. The chronology of Jesus' conception and birth can allow us to glimpse too at her being misunderstood—and being misunderstood will always be the lot of one who seeks to follow Jesus with sincerity.

It may be of interest to add a note about the irregularity of Jesus' birth from a time perspective. We see in John 8:41 a response of the Jews to Jesus: "we were not born illegitimate" which may have been intended as a slur on Jesus. Also noteworthy is the Jewish charge in the 2nd century that Jesus was the illegitimate child of a Roman soldier called Panthera. Origen replied to the Jew Celsus that this was street-corner abuse.[9] But the slander was sufficiently widespread to occasion the polemic of the *Protoevangelium* in favor of Mary's virginity.[10]

There is another important way of discovering the humanness of Mary, namely the writing of women about her. The exhortations of Paul VI (MC 37) and of John Paul II (RM 46) remind us of the necessity of looking at Mary through the eyes of celibate women, married women, mothers and widows. Each of these classes will have its own insights into Mary, ones that can be expected to be a good deal richer than the popes as celibate males could offer in their reflections on Mary as woman.

Currently we can note several approaches. There are in the first place male studies on Mary's femininity: these are interesting but will be of limited value.[11] Then we have women writing on Mary within the broad tradition of mariology.[12] We also have

[9]See *Contra Celsum* 1:39 PL 11:753/SC 132:182.

[10]See Burghardt, "Mary in Eastern Patristic Thought," Carol 2:102-103; Cullmann, op. cit. (n. 6) 367, 373; Brown 526-527, 534-542.

[11]E.g. L. Boff, *The Maternal Face of God. The Feminine and its Religious Expression* (San Francisco-London, Harper & Row, 1987). There are in addition some theological problems with this work in its view of the relation between Mary and the Holy Spirit, see n. 47 of chapter three above.

[12]E.g. M.T. Malone, *Who is my Mother? Rediscovering the Mother of Jesus* (Dubuque, Brown, 1984).

theologians more explicitly feminist.[13] These latter are acutely aware of the past flaws in male presentations of Mary. It is not very helpful, however, to see in the history of marian theology and piety a deliberate ploy to distract women by means of Mary, and so keep them in subjugation to a patriarchal Church.[14] We have argued in chapter six for the urgent need on the part of all to find a model in Mary. It could be suggested indeed that it was devotion to Mary that kept some feminine intuition and feelings alive in the patriarchal leaders and theologians of the Church up to the present. The service which feminist and other women writers on Mary can render the Church is to help both men and women to understand Mary more deeply, and in so doing to understand also themselves.

Finally, the liturgical celebration of Mary's Birthday should be seen as an important illustration of a vital teaching of Vatican II:

> In celebrating this annual cycle of the mysteries of Christ,
> Holy Church honours the Blessed Mary, Mother of God,
> with a special love. (*Liturgy* 103).

It is as we focus on Christ that we find his Mother. To honour Mary with a special love is only to acknowledge the divine plan in which she played an important, though subordinate role. If we sing hymns and pray to Mary with special affection on her birthday, we are only echoing her own thanksgiving: "the Almighty has done great things for me. Holy is his name" (Lk 1:49).

[13]E.g. C. Halkes, "Mary and Women," *Concilium* 168 (1983) 66-73; C.F. Jegen, ed., *Mary According to Woman* (Kansas City: Leaven, 1985); C. Checcacci, "Maria e la donna, oggi" in (various authors) *Maria nel mistero di Cristo e della chiesa* (Bari: Ecumenica Ed.: 1979) 181-192; A.M. Campanile, "Maria e la donna consacrata, oggi" ibid. 193-200. Harsher expositions are: R.R. Reuther, *Sexism and God-talk. Towards a Feminist Theology* (London: SCM, 1983), ch. 6 "Mary as Symbolic Ecclesiology: Repression or Liberation?" 139-158; R. Haughton, *The Recreation of Eve* (Springfield, Ill.: Templegate, 1985) 109-122.

[14]This would seem to be a thesis of the flawed and ultimately unhelpful work of M. Warner, *Alone of All her Sex: The Myth and Cult of the Virgin Mary* (New York: Knopf, 1976).

PRAYER OF THE FAITHFUL

We come to the creator of all, who is also Father, and we present our prayers to him confidently in the name of his Son and relying on the intercession of Mary.

- You willed from all eternity to have Mary as the mother of your Son; send your Spirit upon the Church that it may know how to insert itself into your divine plan.
- You place in women's hearts the desire for equality and justice; give your guidance and support to all who work for the rights of women.
- You create man and woman equal in dignity; give us a true appreciation of the beauty and varying gifts of women and men in our midst.
- You brought Mary into the perfection of humanity; through your healing Spirit may we have life to the full in your Son, Jesus Christ.
- You love the Churches of East and West; as they celebrate together the Birthday of Mary, may they come into closer unity.

  You reveal your power, Father, in the beauty of the Virgin; grant us grace to live according to the wisdom taught by your Son, who is Lord for ever and ever. Amen.

ADDITIONAL READING

W. Beinert, "Maria und die Frauenfrage," *Stimmen der Zeit* 201 (1983) 31-44.

M.T. Bellenzier, "Donna," *NDizM* 499-510.

S. Cipriani, "Credente," *NDizM* 417-425.

De Fiores 398-435.

M. O'Carroll, "Woman and Our Lady," *Theotokos* 369-370.

J. Massyngberde Ford, "Mary and the Ministry of Women," *Marian Studies* 23(1972) 72-112.

A. Sanz, "Maria y la mujer en el N.T.", *Ephemerides mariologicae* 35 (1981) 189-194.

OUR LADY OF SORROWS
(Memorial—15 September)

LITURGICAL HISTORY[1]

The celebration of Our Lady of Sorrows dates from medieval times. We first find an oratory dedicated to Mary at the Cross near Paderborn, Germany, in 1011 A.D. Devotion to Mary as the Sorrowful One is found during the 12th and 13th centuries in the Cistercian and Franciscan traditions. Later there were two feasts of Mary's Sorrows or Dolours. One appeared in Servite communities in 1668 and was celebrated on the third Sunday of

---

[1]See S. Maggiani, "Addolorata," *NDizM* 3-16; W.M. McLoughlin, "Our Lady of Sorrows—A Devotion within a Tradition" in A. Stacpoole, ed., *Mary and the Churches* (Dublin: Columbia, 1987) 114-121.

September. It was extended to the universal Church by Pius VII (1814), and the date was fixed by Pius X as the day after the feast of the Exaltation of the Holy Cross, that is 15 September. The other was established by the Synod of Cologne (1423) as an expiation for the actions of the iconclastic Hussites against images of the Crucified and his Mother. In 1727 it was extended to the universal Church, notably through the efforts of the Servites. This feast celebrated on the Friday before Palm Sunday was dropped in the 1969 revision of the calendar.

THEMES

Mary shares in the sufferings of Christ (opening prayer), and at the cross she was given to us as Mother (prayer over the gifts). As we look to this compassionate Mother, we wish in our turn to make up in our lives what is lacking in the suffering of Christ (post-communion prayer, cf. Col 1:24).

> Rejoice, grief-stricken Mother, for now you share the triumph of your Son. Enthroned in heavenly splendour, you reign as Queen of all creation. (Morning Prayer)

> Jesus, seeing his mother and beloved disciple standing by the cross, said, 'Woman, behold your son!' And to the disciple, 'Son, behold, your mother.' (Evening Prayer)

The Byzantine rite does not celebrate this feast, but regularly in worship says,

> O Virgin all-immaculate, Mother of Christ God, a sword pierced your all-holy soul when you saw your Son and God wilfully crucified. Wherefore, O Blessed One, never cease to pray to Him that He may grant us forgiveness of our sins (*Byzantine Daily Worship* 416-417)

When the Mother beheld upon the cross the Lamb, the Shepherd, the Saviour of the World, she exclaimed tearfully:

'The world rejoices at the sight of its redemption, but my heart is afire as I see your pain on the cross which You accept for the sake of all, O my Son and my God!' (*Byzantine Daily Worship* 425)

SCRIPTURE READINGS

After the first reading, there is a choice between two gospel passages.

a) Hebrews 5:7-9

This text comes from a central part of the Letter to the Hebrews which deals with the compassionate *high priest,* Jesus, *during his life on earth.* It is because of his humanity that he can represent human beings, and sharing their sufferings be compassionate. *During his life on earth,* and especially in Gethsemane, *he offered up prayer and entreaty . . . to the one who had the power to save him from death;* his death was not prevented, but it was overcome by his being raised to glory (see Ph 2:9-11; Hb 2:9). *He learnt obedience* through total submission to his heavenly Father, and was *perfected* in his office of priest and victim. The use of this passage points to Mary's greatest sorrow, the cruel death of her Son. It can be seen also to imply that, since Mary suffered so much, she too is compassionate.

The *response* to this reading is "Save me Lord in your love."

b) Luke 2:33-35

Mary and Joseph *were wondering* at Simeon's prophecy about Jesus being *a light of revelation for the gentiles and glory* for *Israel.* Then *Simeon blessed them* and gave a prophecy to Mary: her Son *is destined for the fall and for the rise of many in Israel.* Here *many* is an inclusive word: all Israel will be affected by him. He will be *a sign that is opposed.* A sign is an invitation to be open to God's plan, and is often an appeal to conversion.[2] It can also be a standard or banner, in which case it is a prophecy that Jesus' invitation to follow him will be rejected.[3]

There is a problem about the meaning of the *sword* which will *pierce* the *soul* of Mary. It is an apparent aside on the part of Simeon. The most obvious Old Testament reference point is Ez 14:17, where the sword is the judgement of God. Jesus will later say that he came not to bring peace but division (Mt 10:34-36 has sword—*machaira* not *rhomphaia* of Lk 2:35; the parallel in Lk 12:51-53 has no reference to sword). Thus the word and the person of Jesus like a sword will divide families and will demand commitment. Mary will be one of those who will prove faithful (see Lk 8:19-21; 11:27-28). R.E. Brown observes here:

> Her special anguish, as the sword of discrimination passes through her soul, will consist in recognising that the claims of Jesus' heavenly Father outrank any human attachments between him and his mother, a lesson she will begin to learn (in the Temple scene 2:48-50).[4]

Pope John Paul takes a somewhat wider view of the sword:

> Simeon's words seem like a second Annunciation to Mary for they tell her of the actual historical situation in which her Son is to accomplish his mission, namely in misunderstanding and sorrow. (RM 16)

Similarly K. Stock also develops more explicitly the basic thought of R. Brown:

> The sorrowful events that Jesus will encounter are directly linked to the sorrowful events that will happen to Mary.

[2]See P. Ternant, "Sign" in X. Léon-Dufour, ed., *Dictionary of Biblical Theology* (London: Chapman, 1973²) 545-548.

[3]See Brown 461, n. 49.

[4]Ibid. 465.

Simeon says: the opposition that will be manifested, will not leave Mary indifferent; she too will be struck by them and will be painfully wounded in her heart and in her inmost being ... the union between mother and Son will above all be a communion in sorrowful experiences.[5]

The text will have a deeper meaning still if one accepts an identification of Mary and the personified Daughter of Sion (see discussion at 21 November). In this case the sword of Simeon becomes symbolic of the division of the whole land by the challenge of Jesus. Even if one rejects the identification, one can still see a profound suffering of Mary at the foot of the cross. She was witnessing not only the terrible death of her Son, but also the rejection of the Messiah by her own people. When we read the anguish of Paul at the failure of his people to accept the Saviour (see Rm 9:1-4), we can grasp something of Mary's double grief— for her Son and for her people.

c) John 19:25-27[6]

The alternative gospel for the celebration of Our Lady of Sorrows shows Mary at the foot of the cross. As at Cana (see Jn 2:4) Jesus calls her by the title "Woman." It is a usual respectful form of address (e.g. Jn 8:11) but quite unusual from a son to his mother.[7] Mary was to have had no active share in the ministry of Jesus,[8] but she appears as the New Eve (see Gen 3) in the climax of Jesus' hour.[9]

---

[5]K. Stock, "Maria nel tempio (Lc 2:22-52)" in *Parola Spirito e vita. Quaderni di lettura biblica. 6: La Madre del Signore* (Bologna: Ed. Dehoniana, 1986) 114-125 at 118.

[6]See R.E. Brown, *The Gospel According to John.* "The Anchor Bible." 2 vols. (Garden City, NY: Doubleday, 1966-London: Chapman, 1971) 2:904-906, 922-927; A. Serra, *Maria a Cana e presso la croce* (Rome: Centro di Cultura Mariana "Mater Ecclesiae, 1985) 79-121 with bibliography; *MaryNT* 206-218.

[7]Brown op. cit. (n.6) notes that it is without precedent in Greek or Hebrew literature, 1:99.

[8]Ibid. 1:109.

[9]Ibid. 2:926.

To the disciple Jesus says, *This is your mother.* The *disciple whom Jesus loved* may have been one of the apostles, John, or somebody else called John, or an idealized figure.[10] Whichever we accept it is important to note that *the disciple took her into his home.*

There is more involved than a filial act on the part of Jesus, who sees to it that his mother will be looked after. When we read the verse which follows we are alerted to some deeper significance: *After this, Jesus knew that everything was now fulfilled* (Jn 19:28a. This verse does not unfortunately form part of the reading in the Lectionary.) The words from the cross are part of the mission which Jesus must accomplish. We should look at the title "Woman." As in Jn 2:4 we must understand that Jesus is *seeing through* his Mother to her more generalized role. (See above 11 February). The destiny of Mary is to be the New Eve and Mother of those who would be the disciples whom Jesus loved.

But there can also perhaps be another level of significance if we follow the tradition of Matthew and Mark in their account of the death of Jesus. On the cross Jesus feels himself abandoned by the Father. St. Paul tells us that Christ was made to be sin (2 Cor 5:21). He experiences the utter chasm between God and sin as he hangs on the cross at the greatest possible distance from his Father, "My God, my God, why have you forsaken me?" (see Mt 27:46 par.). Mary shares in this abandonment as she is asked to look, not to Jesus, but to another as her son. She is thus absolutely stripped of what is most dear to her. Like Abraham she has to offer her Son; unlike Abraham there is no last minute reprieve; she has to see him die. We can see the words, *behold your son,* as a profound challenge to Mary's faith. In darkness she surrenders Jesus and accepts the beloved disciple.

[10]Ibid. 1:1xxxviii-xcviii where Brown with some hesitation settles for John, son of Zebedee.

Jesus feeling himself abandoned by the Father, abandons also his mother, so that she could share as deeply as possible in his sacrificial emptiness on the Cross."[11]

CHURCH DOCUMENTS

In his exhortation *Marialis cultus* (n. 7) Pope Paul VI writes:

there is the commemoration of Our Lady of Sorrows (15 September), a fitting occasion for re-living a decisive moment in the history of salvation and for venerating, together with the Son 'lifted up on the Cross, his suffering Mother' (Prayer of Mass, 15 September).

We take two passages from John Paul II, the first already cited earlier in this chapter:

Simeon's words seem like a second Annunciation to Mary, for they tell her of the actual historical situation in which the Son is to accomplish his mission namely in misunder-standing and sorrow. (RM 16)

The second passage is from the apostolic letter, *Salvifici dolores* (1984) about suffering, which in paragraph 25 speaks of Mary's sufferings. In the section on Calvary we read:

And again, after the events of Her Son's hidden and public life, events which she must have shared with acute sensitivity, it was on Calvary that Mary's suffering, beside the suffering of Jesus, reached an intensity which can hardly be imagined from a human point of view, but which was mysterious and supernaturally fruitful for the redemption of the world. Her ascent of Calvary and her standing at the foot of the Cross together with the Beloved Disciple were a special sort of

[11]H. Urs von Balthasar in J. Ratzinger and H. Urs von Balthasar, *Marie première Eglise* (Paris: Apostolat des Editions-Montreal: Ed. Paulines, 1981) 54-55.

sharing in the redeeming death of her Son. And the words which she heard from his lips were a kind of solemn handing-over of this Gospel of suffering so that it could be proclaimed to the whole community of believers.

As a witness to her Son's Passion by her *presence,* and as a sharer in it by her *compassion,* Mary offered a unique contribution to the Gospel of suffering, by embodying in anticipation the expression of Saint Paul which was quoted at the beginning (cf. Col 1:24). She truly has a special title to be able to claim that she 'completes in her flesh'—as already in her heart—'what is lacking in Christ's affliction.'

REFLECTIONS

There are different lists of the sorrows of Mary. In the 14th century there were seven sorrows that began with the passion, and another list with sorrows belonging also to the infancy of Jesus. What we would think of as the traditional list goes back to the general chapters of the Servite Order in 1646 and 1652: Simeon's prophecy, the flight into Egypt, the loss of Jesus, the meeting with Jesus on the road to Calvary, the crucifixion, the taking down from the cross and the burial of Jesus. In recent years there is a new list, which comes to us again from the Servites. It emphasizes above all the biblical theme of the rejection of Jesus: his birth in poverty, the prophecy of Simeon, the flight into Egypt, the rejection of the testimony of Jesus (see Lk 4:28-29), the arrest of Jesus and his abandonment by the disciples (see Mt 26:49-50.56b), the crucifixion, the sharing by Mary in the sufferings of the infant Church (see Acts 12:1-3a.5b).[12]

In addition there are the two well known devotions, namely the Stations of the Cross and the Rosary, both of which are ways in which we can reflect with Mary on the Passion. Following some thoughts of H. Urs von Balthasar, we can outline the passion

[12]See Maggiani, art. cit. (n. 1) 3-5.

through the mysteries of the Rosary.[13] In the Garden of Olives the apostles, who represent the official institutional Church, failed Jesus. The Mary who anointed the feet of Jesus (see Jn 12:7) shows the generous love that was called for; it is found in Mary his Mother, who was constant to the foot of the Cross. The scourging calls on Mary to say a yes to the unimaginable suffering of her child. Though she knew he was king, the Jews wanted only Caesar as their king (see Jn 19:15). Yet it is in the passion that the glory of God's love is being fully revealed. It is also the imperious will of the Father which Mary met first when Jesus was twelve years old. Jesus carries his own cross (see Jn 19:17), but he allows others to carry it along with him as Simon did (see Mk 23:26). He alone bore the sins of the world, yet he left a space for others to suffer along with him (see Col 1:24; Gal 2:19; 6:17). Mary cannot relieve her Son's sufferings; she can only let the passion happen. It is an outcome that she could never have envisaged in her initial *fiat* (see Lk 1:38). An ancient tradition would have us believe that Jesus and Mary met on the road to Calvary. It is not recorded in scripture, though it is by no means unlikely that in the milling crowd their eyes could have met. It would be a meeting in which the yes of each of them to the Father's will would have been most painful, but supportive. On Calvary the divine anger against sin crushes Jesus, who was made to be sin (see 2 Cor 5:21). Yet this anger is but another side of the mutual love of Father and Son, and the love of each of them for the world which is now being saved. Mary stands beneath the cross, silent, but joining with her Son's destiny.

The Stations of the Cross are another way in which we can enter into the mind and heart of Mary in the passion. The Stations became widespread in the 15th century and their number, four-teen, general from the following century. One of the loveliest hymns of the Middle Ages is the *Stabat Mater* probably the work

[13]See *The Threefold Garland* (San Francisco: Ignatius, 1982) 71-105.

of Jacopone da Todi (d. 1306). Since it is not nearly so accessible now as in former years, we give the text for reflection.[14]

Stabat Mater dolorosa

STABAT Mater dolorosa
Juxta Crucem lacrymosa,
  Dum pemdebat Filius.

Cujus animam gementem,
Contristatam et dolentem,
  Pertransivit gladius.

O quam tristis et afflicta
Fuit illa benedicta
  Mater Unigeniti!
Quae moerebat, et dolebat,
Pia Mater, dum videbat
  Nati poenas inclyti.

Quis est homo qui non fleret,
Matrem Christi si videret
  In tanto supplicio?
Quis non posset contristari,
Christi Matrem contemplari
  Dolentem cum Filio?

Pro peccatis suae gentis
Vidit Jesum in tormentis,
  Et flagellis subditum:
Vidit suum dulcem Natum
Moriendo desolatum,
  Dum emisit spiritum.

AT the Cross her station keeping,
Stood the mournful Mother
  weeping,
Close to Jesus to the last:
Through her heart, His sorrow
  sharing
All His bitter anguish bearing,
Now at length the sword had
  passed.

Oh, how sad and sore distressed
Was that Mother highly blest
Of the sole-begotten One!
Christ above in torment hangs;
She beneath beholds the pangs
Of her dying glorious Son.

Is there one who would not weep,
Whelmed in miseries so deep
Christ's dear Mother to behold?
Can the human heart refrain
From partaking in her pain,
In that Mother's pain untold?

Bruised, derided, cursed, defiled,
She beheld her tender Child
All with bloody scourges rent;
For the sins of His own nation,
Saw Him hang in desolation,
Till His Spirit forth He sent.

---

[14]From *The Hymns of the Breviary and Missal,* edited by M. Britt (London: Burns, Oates and Washbourne—New York: Benziger Brothers, 1924[2]). The translation is by Fr. Caswall, pp. 132-134.

Eja Mater, fons amoris,
Me sentire vim doloris
    Fac, ut tecum lugeam:
Fac, ut ardeat cor meum
In amando Christum Deum
    Ut sibi complaceam.

Sancta Mater, istud agas,
Crucifixi fige plagas
    Cordi meo valide:
Tui Nati vulnerati,
Tam dignati pro me pati,
    Poenas mecum divide.

Fac me tecum pie flere,
Crucifixo condolere,
    Donec ego vixero:
Juxta Crucem tecum stare,
Et me tibi sociare
    In planctu desidero.

Virgo virginum praeclara,
Mihi jam non sis amara,
    Fac me tecum plangere:
Fac ut portem Christi mortem,
Passionis fac consortem,
    Et plagas recolere.

Fac me plagis vulnerari,
Fac me Cruce inebriari,
    Et cruore Filii.
Flammis ne urar succensus,
Per te, Virgo, sim defensus
    In die judicii.

Christe, cum sit hinc exire,
Da per Matrem me venire
    Ad palmam victoriae.
Quando corpus morietur
Fac ut animae donetur
    Paradisi gloria.

O thou Mother! fount of love!
Touch my spirit from above,
Make my heart with thine accord:
Make me feel as thou hast felt;
Make my soul to glow and melt
With the love of Christ my Lord.

Holy Mother! pierce me through;
In my heart each wound renew
Of my Saviour crucified:
Let me share with thee His pain,
Who for all my sins was slain,
Who for me in torments died.

Let me mingle tears with thee,
Mourning Him who mourned for
    me,
All the days that I may live:
By the Cross with thee to stay;
There with thee to weep and pray
Is all I ask of thee to give.

Virgin of all virgins blest!
Listen to my fond request:
Let me share thy grief divine;
Let me, to my latest breath,
In my body bear the death
Of that dying Son of thine.

Wounded with His every wound,
Steep my soul till it hath swooned
In His very Blood away;
Be to me, O Virgin, nigh,
Lest in flames I burn and die,
In that awful Judgment day.

Christ, when Thou shalt call me
    hence,
Be Thy Mother my defence,
Be Thy Cross my victory;
While my body here decays,
May my soul Thy goodness praise,
Safe in Paradise with Thee.

Finally, it is necessary to say something about Mary's universal motherhood. The tradition of the Roman Church sees in the text of John 19:25-27 the basis for this role of Mary. But the evidence is rather late, the first clear indications would seem to be from George of Nicomedia (d. after 880) in the East, and from the 11th century in the West.[15] But once it was introduced, it quickly became established in both East and West, though with different nuances.[16] From medieval times the text of John has been supplemented with other patristic and later reflections so that the idea of Mary as Mother of all Christians can be said to belong in some sense to the faith of the Church, even before Paul VI explicitly proclaimed Mary as Mother of the Church when closing the third session of Vatican II on 21 November 1964. We can see a mature presentation of the idea of Mary's universal motherhood in the marian encyclical of Pope John Paul II:

> Motherhood always establishes a unique and unrepeatable relationship between two people: between mother and child and between child and mother. Even when the same woman is mother of many children, her personal relationship with each one of them is of the very essence of motherhood....
> It can be said that motherhood 'in the order of grace' preserves the analogy with what 'in the order of nature' characterizes the union between mother and child. In the light of this fact it becomes easier to understand why in Christ's testament on Golgotha his Mother's new motherhood is expressed in the singular, in reference to one man: 'Behold your son.'
> It can also be said that these same words fully show the reason for the Marian dimension of the life of Christ's disciples. This is true not only of John, who at that hour

---

[15]Se. T. Köhler, "Les principales interprétations traditionelles de Jn 19:25-27 pendant les douzes premiers siècles," *Études mariales* 16 (1959) 112-155; H. Barré, "La maternité spirituelle de Marie dans la pensée médiévale," *Études mariales* 16(1959) 87-118; a fine summary in M. Thurian, *Mary. Mother of the Lord. Figure of the Church* (London: Faith Press, 1963) 144-175.

[16]See M. O'Carroll, *Theotokos* 253-256.

stood at the foot of the Cross together with his Master's Mother, but it is also true of every disciple of Christ, of every Christian. The Redeemer entrusts his mother to the disciple, and at the same time he gives her to him as his mother. Mary's motherhood which becomes man's inheritance is a gift: a gift which Christ himself makes personally to every individual. The redeemer entrusts Mary to John because he entrusts John to Mary. At the foot of the Cross there begins that special entrusting of humanity to the mother of Christ, which in the history of the Church has been practised and expressed in different ways ... entrusting is the response to a person's love, and in particular to the love of a mother. . . . Thus the Christian seeks to be taken into that maternal charity with which the Redeemer's Mother 'cares for the brethren of her Son' (LG 62), 'in whose birth and development she cooperates' (LG 63) in the measure of the gift proper to each one through the power of Christ's Spirit. (RM 45)

It is then in the sorrow of the cross that we receive the unique gift of our spiritual Mother. From the pain of Calvary comes salvation from sin, and the grace of a Mother in the new family born from the pierced side of Christ.

PRAYER OF THE FAITHFUL

As we celebrate the Sorrows of Mary we bring to our Father the needs and difficulties of his people.

- Mary was given a dark prophecy by Simeon; we pray for all who have received sorrowful news concerning themselves or their loved ones, that they may face the future with confidence.
- Mary knew exile in Egypt; we pray for refugees and for the work of the United Nations Commission for Refugees, that politicians may be courageous and generous in dealing with the stateless.

- Mary suffered the loss of Jesus; we pray for parents who see that their children have apparently lost Jesus, that they may find him in renewed faith.
- Mary met Jesus on the road to Calvary; we pray for those involved in the sufferings of others that they may be ministers of healing.
- Mary saw the death of her Son; we pray for those soon to be bereaved, that they may have strength and hope.
- Mary saw her Son taken down from the Cross; we pray for all concerned with the dying, especially nurses and pastoral persons, that they may find words and actions that are truly comforting.
- Mary saw Jesus buried; we pray for funeral directors and for those employed in graveyards and crematoria, that their work and attitudes may be a sensitive help to the bereaved in their time of anguish.

  Father in heaven, you changed Mary's sorrow into joy at the resurrection of your Son Jesus; grant to those who suffer, the grace and peace of your Holy Spirit, who is Lord for ever and ever. Amen.

ADDITIONAL READING

M. Balagué, "La hora de Maria," *Ephemerides mariologicae* 23(1973) 129-143.

E.R. Carroll, "Mary in the Documents of the Magisterium" in Carol 1:40-44.

R. Casanova Cortés, "El título 'Madre de la Iglesia' en los textos y las actas del Vaticano Concilio Vaticano II," *Ephemerides mariologicae* 32 (1982) 237-264.

C.P. Ceroke, "Mary's Maternal Role in John 19:25-27," *Marian Studies* 11(1960) 123-151.

B. de Margerie, "L'Église peut-elle définir dogmatiquement la maternité spirituelle de Marie? Objections et réponses," *Marianum* 43 (1981) 394–418.

D. Fernandez, "Origenes históricos de la expresión *Mater Ecclesiae*," *Ephemerides mariologicae* 32(1982) 189–200.

J. Galot, "Théologie du titre 'Mère de l'Église'", *Ephemerides mariologicae* 32 (1982) 159–173.

K. Mansell, "Mary, Mother of the Church in the Writings of some Early Eastern Fathers," *Diakonia* (USA) 18 (1983) 147–162.

Roschini, 2:256–343.

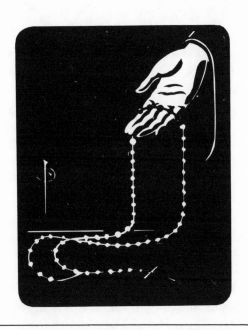

OUR LADY OF THE ROSARY
(Memorial—7 October)

LITURGICAL HISTORY

The Rosary grew out of the practice of reciting the Our Father and Hail Mary 150 times in a devotion that parallels the Liturgy of the Hours in which each week all 150 psalms were said. There is evidence of this devotion from about the 12th century. The Dominican Order had the legend that the Rosary was given by Our Lady to Dominic as a weapon against the Albigensians. Though a vision may have been granted to St. Dominic, it could not have been about the Rosary in its present form. Prior to 1483 only the first part of the Hail Mary was in common usage. In time the 150 Our Fathers and Hail Marys would be reduced to one Our Father and ten Hail Marys. The number of events in the lives of Christ and Mary were also reduced from 150 to 15. The Rosary became more standardized during the 15th century and was approved in 1569 by Pope St. Pius V in a form substantially the same as the present Rosary, viz. with the second part of the Hail Mary ("Holy Mary, Mother of God...), and with a Gloria after each of the fifteen decades. In 1573 this same Pope established the feast of the Rosary in thanksgiving for the victory at Lepanto against the Turks.[1]

THEMES

The translation of the opening prayer of the Mass is quite unfortunate, and it does not even mention Mary. The translation in the Liturgy of the Hours of the prayer of the feast is much better. It is a version of the prayer familiar to many as the prayer at the end of the Angelus with however one important addition. It recalls the incarnation, passion and resurrection of Christ; we ask that grace be poured into our hearts and that we may come to the glory of the resurrection *through the intercession of the Blessed Virgin Mary* (opening prayer with the conclusion in italics added to the Angelus prayer). We ask too that the recollection of the mysteries of Christ may bring us to share in them (prayer over gifts and after communion).

> Blessed Mother and pure Virgin, renowned queen of creation, may all who keep your festival experience the power of your intercession. (Morning Prayer)
> Mary treasured all these things and pondered them in her heart. (Evening Prayer)

---

[1]See M. O'Carroll, "Rosary," *Theotokos* 313-314; E.D. Staid, "Rosario," *NDizM* 1207-1215.

SCRIPTURE READINGS

a) Acts 1:12-14.[2]

This passage gives us an account of the early Church at prayer in Jerusalem. There are three groups present, the key witnesses of the life of Jesus. The *apostles* are witnesses from the baptism of John to the ascension (see Acts 1:21-22). The *women* are witnesses to the empty tomb (see lk 24:22-24). *Mary and the brothers*, that is, his Mother and his close family relatives, are witnesses to the infancy. *With one heart all these joined constantly in prayer.* We are thus invited to see on this day the Rosary as a prayer in imitation of Mary, and as a means of joining with her to penetrate the mystery of her Son.

The *response* is "The Almighty works marvels for me. Holy is his name."

b) Luke 1:26-38

The story of the Annunciation is the first of the mysteries of the Rosary. But there is a more profound reason for choosing it for this celebration. This lies in the conclusion of the passage: *You see before you the Lord's servant, let it happen to me as you said.* The woman who was told that she *enjoys God's favour*, had also been reminded that *nothing is impossible to God.* She then says a yes to God's plan and she becomes the mother of the Messiah.

We can recall here the lovely phrase used by Vatican II about Mary's subsequent life, "the Blessed Virgin advanced in her pilgrimage of faith" (LG 58). As we have earlier observed, a pilgrimage is a journey to a holy place: Mary would journey to Calvary, the place of sacrifice; she would later join the nascent Church in the Upper Room awaiting the Spirit. The Annunciation

---

[2]See B. Buby, "Mary, Model of *Ecclesia orans* in Acts 1:14," *Marian Studies* 35 (1984) 87-99; Laurentin 541-544; R. Laurentin, *Catholic Pentecostalism* (London: Darton, Longman and Todd, 1977) 195-196; A. Serra, "Bibbia," *NDIzM* 231-311 at 271-274; Brown 431, n. 76; *MaryNT* 173-177.

and Mary's life afterwards show us a model of faith in its three aspects: she believed God; she trusted him; she lived according to his plan. Faith in the full sense of the word is not intellectual, but a full yes, and Amen, to the words, promises and commands of God.

CHURCH DOCUMENTS

From the bull of Pius V in 1569, *Consueverunt Romani Pontifices* to the present day, there has been an enormous number of papal statements about the Rosary. We can begin with a synthesis of the teaching of Pius V: the necessity of prayer to overcome the difficulties of wars and other calamities; the simplicity of the Rosary as a prayer within the reach of all; the help the Rosary has been against heresies; the instrumentality of the Rosary in many conversions. The recitation of the Rosary is therefore commended to all.

Pope Paul VI observes in *Marialis cultus* that the feast of Our Lady of the Rosary is one of those which were

> originally celebrated by particular religious families, but
> ... today by reason of the popularity they have gained, can
> truly be considered ecclesial. (MC 8)

The religious family here is, of course, the Dominican Order for as Pope Paul later notes, "the sons of St. Dominic (are) by tradition the guardians of this very salutary practice" (MC 43).

REFLECTION

There are several meanings to the word "mystery": a revealed truth that we cannot fully understand; the divine plan unfolded in Christ Jesus (see Eph 1:9; 3:9; LG ch. 1); events in the life of Christ. It is this third meaning that underlies the use of the word in the context of the Rosary, a usage that goes back to apostolic

Fathers such as Justin (d. c. 165). This clarification apart, there are two main considerations that suggest themselves for our consideration: the value of the Rosary; the role of Mary in the saving mission of her Son.

Pope Paul VI devoted the last part of his Exhortation *Marialis cultus* to the Angelus and the Rosary (MC 40-55). The former needed no revision for modern times; it retains "an unaltered value and an intact freshness" (MC 41). We can summarize the main points he then makes about the Rosary. It is, in the traditional phrase used by Pius XII "a compendium of the entire Gospel." It is moreover a prayer of praise and petition, it fosters contemplation and it has an intrinsic effectiveness for promoting christian life and apostolic commitment.

As a devotional exercise the Rosary has a unique character, since it considers all the principal salvific events accomplished in Christ from his virginal conception to the effects of his paschal mystery radiating out into the Church and upon Mary. Pope Paul recalls that the Rosary follows the mystery of Christ outlined in the primitive christian hymn of Philippians 2:6-11: he emptied himself, he died and he was glorified.

The Rosary is a prayer the centre of which is not Mary but Christ. Each Hail Mary focuses on Jesus, born into our world, who suffered and was glorified. Through its quiet lingering recitation we are drawn along with Mary into contemplation of the mysteries of Christ. Without this contemplative aspect, the Rosary can be a mechanical repetition. The Pope then studies carefully the relation between the liturgy and the Rosary, "which is, as it were, a branch sprung from the ancient trunk of the christian liturgy" (MC 48). There should be no conflict between the liturgy and devotions. Indeed the Rosary harmonizes easily with the liturgy: in the liturgy and in the Rosary the same mysteries of Christ are celebrated and the Word of God is pondered. The Rosary "can be an excellent preparation for the celebration of these mysteries in the liturgical action and can also be their continuing echo" (MC 48)

He then reflects on the prayers that make up the Rosary and

give it its varying moods or tones: the Our Father, a grave and suppliant prayer; the tranquil succession of Hail Marys which are lyrical and full of praise, leading to the adoration of the Glory be to the Father. He goes on to say that after the Liturgy of the Hours, "the Rosary should be considered as one of the best and most efficacious prayers in common that the christian family is invited to recite" (MC 54).

In an important conclusion Paul VI warns against propagating the Rosary

> in a way that is too one-sided or exclusive. The rosary is an excellent prayer, but the faithful should feel serenely free in its regard. They should be drawn to its calm recitation by its intrinsic appeal. (MC 55)

Here he is saying at the very least that people should not feel guilty if for a time they find the Rosary difficult. There are other forms of marian piety, especially ones based on the Rosary (MC 54). This freedom advocated by the pope is reflected in the new Code of Canon Law. Whereas the old Code of 1917 laid down for clerics the daily recitation of the Rosary (canon 125), the new Code states only that clerics should cultivate a special devotion to the Blessed Virgin (canon 276).

The second issue suggested by the memorial of Our Lady of the Rosary is the relationship of Mary to her Son's saving mission. The Rosary, Pope Paul notes, helps us

> to meditate on the mysteries of the Lord's life as seen through the eyes of her who was closest to the Lord. In this way the unfathomable riches of these mysteries are unfolded. (MC 47)

Such a statement recalls the prayer attributed to St. Ignatius, "Jesus, show me your Mother; Mary, show me your Son"—a prayer which we have already suggested as being helpful for those whose affective relationship with Mary is weak, often because of inadequate relationship with their own human mothers.

The prayer of the Rosary then in inviting us to contemplate Christ with Mary, raises the larger question of Mary's relationship to the saving mystery of her Son, and in particular the issues of Mary's mediation and the title "Mediatrix." The Catholic Church cannot but hold firm the teaching of scripture:

> For there is only one mediator between God and humanity, himself a human being, Christ Jesus, who offered himself as a ransom for all. (I Tm 2:5)[3]

The same idea is also expressed by Peter:

> for of all the names in the world given to men, this is the only one by which we can be saved (Acts 4:12).

We have already alluded briefly to the difficulty which Protestants have with asking Mary's intercession. They fear that it would derogate from the mediation of Christ Jesus. We can repeat our earlier response following K. Rahner who alludes to such scripture texts as we have just quoted. Yet despite these clear assertions of scripture, Christians of all Churches practise mediation; they pray for one another. When one prays for another one is coming before God on behalf of that person. This is not to say that one is denying that Jesus is the one mediator between God and humanity: he has already provided all grace through his passion and death. In the Roman Catholic and Orthodox Churches there is a strong conviction that such intercession continues beyond the grave, that the saints continue to pray for us in the communion of saints. Preeminent amongst these saints is Mary.[4]

---

[3]The text might also be given as follows: "There is one and the same God (for all) and there is also one and the same mediator (for all)." See M. Miguens, "One God, One Mediator," *Marian Studies* 25 (1974) 44-64, where it is argued that the point of the text is *not* the *uniqueness of God* and the *uniqueness of the mediator*, but rather *the universality of salvation*.

[4]See "Mediatrix of Graces" in *Mary Mother of the Lord. Theological Meditations* (Freiburg: Herder-Edinburgh/London: Nelson, 1963) 93-103.

We should note then that the notion of Mary's intercession is very early, being found in the 3rd century prayer *Sub tuum* (We fly to thy patronage ...), in which Mary is asked to deliver us (*rhysai* as in the Our Father, Mt 6:13) from evil.[5] Similar positive roles are ascribed to Mary in the New Eve theology, "Death through Eve, life through Mary."[6] The term "mediatrix" began to appear in the 6th century.[7] It became widespread in the 12th century, and is found for example in St. Thomas.[8] Theologies of mediation soon followed, being particularly abundant from the 17th century.

The term Mediatrix applied to Mary involves several ideas. It was originally applied to her intercession for, and her distribution of graces. It also involves her role in redemption itself, hence we find the other words coredemption and coredemptrix.[9]

In the preparatory stages of Vatican II there were 382 requests for a definition of Mary's mediation. After rather torturous work the Council made a somewhat limited statement on various marian titles:

> By her maternal charity, she cares for the brethren of her Son, who still journey on earth surrounded by dangers and difficulties, until they are led into their blessed home. Therefore the Blessed Virgin is invoked in the Church under the titles of Advocate, Helper, Benefactress, and Mediatrix. This, however, is so understood that it neither takes away anything from nor adds anything to the dignity and efficacy of Christ the one Mediator. (LG 62)

[5]See M. O'Carroll, "Sub tuum," *Theotokos* 336.

[6]Jerome, *Epist.* 22, 21—PL 22:408, and LG 56 with notes.

[7]See M. O'Carroll, "Mediation," *Theotokos* 239-242 for patristic and later evidence; S. Meo, "Mediatrice," *NDixM* 920-935 at 921; for earlier texts of the magisterium see E.R. Carroll, "Mary in the Documents of the Magisterium" in Carol 1:32-40; as overall study M. O'Carroll, *Mediatress of all Graces* (Dublin: Golden Eagle Books, 1958).

[8]See *In Ioan* 2, lect. 1 (344) where the word is used, and 345-354 for the exercise of mediation.

[9]See J.P. Carol, "Our Lady's Coredemption" in Carol 2:377-425; Roschini 2:116-198;

We know from the *Acts* of the Council[10] that this passage presented innumerable difficulties and was a compromise.[11] The text supports the use of the word "Mediatrix" in the context of Mary's maternal care for the brethren of her Son. Elsewhere we can find in Vatican II an important theological underpinning which could be used to support this statement. It frequently speaks of the sharing by all christians, laity and the hierarchy in the one priesthood of Christ (e.g. LG 10-11, 21, 34. . .). Mary's mediation cannot be seen as another mediation separate from her Son's, but a sharing in his unique mediation. Or as Pope John Paul II notes, Mary's mediation is mediation in Christ (RM 38).

This text of LG 62 is not however the only one we should examine for an insight into the Council's teaching on Mary's role in salvation; elsewhere though avoiding the word "mediation" the Council develops the matter further:

> She was the gracious Mother of the divine Redeemer here on earth, and above all other and in a singular way, the generous associate and humble handmaiden of the Lord. (LG 61)
>
> Mary, consenting to the word of God, became the Mother of Jesus. Committing herself whole-heartedly and impeded by no sin to God's saving will, she devoted herself totally, as a handmaiden to the Lord to the person and work of her Son, under him and with him, serving the mystery of redemption, by the grace of Almighty God. Rightly, therefore, the Fathers see Mary not merely as passively engaged by God, but as freely cooperating in the work of man's salvation through faith and obedience. (LG 56)
>
> (In the words of Augustine) 'she is clearly the mother of the members of Christ . . . since she has by her charity joined in bringing about the birth of believers in the Church, who are

---

[10]See G. Alberigo and F. Magistretti, *Lumen gentium synopsis historica* (Bologna: Istituto per le Scienze Religiose, 1975) 501-502, 562-563.

[11]See M. O'Carroll, "Mediation" (n. 7) 242-245; id. "Vatican II and Our Lady's Mediation," *Irish Theological Quarterly* 37 (1970) 24-55.

members of its head.' Wherefore she is hailed as pre-eminent
and as a wholly unique member of the Church, and as its
type and outstanding model in faith and charity ... taught
by the Holy Spirit (the Church) honours her with filial
affection and devotion as a most beloved mother. (LG 53)

These three texts teach that Mary truly cooperated in the saving
work of her Son, though in a secondary way, which is explained
by her faith and obedience. There is an important distinction
made by the eminent Roman theologian J. Alfaro:

We have to remember that the action that constituted the
redemptive power of the death of Christ was his personal
offering to the Father on behalf of humanity. This act was
exclusively his. But it places the kernel of redemption in his
self-offering, rather than in the sufferings that were the
form this offering took, then we can see that Mary's obedience and faith are a reflection of Christ's; she too offered
herself to the Father.[12]

Nothing need nor could be added to the perfect act of redemption
which lies in the self-offering of the Son. At most we can say that
Mary joined this offering with her own self-offering and with her
sacrifical offering of her own sufferings at the death of Jesus. As
the liturgy and theology of the Immaculate Conception make
clear, Mary herself was redeemed (see 8 December). It was in
being fully redeemed from sin through the merits of her Son that
Mary was a fit person to cooperate in her Son's victory over sin
and evil. Prior to Vatican II theologians saw Mary's role in the
redemption primarily, indeed almost exclusively, in terms of the
Annunciation and of her standing by the foot of the cross. The
Council, however, prefers to speak of her as being in her whole
life an associate or companion to Jesus (see LG 56-59, 61).

The encyclical of John Paul II takes the same approach. Her

---

[12]J. Alfaro, *Maria la bienaventurada porque ha creído*. Italian tr. *Maria. Colei che è beata perché ha creduto* (Casale Monferrato: Ed. Pienne, 1983) 33-34.

cooperation with Christ's work is mediation (RM 39-40), and her maternal care continues in heaven (RM 40). Humanity has been entrusted to her from the cross (Rm 45) and she continues to show motherly care for all from her state of glory (RM 40). In a long section (RM 38-47) the Pope develops the maternal character of Mary's mediation. It is her motherhood

> completely pervaded by her spousal attitude as 'handmaid of the Lord' (that) constitutes the first and fundamental dimension of that mediation which the Church confesses and proclaims in her regard. (RM 39)

It is noteworthy that neither Vatican II in its final draft nor John Paul II used the term "Mediatrix of all Graces." Despite his elaborate treatment of Mary's mediation, the basic assertions of Pope John Paul II are quite limited: it is a maternal mediation; Mary was the noble associate of her Son in the redemption; she can therefore be said to cooperate in a subordinate way in his mediation; she joined in her Son's saving work by faith and obedience; her mediation in heaven is described only in terms of maternal care and intercession,

> After her Son's departure, her motherhood remains in the Church as maternal mediation: interceding for all her children, the Mother cooperates in the saving work of her Son, the Redeemer of the world (RM 40).

The theological task of understanding this mediation is not an easy one. As ascending it is clearly intercession, as the Pope points out. But can we see this mediation also in a descending direction? As long as grace was seen as a "thing," it was easy to envisage Mary as "handing on" graces, as the "neck" of the mystical body, or as it were an "aqueduct." These are symbolic, imaginative ways of stating that Mary has some role in the distribution of grace. But recent theology, returning to biblical and patristic roots sees grace as a relationship in which God bestows his love on us by changing us and giving us his Spirit. Such a view of grace can be seen in a paragraph of K. Rahner:

> Grace is light, love, receptive access of a human being's life
> as a spiritual person to the infinite expanses of the Godhead.
> Grace means freedom, strength, a pledge of eternal life, the
> predominant influence of the Holy Spirit in the depths of the
> soul, adoptive sonship and an eternal inheritance.[13]

The imaginative picture of handing out graces like jewels from a
treasury does not harmonize with this more accurate and more
profound theology of grace as God's self-communication. Yet it
would seem that there is some conviction in the Church that
Mary has a role in the distribution of grace, that her maternal
role might not be confined to intercession.

An earlier draft of *Lumen gentium*, chapter 8, did state that
Mary is called "Mediatrix of all Graces" because she was associated with Christ in acquiring them; she remains the associate
(*socia*) of Christ in heaven, "so that in conferring all graces on
men the maternal charity of the Blessed Virgin is present."[14]
Though one should not perhaps use the term "Mediatrix of all
Graces," one can ask what such a title might mean.[15] We ask
therefore if there is in any sense a descending dimension to Mary's
maternal care. The statements of Vatican II and of John Paul II
about Mary's being Mother in the order of grace, as well as some
general, if a trifle confused, feeling among the faithful, all suggest
that there might be such a role. Grace we have said is a relationship with God. Its best human analogy is friendship. God looks

---

[13]Op. cit. (n. 4) 48. The point is made more technically in a later work primarily in
terms of God's self-communication, see *Foundations of Christian Faith. An Introduction to the
idea of Christianity* (New York: Seabury—London: Darton, Longman & Todd, 1978)
116-133.

[14]Alberigo-Magistretti, op. cit. (n. 10) 273 col. 1.

[15]See A.J. Robichaud, "Mary, Dispensatrix of all Graces" in Carol 2:426-460 with
bibliography of pre-Vatican II literature; see further the series of articles in *Ephemerides
mariologicae* 25.26 (1975-1976) and the summary in A.J. Tambasco, *What are they Saying
about Mary?* (New York: Paulist, 1984) 46-48.

upon us, and by the mission of the Holy Spirit we are changed and become in some real sense his children, brothers and sisters of his Son. The point of insertion of Mary in this divine action is that the change wrought in us is for the purpose of making us more marian. She is the model which God uses in gracing us. Her person, her loveliness thus directly influence us, because God is acting in accordance with her image. In technical theological terms we would say that Mary is Mediatrix of all Graces by being the proximate exemplary cause in the divine work of producing graced persons.[16] As exemplar she is truly involved in our salvation. The term "Mediatrix of all Graces" means therefore that Mary intercedes for all graces, and that all grace comes to us with a marian character, because God gives us grace so that we can be more deeply imbued with the marks of her perfect discipleship of Jesus. Mediatrix of Grace in this view would be a statement about the marian character of the Church, about the receptivity that is its essential hallmark (see above on the Immaculate Heart of Mary). The explanation offered has the additional advantage of maintaining an ecclesial dimension both of grace itself, and of Mary's mediation.[17] If it be asserted that this notion of exemplary causality seems rather minimal, several responses would be in order: exemplarity, fully understood, is a deep and beautiful concept; one has to take account of the fact that the Council and the present Pope have not pursued the pre-Vatican II theories of physical and instrumental causality; it is better to attempt some explanation of a phrase which has been in use for quite some time, and seems to have echoes in the *sensus fidelium* than to pass by the issue in silence.

But however one understands the mediation of Mary, the memorial of the Rosary does encourage us to see the life of Jesus through the eyes of Mary, and further to see Mary as somehow joined with her Son in the plan of redemption.

---

[16]I hope to develop these points in a 1988 issue of *Milltown Studies*.

[17]See S. Meo, "Mediatrice," *NDizM* 920-935 at 930-31.

PRAYER OF THE FAITHFUL

Celebrating the mysteries of Christ in the Rosary, we pray for the gift of the Spirit for the Church.

- That the Church may learn to penetrate more deeply the mysteries of Christ.
- That the world may recognize that only in love and peace can nations prosper.
- That we may learn the lessons of the humble infancy of Jesus.
- That we may glory in the cross of our Lord Jesus Christ.
- That we may be an Easter people, filled with the Holy Spirit.
- That we may always see Mary in company with her Son.

Father in heaven, your Spirit makes us your children, reflecting your Son Jesus and draws us into that perfect discipleship which was Mary's. Open our hearts to the plan of our salvation revealed in him, who is Lord for ever and ever. Amen.

ADDITIONAL READING

a) The Rosary

W.J. Harrington, *The Rosary. A Gospel Prayer* (Canfield, Ohio: Alba, 1975).

G. Martin, "The Origins of the Rosary," *God's Word Today* 9/10 (October 1987) 44–48.

E.D. Staid, "Valore e attualità del Rosario" in (various authors) *Maria nel mistero di Cristo e della Chiesa* (Bari: Ecumenica Ed., 1979) 201–216.

Seventeen Papal Documents on the Rosary (Boston: Daughters of St. Paul, 1980).

b) Mediation

C. Andronikof, "La Theotokos médiatrice du salut dans la liturgie" in A.M. Triacca and A. Pistoia, eds., *La Mère de Jesus-Christ et la Communion des Saints dans la liturgie*. "Conferences Saint-Serge 1985." (Rome: CLV, 1986) 29-44.

A. Bandera, *La Virgen Maria y los sacramentos*. "Patmos 171" (Madrid: Ed. Rialp, 1978).

F.M. Butler, "Our Lady and Salvation in the Twentieth Century," *Marian Studies* 20 (1969) 49-69.

J.B. Carol, "Our Lady's Coredemption," Carol 2:377-428.

B.J. Cooke, "Our Lady and the Sacraments," *Marian Studies* 17 (1966) 110-120

J. Galot, *Dieu et la Femme. Marie dans l'oeuvre du salut*. (Louvain: Ed. Sintal, n.d.).

P.G. Hinnebusch, "Mary and Salvation in the Twentieth Century," *Marian Studies* 21 (1969) 401-464 with a response by F.M. Butler (see above).

"Rescherches sur l'intercession de Marie," *Études mariales* 23 (1966) 9-104.

G.F. Kirwin, "Mary's Salvific Role Compared with that of Christ," *Marian Studies* 25 (1974) 29-43

S. Meo, "Nuova Eva," *NDizM* 1021-1029.

J. Ordoñes Márquez, "Mediación e intercesión de Maria," *Estudios marianos* 48 (1983) 129-164.

id., Ministerio maternal de Maria en la liturgia," *Ephemerides mariologicae* 31 (1981) 267-296.

c) Vatican II

All the commentaries commonly in use date from the 1960s, that is, before the *Acta* of the Council were published. Among the best of these is S. de Fiores, *Maria nel mistero di Cristo e della Chiesa. Commento teologico-pastorale al capitolo VIII della Constituzione* "Lumen Gentium" (Rome: Centro Mariano Monfortano, 1968).

There is a series of commentaries on *Lumen gentium* ch. 8 in *Marian Studies* 37 (1986) which take account of the *Acta* of the Council, and for the moment must be considered the most definitive.

d) Acts 1:14

X. Pikaza, *Maria el el Espiritu Santo (Hech 1:14). Apuntes para una marología pneumatologica* (Salamanca: Secretariado Trinitario, 1981).

J. Schlosser, "Marie et la prière de l'Église d'asprès Lc 1:48 et Ac 1:14," Études mariales 39 1985-86) 13-22.

THE PRESENTATION OF THE
BLESSED VIRGIN MARY
(Memorial—21 November)

LITURGICAL HISTORY

If many of the feasts of Mary have historical obscurities, the Presentation in the Temple is more enigmatic than most.[1] In the Eastern Church it is one of the twelve great feasts (*Dodecaorton*) of the liturgical year; in the West it is now a memorial. We know that the Emperor Justinian had a splendid church, the "New Church" erected in honour of Mary in the Temple area in Jerusalem. It was dedicated on 21 November 543, but within a century it was destroyed by the Persians. The feast would not seem to have been established in Rome when Pope Sergius (687-701) gave special prominence to four feasts (Purification, Annunciation,

---

[1]See G. Gharib, "Presentazione di Maria," *NDizM* 1155-1161 at 1155-1158.

Dormition and Birthday of the Virgin). The first reference to the feast apart from the church built in Jerusalem is from St. Germanus, patriarch of Constantinople (715-730) who preached two homilies for the feast.[2] Homilies are abundant in the East from the 9th century, from which time also we have the liturgy of the feast composed by George of Nicomedia (d. after 880) on the basis of some existing materials.

Since it was not one of Pope Sergius' feasts, and it seemed to be based on an apocryphal gospel, the acceptance of this feast in the West was slow. It appeared in eastern monasteries in Southern Italy in the 9th century and in England in the 14th century. It was celebrated by the papal court at Avignon only from 1373. In 1472 it was extended to the universal Church by Sixtus IV, but it was later dropped for two decades under Pius V, being restored by Sixus V in 1595.

THEMES

As we honour the glorious memory of the Virgin Mary we pray that through her intercession, we too may receive from the fullness of divine life and love (prayer of the Mass).

> Blessed are you, Mary, because you believed that all those things which were said to you by the Lord would be fulfilled. (Morning Prayer)
> Holy Mother of God, Mary ever Virgin, temple of the Lord, sacred dwelling place of the Holy Spirit, you alone without equal found favour with our Lord Jesus Christ. (Evening Prayer)
> O Faithful, let us exchange glad tidings today, singing psalms to the Lord and hymns of praise in honour of Mary his Mother, his Holy Tabernacle, the Ark that contained the

---

[2]Homilies ascribed to Gregory Nyssa (d. 394), Gregory Nazianzus (d. c. 390), John Chrysostom (d. 407) and Epiphanius (d. 403) on the Presentation are of doubtful authenticity. Moreover, they refer to the event of Mary's Presentation rather than to the feast.

Word whom nothing can contain. She is offered to God in a marvellous way and Zachary, the high priest, receives her with great joy, for she is the dwelling place of the Most High. Today the living Temple of the holy glory of Christ our God, Mary, the pure and blessed one, is presented to the Temple of Moses to live in its holy precincts. Joachim and Anne rejoice with her in the spirit, and all the virgins sing hymns of praise to the Lord in honour of his Mother. (*Byzantine Daily Worship* 516)

SCRIPTURE READINGS

a) *Zechariah 2:14-17*

The first part of the prophecy of Zechariah (cc. 1-8) is concerned with the situation of the exiles after they had returned from captivity in 538 b.c. The vision of this part can be precisely dated as 520-519 b.c.

Jerusalem, the *Daughter of Zion*, is to *sing* and *rejoice* for the Lord is *coming* to *live amongst* her. The prophet then breaks out of the narrow theological vision of earlier Old Testament writings and sees *many nations coming to the Lord's people*. Judah is called the *Holy Land*—the first occurrence of this expression in the bible. *All peoples* are to be *silent* to await the Lord's word, *now that he is stirring from his holy Dwelling*.

This text is one of several which some exegetes believe lies behind the infancy gospel of Luke. The notion of rejoicing is present (though with *euphrainou* in the LXX rather than *chaire* of Lk 1:28); the idea of the Lord's coming to live among his people is also present (see Lk 1:28, "the Lord is with you"). Other texts, such as Zeph 3:14; Jl 2:21 and Zech 9:9, especially the first of these, are seen by these exegetes as being deliberately evoked by Luke.[3] These references coalesce in a picture of Mary as the

---

[3]See Laurentin 63-69; McHugh 37-52, 150-153; E.G. Mori, "Figlia di Sion," *NDizM* 580-589.

personification of the Daughter of Sion.[4] Sion itself was probably a refugee camp outside the northern walls of Jerusalem, that is facing the country of oppression, Assyria. Since it was the place of the homeless and dispossessed, the image of the Daughter of Sion became in time blurred with the notion of the "faithful remainder," that is the *anawim* or the poor whose confidence lay in God alone. This transposition would appear to have first occurred in Micah 4:9-10. If Luke is intending to present Mary as the eschatological Daughter of Sion, he would be implying that she personifies an ideal of Old Testament spirituality: it is the attitude of those who wait humbly and patiently on God and are confident that he will deliver them.

It must be said at once that there are exegetes who will not agree that Luke is thinking of the Daughter of Sion in his picture of Mary. A middle position is taken by Vatican II, but only in one of the final drafts of *Lumen gentium* ch. 8:

> (Mary) stands out among the poor and humble of the Lord, who confidently hope for and receive salvation from him. After a long period of waiting the times are fulfilled in her, the exalted (*praecelsa*) Daughter of Sion and the new plan of salvation is established . . . (LG 55).

G. Philips, a main author of *Lumen gentium*, notes that neither "poor" nor "humble" carries scriptural references, since they are commonplaces of Old Testament spirituality.[5] The *Acts* of Vatican II make clear that the Doctrinal Commission noted explicitly that there was no consensus amongst the exegetes for the literal meaning of the Old Testament texts.[6] Hence we can only say

[4]See McHugh 438-444 following H. Cazelles. On "Mother Sion" see G. Ravesi, "La madre Sion" in *Parola spirito e vita. Quaderni di lettura biblica. 6—La Madre del Signore* (Bologna: Ed. Dehoniana, 1979) 36-52.

[5]*L'Eglise et son mystère au deuxième concile du Vatican. Histoire, textes, et commentaire de la constitution 'Lumen gentium.'* 2 vols. (Paris: Desclée, 1968) 2:231.

[6]G. Alberigo and F. Magistretti, *Lumen gentium synopsis historica* (Bologna: Istituto per le Scienze Religiose, 1975) 560.

with D. Flanagan: that Mary in this text

> in a certain sense incorporates the whole people, embodies them in herself. She is, in a word, Israel awaiting the Messiah, accepting the Messiah when he comes.[7]

We are thus not dealing with the literal meaning, such as would be established by exegetes seeking the intention of Luke, but with the Church's ongoing reflection on the relationship between the two Testaments.

The *response* to this reading is either "The Almighty works marvels for me. Holy is his name" or "Blessed is the Virgin Mary, who bore the Son of the Eternal Father."

b) Matthew 12:46-50

This is one of the texts that used to be called "anti-mariological"—one moreover avoided in the quite voluminous marian writings of the popes from Leo X111 to John XXIII. The *Mother and the brothers* were outside and *were anxious to have a word with him.* Jesus points *towards his disciples* and says that they are his *mother* and his *brothers.* Jesus demanded in his preaching that his disciples be prepared to set aside family ties in order to be disciples (see Mt 8:22; 10:37). He asserts that the *will of the Father* is the decisive way of relating to him, and one which surpasses blood ties. This gospel text is thus very apt for the liturgical celebration of the Presentation which stresses that Mary belonged fully to God even from her childhood. The *will of the Father* was an absolute for her, the deepest reality of her whole life and being.

---

[7] In K. McNamara, ed., *The Church. A Theological and Pastoral Commentary on the Constitution on the Church.* (London: Chapman, 1968—Dublin: Veritas, 1983) 335. See Roschini 4:74-76.

DOCUMENTS OF THE CHURCH

In *Marialis cultus* Pope Paul VI observes

> There are still others which, apart from their apocryphal
> content, present lofty and exemplary values and carry on
> venerable traditions having their origin especially in the
> East, e.g. 21 November, the Presentation of the Blessed
> Virgin. (MC 8)

REFLECTION

The feast of the Presentation of the Blessed Virgin seems to
celebrate an event which we know only from the apocryphal
Protoevangelium of James (nn. 7:2—8:1), which predates 200 A.D. by
some decades.[8] It tells us that Joachim and Anne were childless.
When an angel appeared to her in answer to her lamentation, she
promised that, if she bore a child, it would belong to the Lord.
Anne sought to keep the baby free from any ritual impurity.[9] The
text continues:

> The months passed and the child grew. When she was two
> years old, Joachim said to Anna, 'Let us bring her up to the
> temple of the Lord, so that we may fulfil the promise which
> we made, lest the Lord send (some evil) upon us and our gift
> become unacceptable.' And Anna replies: 'Let us wait until
> the third year, that the child may then no more long after
> her father and mother.' And Joachim said: 'Very well.' And
> when the child was three years old, Joachim said: 'Let us call
> the undefiled daughters of the hebrews, and let each take a
> lamp, and let it be burning, in order that the child may not
> turn back and her heart be enticed away from the temple of

[8]See M. O'Carroll, "Apocrypha," *Theotokos* 37-44 at 39.

[9]See *Protoevangelium of James* 6:1 in O. Cullmann, "Infancy Gospels" in E. Henecke,
edited by W. Schneemelcher, *New Testament Apocrypha*. 2 vols. (London: SCM, 1963)
1:377.

the Lord.' And he did so until they went up to the temple of the Lord. And the priest took her and kissed her and blessed her, saying: 'The Lord has magnified your name among all generations; because of you the Lord at the end of days will manifest his redemption to the children of Israel.' And he placed her on the third step of the altar, and the Lord God put grace upon the child, and she danced for joy with her feet, and the whole house of Israel loved her. And her parents went down wondering, praising and glorifying the almighty God because the child did not turn back to them. And Mary was in the temple nurtured like a dove and received food from the hand of an angel.[10]

The story is a legend and without foundation in history. Very few scholars would accept that young children were offered at and remained in the Temple.[11] Indeed it is the legendary character that led to the brief suppression of the feast in the 16th century. It is important, however, to look for the theological motifs that lie behind the legend. And these are patently clear. The point of the whole narrative is to show that even in her childhood Mary fully belonged to God. The symbol for God's possession of Mary at all times is Anne's care to avoid impurity touching Mary, and her later presence in the Temple even as a child. One could say with G. Gharib that for the East to have the Presentation as a major feast is a celebration of more or less the same values as the Western Church finds in the Immaculate Conception. In this way we can consider the two feasts to be complementary.[12]

Earlier (5 August) we alluded to the notion of Mary as Temple of the Lord. Mary is truly where God chose to dwell through his Spirit by grace, and through the Son in the Incarnation. Mary is also the perfect response to God's grace and his dwelling in her. In Mary God is worshipped in spirit and in truth (see Jn 4:23). She

[10]*Protoevangelium of James* 7:1—8:1. ibid. 1:378.

[11]Roschini would seem to be an exception at least in his early work. See Gharib, art. cit. (n. 1) 1159.

[12]Ibid. 1160.

makes her own the Israelite promise, "we shall do everything that Yahweh has said" (Ex 24:7). Her last recorded words were to teach her own people and the Church to obey her Son: "Do whatever he tells you" (Jn 2:5).

The memorial of the Presentation also invites us to consider more profoundly truths about Mary's holiness[13] and consequently about our own. In the not so distant past two false notions concerning holiness were current: it was something extraordinary and therefore for the few; it depended on what people did. With Vatican II there came a deeper grasp of the nature of biblical holiness. In the fifth chapter of the Constitution on the Church we see that holiness is a quality that in strict truth belongs only to God ("You alone are holy"—Gloria at Mass). When we say that people are holy, we mean two things: God has consecrated them so that they share somehow in his holiness; they have responded to this act of God.

We leave to the following chapter (8 December) more detailed treatment of Mary's holiness, being content here to stress that her holiness lies above all in God's gift to her. Her part is to be the receptive Virgin who receives and then responds to God's love for her. It is this idea of holiness and the attendant notion of Mary as belonging wholly to God that lies behind the celebration of the Presentation. They are lessons about holiness also for us. God has made us his own through baptism and confirmation. He strengthens divine life in us by the Eucharist through which we become joined to his Son and to others. As a result of the divine graciousness that we meet, we can then serve God and love others.

Holiness is not the preserve of a few:

> The forms and tasks of life are many, but holiness is one—
> that sanctity which is cultivated by all who act under God's

[13]See L. De Candido, "Santa Maria," *NDizM* 1242-1253; F.P. Calkins, "Mary's Fullness of Grace" in Carol 2:297-312; M. O'Carroll, "Holiness of Mary," *Theotokos* 172-174; E.R. Carroll, "Theological Reflections on Our Blessed Lady's Impeccabilitas," *Primordia cultus mariani*. "Proceedings of the Lisbon International Mariological Congress 1967" 2:371-385 and *The University of Dayton Review* 5 (1968) 21-31

Spirit and, obeying the Father's voice and adoring God the Father in spirit and in truth, follow Christ, poor, humble and cross-bearing, that they may deserve to be partakers of his glory. Each one, however, according to his own gifts and duties must steadfastly advance along the way of a living faith, which arouses hope and works through love. (LG 41)

This teaching of Vatican II can be seen as an admirable summary of the life of Mary and of the path we are to tread. Mary was consecrated to God from her conception, she grew in discipleship, and following the word of God, she added a deepening relationship in the Spirit to the existing blood relationship to the Son of God; she was one who truly did the will of the Father in heaven. (see Mt 12:50 and the gospel of the memorial).

PRAYER OF THE FAITHFUL

We come on the Presentation of Mary to offer our prayers to our Father in heaven as we rely on her intercession.

- We pray for the Churches of the East which have such great devotion to Mary; that we be one with them.
- We pray for the children of the world, and especially for the work of UNICEF for deprived children; that the rights of children to life, education and food may be guaranteed by governments.
- We pray for the homeland of Mary; that there may be peace based on justice there and in the surrounding countries.
- We pray for a deeper commitment to holiness; that we may come to that perfection to which the Spirit is drawing us. Father in heaven, the Virgin Mary belonged to you from the time of her conception; by your Holy Spirit trace in our lives the pattern of her humble holiness, so that glory may be given to you and to your Son, Jesus our Lord. Amen.

ADDITIONAL READING

G.M. Ellero, "Le culte de la Theotokos dans la liturgie byzantine" in (various authors) *La Vierge dans la prière de l'Eglise* (Paris: Mame, 1968) 107-121.

J. Galot, *Dieu et la Femme. Marie dans l'Oeuvre du salut* (Louvain: Ed. Sintal, n.d.) 184-235.

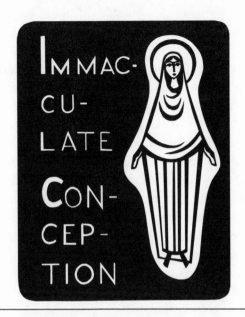

THE IMMACULATE CONCEPTION
OF THE BLESSED VIRGIN MARY
(Solemnity—8 December)

LITURGICAL HISTORY[1]

More than any other feast the Immaculate Conception spurred on and anticipated doctrinal development. And it was a slow development. A feast of Mary's nativity was celebrated in the East in the late 6th century. In the 7th century there arose a feast of the Conception of Mary. In the West a feast of the Conception of Mary appears in England towards 1060 introduced possibly through an Eastern monk. After the Norman conquest the feast revived and passed into Europe, and within the century it had become a feast of the Immaculate Conception. St. Bernard in a

[1] S. De Fiores, "Immaculata," *NDizM* 679-688 M. O'Carroll, "Immaculate Conception," *Theotokos* 179-182.

celebrated letter to the Canons of Lyons protested against the introduction of this feast there.[2] Like many theologians of his time, Bernard thought that original sin was transmitted by the concupiscence which he saw as being inherent in sexual intercourse.[3] After some centuries of controversy a Mass, Office and octave were approved for the whole Church by Innocent XII (1695), and the feast was made a holy day of obligation by Clement XI (1708). The Miraculous Medal apparitions to St. Catherine Labouré in 1830 lent further support with its invocation, "O Mary, conceived without sin, pray for us who have recourse to thee." Four years after the 1854 definition of Pius IX, we have Mary giving her name at Lourdes. "I am the Immaculate Conception." In the revised liturgy the celebration has the rank of solemnity.

THEMES

In the Mass there are two themes, a christological one which relates the Immaculate Conception to Christ and the Divine Maternity, and an ecclesiological one which relates the Immaculate Conception to the Church and to us. Thus we recall that Mary was kept free from sin from the first moment of her conception in order to be a worthy Mother of the Son (opening prayer) and we pray that we be set free from sin (opening prayer, prayers over gifts and after communion). The two themes are interwoven in the preface:

> You allowed no stain of Adam's sin
> to touch the Virgin Mary.
> Full of grace she was to be a worthy mother of your Son,
> your sign of favour to the Church at its beginning,
> and the promise of its perfection as the bride of

---

[2]See *Epist.* PL 182:335-336. English tr. by B. Scott James, *The Letters of St. Bernard* (London, 1953) 289-293.

[3]M. O'Carroll, "St. Bernard," *Theotokos* 75-76.

Christ, radiant in beauty.
Purest of virgins, she was to bring forth your Son,
the innocent lamb who takes away our sins.
You chose her from all women to be our advocate with you
and our pattern in holiness.

The main thrust of the Liturgy of the Hours is a celebration of the beauty of God's work in Mary.

All generations will call me blessed, for the Almighty has done great things for me, Alleluia. (Evening Prayer I)
Blessed are you, O Virgin Mary, above all women on earth.
The Lord God himself has chosen you. (Morning Prayer)
You are the glory of Jerusalem, you are the joy of Israel!
You are the highest honour of our race. (Evening Prayer 2)

The Byzantine Orthodox Church does not recognize the Immaculate Conception. The Uniate Byzantine Rite Church, which is in communion with Rome, celebrates on 9 December a feast of the Maternity of St. Anne:

Today the great mystery which has been announced from eternity, whose depths angels and human beings cannot gauge, appears in the arms of Anne; Mary, the Maiden of God is prepared to be the dwelling of the King of Eternity, who will renew our human nature. Let us entreat her with a pure conscience and say: 'Intercede for us with your Son and your God, that He may save our souls, for you are the intercessor.' (*Byzantine Daily Worship* 538)

SCRIPTURE READINGS

c) Genesis 3:9-15.20

We have here the consequences of the Fall. It is clear that the author of Genesis had no idea about Mary, much less of her Immaculate Conception, and so the text has to be handled with some care. The choice of this passage is to show the sin from which Mary was preserved and to hint at the idea of Mary's being the New Eve. The man and woman were *afraid*: in their sin they knew that they were despoiled and vulnerable; they were *naked*. The *woman* was *tempted* by the *snake*. She listened to the temptation and *gave* the man *some fruit from the tree* and he *ate it*. The serpent is to continue his enmity throughout history. God will put *enmity between* it *and the woman* and between their *offspring*. The offspring of the woman *will bruise* the snake's *head*, whilst the snake will continue to attack, to *strike the heel* of the woman's offspring. The woman is called by Adam *Eve because she was the mother of all those who live*.

The early Fathers of the Church, beginning with Justin would see in the Annunciation story the reversal of the process of sin: Mary *listened to the Angel*; she was *obedient* to God's word; in a more profound sense she is *the mother of all those who live* through the redeeming death of her Son who finally conquers evil, Satan and death.

The *response* is praise: "Sing a new song to the Lord, for he has worked wonders.

b) Ephesians 1:3-6.11-12.

The first chapter of this letter is a majestic overview of the eternal plan, the *mystery* (v. 9) hidden for ages and now revealed in Christ. This opening section of Ephesians is extensively used in the early pages of the Marian encyclical of Pope John Paul II (nn. 7-11) for as the Pope observes, "Only in the mystery of Christ is the mystery of Mary made clear" (RM 4). Like all of us God *chose* Mary *in Christ* from eternity *to be holy and faultless before him in love*. In the case of Mary *all the spiritual blessings of heaven in Christ* were of a special kind: she was never under the reign of sin, being at all times Spirit-filled. Since God has blessed us in Christ, *we are marked out beforehand*. The reference here is probably to our baptism; Mary was sealed with the Holy Spirit and her response was perfect. She belongs to God in a singular manner. The author of Ephesians looks back at the Old Testament and sees *the people who would put their hopes in Christ before he came.* Mary in the words of Vatican II, "stands out among the poor and humble of the Lord, who confidently hope for and receive salvation from him" (LG 55). Though the opening of Ephesians is concerned with the whole of humanity, we can, with Pope John Paul II, see that the *praise of God's grace* "determines the extraordinary greatness and beauty of (Mary's) whole being" (RM 11).

c) Luke 1:26-38

At the level of historical critical exegesis the Annunciation story is seen in terms of a divine invitation to which Mary responds. The details of the text do not carry the same certainty. But since it is the gospel reading for the solemnity of the Immaculate Conception, we have to see what the continual mediation of the Church has discovered in the text. The marian year encyclical observes that Mary is addressed as "Full of grace" (Greek: "highly favored" with the sense that what was begun in the past is continuing into the present) instead of by her own name (RM 8). So "Highly Favored" is almost a new name for Mary; it describes her state and mission. It is a principle of God's dealings with humanity that he is always faithful; he will give grace for each task to which he calls a person. She is assured of God's protection and care: *The Lord is with you.* Mary is presented as being *deeply disturbed by these words*, and the angel says *Do not be afraid; you have won God's favour.* Fear before the divine is normal and it is a regular motif in biblical apparitions.[4] Mary is reassured. The Church under the guidance of the Holy Spirit long meditated on this text as it pondered the holiness of Mary and the consequences of the divine choice of her as Mother of the Eternal Word. Seeing Mary here and in relation to her Son, the Church gradually came to realize that where Mary was concerned there could never have been a taint of sinfulness.

[4]See *MaryNT* 107-113.

CHURCH DOCUMENTS[5]

The Immaculate Conception was defined by Pope Pius IX in the bull *Ineffabilis Deus* (1854):

> ...we declare, pronounce and define that the doctrine which holds that the most Blessed Virgin Mary from the first moment of her conception was, by the singular grace and privilege of Almighty God, in view of the merits of Christ Jesus the Saviour of the human race, preserved immune from all stain of original sin, is revealed by God and is therefore firmly and constantly to be believed by all the faithful.[6]

Quite simply the definition states that Mary was never bound by any guilt of original sin. But in view of many historical difficulties the definition states in technical language the exact meaning of the dogma: *from the first moment of her conception*—the definition seeks to avoid biological questions and to state merely that from the moment she was a person, whenever she came to be she was free from sin, and thus the view that Mary briefly had original sin but was immediately purified is excluded; *a singular grace and privilege*—she is the only case of this privilege of which the Church knows (this terminology is dropped in the definition of the Assumption); *in view of the merits of Christ Jesus the Saviour of the human race*—Mary was truly redeemed by the future merits of Jesus Christ, significantly described as "Saviour" since Mary is not outside the universal need of redemption; *preserved immune*—again it is being stated that she never had original sin, and it is probably implied that had God not intervened she would have been subject to original sin; *from all stain of original sin*—whatever is of sin is excluded in the case of Mary, but the definition does not state what the *stains* are. It is the task of theology to attempt an understanding of what is involved, e.g. Mary still could suffer, be

---

[5]See E.R. Carroll, "Mary in the Documents of the Magisterium" Carol 1:17-24.

[6]DS 2803/TCC 325.

tempted, die.... The definition is thus couched in negative terms to eliminate false views, rather than as a positive statement of Mary's holiness.

The bull of definition went through eight drafts. It was only in the penultimate one that it was decided to drop any attempt to "prove" the doctrine from scripture and tradition. A new process was then adopted. The Immaculate Conception was seen clearly to be the faith of the Church. The bull then re-read the documents of scripture and of tradition and found in them implications and deeper significance than their authors had grasped at the time of writing.[7]

The doctrinal definition came at the end of a long process of development.[8] We outline some of its stages. Firstly, we find the parallel in the Fathers between Eve and Mary. We have already alluded to its origin in Justin and its basic elements. But though we are interested in the New Eve theology for its mariological elements, we have to remember that this theology is at its root christological; it really concerns the New Adam, Christ who has the New Eve, Mary at his side. This emphasis is very clear in Irenaeus. At the centre of his christology, indeed of his whole theology is the idea, borrowed from Ephesians 1:10 of recapitulation (*anakephalaiōsis*): God takes up all from the beginning and renews it in his incarnate Son who thus becomes the New Adam:

---

[7]See A. Serra, "Immaculata," *NDizM* 688-689.

[8]On development see T. P. Rausch, "Development of Doctrine" in J.A. Komonchak et al. eds., *The New Dictionary of Theology* (Wilmington: Glazier-Dublin: Gill and Macmillan, 1987) 280-283; C. Pozo, "Dogma, Development" in *Sacramentum Mundi. An Encyclopedia of Theology* 6 vols. (London: Burns & Oates-New York: Herder & Herder, 1968) 2:98-102; R.E. Brown, "Critical Biblical Exegesis and the Development of Doctrine" in *Biblical Exegesis and Church Doctrine* (New York: Paulist-London: Chapman, 1985) 26-53; W.H. Marschner, "Criteria for Doctrinal Development in Marian Dogmas. An Essay in Methodology," *Marian Studies* 28 (1977) 47-100; F.A. Sullivan, *Magisterium. Teaching Authority in the Catholic Church* (Dublin: Gill and Macmillan—New York: Paulist, 1983) 17-19, 83; K. Rahner, "The Development of Dogma," *Theological Investigations* vol. 1 (London: Darton, Longman and Todd, 1961) 37-77.

> God recapitulates in himself the ancient formation of man
> that he might kill sin, deprive death of its power and vivify
> man.[9]

A complementary principle is that of untying the knot; the procedure of knotting has to be reversed:

> And so it was that the knot of Eve's disobedience was loosed
> by Mary's obedience. For what the virgin Eve bound fast by
> her refusal to believe, this the Virgin Mary unbound by her
> belief.[10]

We can note in passing that the Second Vatican Council takes up the New Eve theme twice: in the context of the Annunciation, which cites the latter text of Irenaeus above (see LG 56) and in the context of the Church:

> Through her faith and obedience she gave birth on earth to
> the very Son of the Father, not through knowledge of man,
> but by the oveshadowing of the Holy Spirit, in the manner
> of a new Eve who placed her faith not in the serpent of old,
> but in God's messenger without wavering in doubt. (LG 63)

The second element in the doctrinal development was the growing awareness of Mary's holiness. Words like "holy," "all-holy," and "spotless" were applied to her by both Eastern and Western Fathers.[11] Ephraem, the Syrian poet and theologian, can be taken as an example of a well developed teaching on Mary's holiness. He says in phrases echoed in the Byzantine liturgy, that the

---

[9]Adv. Haer. 3:18, 7—*EnMar* 51

[10]ibid. 3:22, 4—*EnMar* 45. See further on the New Eve W.J. Burghardt, "Mary in Western Patristic Thought," Carol 1:110-117; id. "Mary in Eastern Patristic Thought," Carol 2:88-110; M. O'Carroll, "Eve and Mary," *Theotokos* 139-141; J.A. de Aldama, *Maria en la patristica de los siglos 1 y 11.* (Madrid: BAC, 1970) 264-299; H. Graef, *Mary: A History of Doctrine and Devotion.* 2 vols. (London and New York: Sheed and Ward, 1965) vol. 1 passim; R. Laurentin and S. Meo, "Nouva Eva," *NDizM* 1017-1029.

[11]See Burghardt, arts. cit. (n. 10) 1:137-139; 2:125-132.

cherubim are not her equal in holiness, the seraphim yield to her in loveliness, the legions of angels are inferior to her in purity.[12] More striking still is his prayer to Christ:

> Indeed you and your Mother alone are beautiful in every respect. In you, Lord, there is no stain; in your Mother there is no spot.[13]

But there are also hesitations: some of the Fathers were not adverse to ascribing faults, if not indeed sins, to Mary.[14] These revolve around four events: the Annunciation, Cana, the "mother and brothers" episode (see Mt 12:46-50), and Calvary. The flaws are portrayed as weakness at the Annunciation, untimely haste, vainglory or disbelief in Cana and the crowd scenes, and some scandal at Calvary. The writers involved are some of the most important names in christian literature: in the East John Chrysostom, Basil, Cyril of Alexandria, Origen; in the West Irenaeus and Tertullian. Besides those who ascribed faults to Mary there were writers such as Hilary of Poitiers and Optatus who held the principle that Christ alone was sinless. These doubts fell away after the 5th century.

There is a third element of the doctrinal development to be considered, namely, the explicit question, did Mary ever have original sin? Here we have to make a distinction between the East and the West. The catholic doctrine of original sin developed in the West in answer to the heresy of Pelagius. Pelagius, reacting against laxity, stressed people's ability to be holy by their efforts assisted by grace. But his idea of grace was purely external: it was the help of the scriptures and the example of Christ. Augustine, on the other hand, drawing no doubt on his own experience as well as on the scriptures, asserted that there was in humanity a sinfulness that required an interior, healing grace that

[12]*Hymn. de B. Maria* 13:5-6—*EnMar* 390.

[13]*Carm. Nisibena* 27:8—*EnMar* 429.

[14]See Burghardt, arts. cit. (n. 10) 1:139-147; 2:132-136.

touches the person and leads to conversion. That wound of human nature requiring grace is original sin. Basically the doctrine of original sin states that grace is not inherited: all who are born are in need of salvation by Christ. In the East these issues did not arise. Once the doctrine of original sin was clarified it was natural that the position of Mary would arise. And it did even during the pelagian controversy. It is still not clear what two complex statements of Augustine actually mean with regard to Mary. The result was that there would remain at least a doubt about the mind of Augustine in relation to Mary and original sin.[15] We might note in passing that the non-acceptance of the Immaculate Conception by the Orthodox East is due more to a difficulty in understanding original sin than to a strict mariological issue.[16]

The high point of the Middle Ages revealed two problems: original sin was thought to have been transmitted by the concupiscence that was supposed to be present in all intercourse—an idea going back to Augustine and very much influencing Bernard; all humanity needed salvation. The first problem would mean that by the very fact that Mary was conceived by her parents, Mary would have been tainted by original sin; the best then that could be said was that Mary was conceived in original sin, but was purified immediately. The more serious difficulty was, however, the second one—the universal need for salvation. It held St. Thomas Aquinas back from asserting the Immaculate Conception. He too took refuge in the idea of an immediate sanctification of Mary after she had incurred original sin.[17] However during all this time of doubt and denial the liturgy was gradually celebrating

[15]See Burghardt, art. cit. (n. 10 "Western") 1:143-147, and M. O'Carroll, "Augustine," *Theotokos* 63 which shows that little advance has been made in two decades since Burghardt's work.

[16]See the remarkable discussion by Bishop Kallistos Ware and Edward Yarnold, *The Immaculate Conception. A Search for Convergence.* "Paper from the Ecumenical Society of the Blessed Virgin Mary Congress" at Chichester, 1986 published as a paper of the Society. See further, K. Ware, "The Sanctity and Glory of the Mother of God: Orthodox Approaches," *The Way—Supplement* 51 (1984) 79-96.

[17]See *Summa theologiae* 3a, q.27, a.2.

in more and more places the feast of the Immaculate Conception.

It was Scotus (d. 1308) who found a way out of the impasse. He made two critical contributions. Firstly, he evolved the idea of preservative redemption as being a more perfect one: to have been preserved free from original sin was a greater grace than to be set free from it. Secondly, he proposed a clear formula according to which Mary did not have original sin, even though had she not been preserved, she would have incurred it. From these two arguments it became clear that Mary was truly redeemed through the merits of Christ the Saviour. The idea of preservation is a familiar one, but in a different context. At Mass we pray for forgiveness at the penitential rite. After the Our Father we pray for a still greater favour from God: "in your mercy keep us free from sin." There were some hints of the final solution of Scotus already to be found in the work of Anselm, but neither he nor his disciple Eadmer developed sufficiently his idea of anticipated redemption.[18]

After Scotus Dominican theologians continued for several centuries to follow St. Thomas, but by the 19th century they too had accepted the doctrine of the Immaculate Conception which continued to grow in popular devotion, religiosity and in liturgy.

Vatican II takes up the Scotist idea and states that Mary was "redeemed in a more excellent fashion, by reason of the merits of her Son" (LG 53). Earlier the Council spoke of her as "the most excellent fruit of redemption" (*Liturgy* 103). The Council also states in the Constitution on the Church:

> It is no wonder then that it was customary for the Fathers to refer to the Mother of God as all holy and free from every stain of sin, as though fashioned by the Holy Spirit and formed as a new creature. (LG 56)

The Fathers in question quoted by the Council here are the later Greek Fathers.

---

[18]See S. De Fiores, "Immaculata," *NDizM* 685-686

Pope Paul VI comments on the aptness of the occurrence of the feast of the Immaculate Conception during Advent:

> ...during Advent there are many liturgical references to Mary, besides the Solemnity of 8 December, which is a joint celebration of the Immaculate Conception of Mary, of the basic preparation (see Is 11:1.10) for the coming of the Saviour and of the happy beginning of the Church without spot or wrinkle. (MC 3)

We can leave the reflection of the magisterium on the Immaculate Conception with this rich and dense passage from Pope John Paul II:

> According to the belief formulated in solemn documents of the Church, this 'glory of grace' (see Eph 1:4) is manifested in the Mother of God through the fact that she has been 'redeemed in a more sublime manner' (Pius IX). By virtue of the richness of the grace of the beloved Son, by reason of the redemptive merits of him who willed to become her Son, Mary was preserved from the inheritance of original sin. In this way, from the first moment of her conception— which is to say of her existence—she belonged to Christ, sharing in salvific and sanctifying grace and in that love which has its beginning in the 'Beloved,' the Son of the Eternal Father, who through the Incarnation became her own Son. Consequently, through the power of the Holy Spirit, in the order of grace, which is a participation in the divine nature, Mary receives life from him to whom she herself, in the order of earthly generation, gave life as a mother. The liturgy does not hesitate to call her 'mother of her Creator' and to hail her with the words which Dante Alighieri places on the lips of Saint Bernard: 'daughter of your Son.' (RM 10)

It could be noted that the Pope develops these reflections in the beginning of his encyclical in which he is considering the opening chapter of Ephesians, from which the second reading of the Solemnity is taken.

REFLECTION

The Immaculate Conception is often misunderstood as referring not to Mary's conception but to the virginal conception of Jesus. Though it is possible to indicate important stages in the development of the doctrine, it is not easy to grasp the internal dynamic of the progression from the New Testament, which is silent about Mary's conception, to the dogmatic definition. One of the critical stages was the writings of Eadmer (d. 1130), a disciple of St. Anselm. He argued that the Immaculate Conception was possible: God certainly could do it; if therefore he willed it, he did it. This form of argument was later sharpened into a three-word aphorism, *potuit, decuit, fecit* (God could, it was appropriate, therefore he did). The results of this maxim in mariology was often unfortunate. The divine power is unlimited. What theologians and preachers deemed appropriate was without controls and frequently both without foundation and unwise, e.g. that Mary should have had the beatific vision whilst on earth. Once then theologians decided what was appropriate, they concluded that God had effected it.

There are several significant points of contrast, at least at first sight, between the two late marian dogmas and the earlier ones. The early dogmas of Mary's virginity and divine motherhood were christological, that is to say that they made statements about Mary in order to preserve truths about Christ. The modern dogmas of the Immaculate Conception and Assumption more directly envisage Mary. At one level they can be seen as privileges and gifts to Mary, to the woman who is Mother of Jesus who is God and man. But their deeper significance is soteriological: they teach us about our end, about the triumphant grace of Christ which overcomes sin and leads to final glory.

The most fundamental thing to say about the Immaculate Conception is the assertion that Mary was redeemed: in this world where sin reigns, she was conceived sinless, that is, she was redeemed by the merits of her Son. Jesus died for all on Calvary. We must thus say that he earned on the cross the grace of his Mother's Immaculate Conception.

All christian theologians will agree that salvation is a free gift of God. The infant is sanctified by baptism; the adult accepts God's gift of justifying grace through faith. When we say that Mary was immaculately conceived we state that she was redeemed in the most perfect possible way; sin was prevented from touching her. This gift of God is pure grace, the most perfect example of "grace alone" (the *gratia sola* so emphasized in the Reformation tradition). She did nothing to merit or to acquire this grace: it is totally gratuitous. Later at the Annunciation she would respond in faith to God's gift.

We can therefore see why this gift is so dear to Mary, why at Lourdes she gave her name in the words: "I am the Immaculate Conception." She rejoices that she was never for an instant outside God's love, that she was never tainted by sin. It is as we reflect on her love for God and on her awareness of how much he loved her that we can have some fleeting insight into Mary's joy at her Immaculate Conception.

In the Immaculate Conception we can see the redemption fully at work. We can say that through this gift Mary is the fully healed one: she never had the spiritual flaws that hold us back from total love of God. Thus the Immaculate Conception allowed Mary's yes at the Annunciation to be limitless, without any unconscious restriction.[19] In several places the liturgy speaks of Mary as the beginning of the Church. She is also where the grace of redemption reaches its highest expression. Already in the Immaculate Conception the Church begins to exist "with no speck or wrinkle . . . but holy and faultless" (Eph 5:27). What the whole Church will one day become is already perfect in Mary

---

[19]See H. Urs von Balthasar in J. Ratzinger and H. Urs von Balthasar, *Marie première Eglise* (Paris: Apostolat des Editions-Montreal: Ed. Paulines, 1981) 47-49.

through her Immaculate Conception and Assumption. These are consoling mysteries since they are

> the real pledge and guarantee that (God's) grace is more powerful than our guilt. So the Immaculate Conception of the Blessed Virgin reveals that God loves humanity as such.... The Immaculate Conception also means that God surrounds this life of humanity with loving fidelity.[20]

It should also be noted that the Immaculate Conception has a further significance in the plan of redemption, as the Anglican-Roman Catholic discussions (ARCIC *Final Report*) have shown. Mary's preservation from original sin can be seen as a sign that the salvation won by Christ was operative among all humanity before his birth. It is only if we see God as being conditioned by time that we will have trouble with the notion of preservative redemption.

All this is not to say that Mary is utterly remote, as if sin is the key to the understanding of humanity. On the contrary sin is abnormal and holiness is normality. A short reflection on our own experience should confirm this assertion. When we are in regular contact with God in prayer, when we take the spiritual life more seriously, we tend to be kinder to others. Indeed we would rightly expect much compassion and understanding for our frailty from enclosed Carmelite sisters. It is Mary's sinlessness that makes her the Mother of Mercy, the compassionate Mother.

As we have seen, the liturgy suggests that Mary was immaculately conceived so that she might provide "a worthy dwelling place for her Son" (preface). This idea surely reflects the intuition of centuries into the mystery of the Mother of God. But more perhaps can be said. We return to the second reading at Mass (Eph 1). The divine plan was that sin should be overcome through the death of the incarnate Son. Salvation, we have also seen, is utter gratuity: only God can save; sinful humanity cannot redeem

---

[20]K. Rahner, *Mary, Mother of the Lord. Theological Meditations* (Freiburg: Herder—Edinburgh/London: Nelson, 1963) 46-47.

itself. Salvation must come from outside the reign of sin. Because Mary was immaculately conceived, she could stand with her Son, thus associating herself with his sinless humanity which makes expiation for all sin.[21] In Mary God has already entered into friendship with humanity, and humanity has already taken the side of God in the battle against evil.[22] Humanity is perfect, fully "normal in the sinlessness of Mary."[23]

PRAYER OF THE FAITHFUL

As a sinful people we come to our Father in confident prayer, relying on the intercession of Mary conceived without sin.

- For the Church: that its members be not overcome by temptation, but may come ever closer to the holiness of God.
- For the world: that the reign of sin in the structures of society may be overcome.
- For all of us: that the Holy Spirit may widen our vision and lead us to rejoice in God's saving plan for us.
- For those in need of special healing: that the prayers of the Virgin may support them and bring them to fullness of life.

Father in heaven, we celebrate the wonders you have accomplished in Mary; may we always be buoyed up by the vision of sinlessness seen in the Mother of your Son, Jesus our Lord. Amen.

[21]See W. Beinert in *HBdMK* 288-289

[22]See L. Scheffczyk, *Mhe* 106.

[23]See ibid. 103.

ADDITIONAL READING

J.A. Alonso, "¿Desmitologización del dogma de la Inmaculada Concepción de Maria?," *Ephemerides mariologicae* 23 (1973) 95-120

A. Carr and G. Williams, "Mary's Immaculate Conception," Carol 1:325-394.

De Fiores 452-477.

B. Gherardini, "L'Immacolata concezione in Luthero," *Divinitas* 30 (1986) 271-283.

J.P. Kenny, "Mary's Immaculate Conception," *Clergy Review* 63 (1978) 456-465.

M. Meilach, *Mary Immaculate and the Divine Plan* (Wilmington: Glazier, 1982).

M. O'Carroll, "Immaculate Conception and Assumption" in J. Hyland, ed., *Mary and the Church Today. Papers of the National Marian Congress 1984* (Athlone: Marist Brothers—Dublin: Veritas, 1988) forthcoming.

E.D. O'Connor, "Modern Theories of Original Sin and the Dogma of the Immaculate Conception," *Marian Studies* 20 (1969) 112-136.

K. Rahner, "The Immaculate Conception," *Theological Investigations*. vol. 1 (London: Darton, Longman and Todd, 1961) 201-213.

Roschini 3:9-267.

G. Söll, *Storia dei dogmi mariani.* "Accademia Mariana Salesiana 15" (Rome: LAS, 1981) 217-225, 230-240, 272-352.

A. Venneste, "Le dogme de l'Immaculée Conception et l'evolution actuelle de la théologie du péché originel" *Ephemerides mariologicae* 23 (1973) 77-93.

EPILOGUE

As we celebrate the festivals of Mary, we constantly hear her words, "The Almighty has done great things for me, holy is his name." Our liturgical celebrations, and our theological and prayerful reflections, allow us to join in Mary's praise of God's goodness to her, and through her also to us.

But the feasts of Mary have perhaps another role also. As we struggle forwards on our pilgrim way, we cannot but be conscious of the cross, of the weight of sin, of difficulties in discipleship. The figure of Mary is a vision of beauty: it does not threaten; it only draws us on. Her feasts are moments of repose and refreshment on our journey. Beauty cannot be possessed; it can only be enjoyed. In a frenetic world, we need moments of tranquillity. In times of stress and anxiety, we need to raise our eyes aloft. The way of beauty is an authentic approach to Mary, as Pope Paul VI told the Seventh Mariological and Fourteenth Marian congresses.[1] It is also a way for all theology and for all spirituality.

Celebration of the feasts of Mary can encourage us to move from admiration of her beauty to marvel also at our own. God's faithful love has enriched us also. In a lower key Mary's song of praise is the Church's as well: "The Almighty has done great things for me, holy is his name."

[1] *AAS* 67 (1975) 338.